Florida Rules of Civil Procedure 2012

Florida Evidence Code 2012

TABLE OF CONTENTS

FLORIDA RULES OF CIVIL PROCEDURE 2012

x

FLORIDA EVIDENCE CODE 2011

TITLE VII
EVIDENCE

CHAPTER 90
EVIDENCE CODE

CHAPTER 92
WITNESSES, RECORDS, AND DOCUMENTS

Florida Rules of Civil Procedure 2012

RULE 1.010. SCOPE AND TITLE OF RULES

These rules apply to all actions of a civil nature and all special statutory proceedings in the circuit courts and county courts except those to which the Florida Probate Rules, the Florida Family Law Rules of Procedure, or the Small Claims Rules apply. The form, content, procedure, and time for pleading in all special statutory proceedings shall be as prescribed by the statutes governing the proceeding unless these rules specifically provide to the contrary. These rules shall be construed to secure the just, speedy, and inexpensive determination of every action. These rules shall be known as the Florida Rules of Civil Procedure and abbreviated as Fla.R.Civ.P.

RULE 1.030. NONVERIFICATION OF PLEADINGS

Except when otherwise specifically provided by these rules or an applicable statute, every written pleading or other paper of a party represented by an attorney need not be verified or accompanied by an affidavit.

Committee Notes

1976 Amendment. Subdivisions (a)–(b) have been amended to require the addition of the filing party's telephone number on all pleadings and papers filed.

RULE 1.040. ONE FORM OF ACTION

There shall be one form of action to be known as "civil action."

RULE 1.050. WHEN ACTION COMMENCED

Every action of a civil nature shall be deemed commenced when the complaint or petition is filed except that ancillary proceedings shall be deemed commenced when the writ is issued or the pleading setting forth the claim of the party initiating the action is filed.

RULE 1.060. TRANSFERS OF ACTIONS

(a) Transfers of Courts. If it should appear at any time that an action is pending in the wrong court of any county, it may be transferred to the proper court within said county by the same method as provided in rule 1.170(j).

(b) Wrong Venue. When any action is filed laying venue in the wrong county, the court may transfer the action in the manner provided in rule 1.170(j) to the proper court in any county where it might have been brought in accordance with the venue statutes. When the venue might have been laid in 2 or more counties, the person bringing the action may select the county to which the action is transferred, but if no such selection is made, the matter shall be determined by the court.

(c) Method. The service charge of the clerk of the court to which an action is transferred under this rule shall be paid by the party who commenced the action within 30 days from the date the order of transfer is entered, subject to taxation as provided by law when the action is determined. If the service charge is not paid within the 30 days, the action shall be dismissed without prejudice by the court that entered the order of transfer.

Court Commentary

1984 Amendment. Because of confusion in some circuits, subdivision (c) is added:

(a) to specify who is to pay the clerk's service charge on transfer;

(b) to provide for the circumstance in which the service charge is not paid; and

(c) to require the dismissal to be by the court which entered the order of transfer.

RULE 1.061. CHOICE OF FORUM

(a) **Grounds for Dismissal.** An action may be dismissed on the ground that a satisfactory remedy may be more conveniently sought in a jurisdiction other than Florida when:

(1) the trial court finds that an adequate alternate forum exists which possesses jurisdiction over the whole case, including all of the parties;

(2) the trial court finds that all relevant factors of private interest favor the alternate forum, weighing in the balance a strong presumption against disturbing plaintiffs' initial forum choice;

(3) if the balance of private interests is at or near equipoise, the court further finds that factors of public interest tip the balance in favor of trial in the alternate forum; and

(4) the trial judge ensures that plaintiffs can reinstate their suit in the alternate forum without undue inconvenience or prejudice.

The decision to grant or deny the motion for dismissal rests in the sound discretion of the trial court, subject to review for abuse of discretion.

(b) **Stipulations in General.** The parties to any action for which a satisfactory remedy may be more conveniently sought in a jurisdiction other than Florida may stipulate to conditions upon which a forum-non-conveniens dismissal shall be based, subject to approval by the trial court. The decision to accept or reject the stipulation rests in the sound discretion of the trial court, subject to review for abuse of discretion.

A forum-non-conveniens dismissal shall not be granted unless all defendants agree to the stipulations required by subdivision (c) and any additional stipulations required by the court.

(c) **Statutes of Limitation.** In moving for forum-non-conveniens dismissal, defendants shall be deemed to automatically stipulate that the action will be treated in the new forum as though it had been filed in that forum on the date it was filed in Florida, with service of process accepted as of that date.

(d) **Failure to Refile Promptly.** When an action is dismissed in Florida for forum non conveniens, plaintiffs shall automatically be deemed to stipulate that they will lose the benefit of all stipulations made by the defendant, including the stipulation provided in subdivision (c) of this rule, if plaintiffs fail to file the action in the new forum within 120 days after the date the Florida dismissal becomes final.

(e) **Waiver of Automatic Stipulations.** Upon unanimous agreement, the parties may waive the conditions provided in subdivision (c) or (d), or both, only when they demonstrate and the trial court finds a compelling reason for the waiver. The decision to accept or reject the waiver shall not be disturbed on review if supported by competent, substantial evidence.

(f) **Reduction to Writing.** The parties shall reduce their stipulation to a writing signed by them, which shall include all stipulations provided by this rule and which shall be deemed incorporated by reference in any subsequent order of dismissal.

(g) **Time for Moving for Dismissal.** A motion to dismiss based on forum non conveniens shall be served not later than 60 days after service of process on the moving party.

(h) **Retention of Jurisdiction.** The court shall retain jurisdiction after the dismissal to enforce its order of dismissal and any conditions and stipulations in the order.

Committee Notes

2000 Amendment. Subdivision (a)(1) is amended to clarify that the alternative forum other than Florida must have jurisdiction over all of the parties for the trial court to grant a dismissal based on forum non conveniens.

Subdivision (b) is amended to clarify that all of the defendants, not just the moving defendant, must agree to the stipulations required by subdivision (c) as well as any additional stipulations required by the trial court before an action may be dismissed based on forum non conveniens.

Subdivision (g) is added to require that a motion to dismiss based on forum non conveniens be served not later than 60 days after service of process on the moving party.

Subdivision (h) is added to require the court to retain jurisdiction over the action after the dismissal for purposes of enforcing its order of dismissal and any conditions and stipulations contained in the order.

<h3 style="text-align:center">Court Commentary</h3>

This section was added to elaborate on Florida's adoption of the federal doctrine of forum non conveniens in *Kinney System, Inc. v. Continental Insurance Co.*, 674 So.2d 86 (Fla. 1996), and it should be interpreted in light of that opinion.

Subdivision (a) codifies the federal standard for reviewing motions filed under the forum-non-conveniens doctrine. Orders granting or denying dismissal for forum non conveniens are subject to appellate review under an abuse-of-discretion standard.

As stated in *Kinney*, the phrase "private interests" means adequate access to evidence and relevant sites, adequate access to witnesses, adequate enforcement of judgments, and the practicalities and expenses associated with the litigation. Private interests do not involve consideration of the availability or unavailability of advantageous legal theories, a history of generous or stingy damage awards, or procedural nuances that may affect outcomes but that do not effectively deprive the plaintiff of any remedy.

"Equipoise" means that the advantages and disadvantages of the alternative forum will not significantly undermine or favor the "private interests" of any particular party, as compared with the forum in which suit was filed.

"Public interests" are the ability of courts to protect their dockets from causes that lack significant connection to the jurisdiction; the ability of courts to encourage trial of controversies in the localities in which they arise; and the ability of courts to consider their familiarity with governing law when deciding whether to retain jurisdiction over a case. Even when the private conveniences of the litigants are nearly in balance, a trial court has discretion to grant a forum-non-conveniens dismissal upon finding that retention of jurisdiction would be unduly burdensome to the community, that there is little or no public interest in the dispute, or that foreign law will predominate if jurisdiction is retained.

Subdivision (b) provides that the parties can stipulate to conditions of a forum-non-conveniens dismissal, subject to the trial court's approval. The trial court's acceptance or rejection of the stipulation is subject to appellate review under an abuse-of-discretion standard.

Subdivisions (c) and (d) provide automatic conditions that shall be deemed included in every forum-non-conveniens dismissal. The purpose underlying subdivision (c) is to ensure that any statute of limitation in the new forum is applied as though the action had been filed in that forum on the date it was filed in Florida. The purpose underlying subdivision (d) is to ensure that the action is promptly refiled in the new forum. Both of these stipulations are deemed to be a part of every stipulation that does not expressly state otherwise, subject to the qualification provided in subdivision (e).

Subdivision (e) recognizes that there may be extraordinary conditions associated with the new forum that would require the waiver of the conditions provided in subdivisions (c) and (d). Waivers should be granted sparingly. Thus, the parties by unanimous consent may stipulate to waive those conditions only upon showing a compelling reason to the trial court. The trial court's acceptance or rejection of the waiver may not be reversed on appeal where supported by competent, substantial evidence.

Subdivision (f) requires the parties to reduce their stipulation to written form, which the parties must sign. When and if the trial court accepts the stipulation, the parties' agreement then is treated as though it were incorporated by reference in the trial court's order of dismissal. To avoid confusion, the parties shall include the automatic stipulations provided by subdivisions (c) and (d) of this rule, unless the latter are properly waived under subdivision (e). However, the failure to include these automatic conditions in the stipulation does not waive them unless the dismissing court has expressly so ruled.

RULE 1.070. PROCESS

(a) **Summons; Issuance.** Upon the commencement of the action, summons or other process authorized by law shall be issued forthwith by the clerk or judge under the clerk's or the judge's signature and the seal of the court and delivered for service without praecipe.

(b) **Service; By Whom Made.** Service of process may be made by an officer authorized by law to serve process, but the court may appoint any competent person not interested in the action to serve the process. When so appointed, the person serving process shall make proof of service by affidavit promptly and in any event within the time during which the person served must respond to the process. Failure to make proof of service shall not affect the validity of the service. When any process is returned not executed or returned improperly executed for any defendant, the party causing its issuance shall be entitled to such additional process against the unserved party as is required to effect service.

(c) **Service; Numerous Defendants.** If there is more than 1 defendant, the clerk or judge shall issue as many writs of process against the several defendants as may be directed by the plaintiff or the plaintiff's attorney.

(d) **Service by Publication.** Service of process by publication may be made as provided by statute.

(e) **Copies of Initial Pleading for Persons Served.** At the time of personal service of process a copy of the initial pleading shall be delivered to the party upon whom service is made. The date and hour of service shall be endorsed on the original process and all copies of it by the person making the service. The party seeking to effect personal service shall furnish the person making service with the necessary copies. When the service is made by publication, copies of the initial pleadings shall be furnished to the clerk and mailed by the clerk with the notice of action to all parties whose addresses are stated in the initial pleading or sworn statement.

(f) **Service of Orders.** If personal service of a court order is to be made, the original order shall be filed with the clerk, who shall certify or verify a copy of it without charge. The person making service shall use the certified copy instead of the original order in the same manner as original process in making service.

(g) **Fees; Service of Pleadings.** The statutory compensation for making service shall not be increased by the simultaneous delivery or mailing of the copy of the initial pleading in conformity with this rule.

(h) **Pleading Basis.** When service of process is to be made under statutes authorizing service on nonresidents of Florida, it is sufficient to plead the basis for service in the language of the statute without pleading the facts supporting service.

(i) **Service of Process by Mail.** A defendant may accept service of process by mail.

(1) Acceptance of service of a complaint by mail does not thereby waive any objection to the venue or to the jurisdiction of the court over the person of the defendant.

(2) A plaintiff may notify any defendant of the commencement of the action and request that the defendant waive service of a summons. The notice and request shall:

(A) be in writing and be addressed directly to the defendant, if an individual, or to an officer or managing or general agent of the defendant or other agent authorized by appointment or law to receive service of process;

(B) be dispatched by certified mail, return receipt requested;

4

(C) be accompanied by a copy of the complaint and shall identify the court in which it has been filed;

(D) inform the defendant of the consequences of compliance and of failure to comply with the request;

(E) state the date on which the request is sent;

(F) allow the defendant 20 days from the date on which the request is received to return the waiver, or, if the address of the defendant is outside of the United States, 30 days from the date on which it is received to return the waiver; and

(G) provide the defendant with an extra copy of the notice and request, including the waiver, as well as a prepaid means of compliance in writing.

(3) If a defendant fails to comply with a request for waiver within the time provided herein, the court shall impose the costs subsequently incurred in effecting service on the defendant unless good cause for the failure is shown.

(4) A defendant who, before being served with process, timely returns a waiver so requested is not required to respond to the complaint until 60 days after the date the defendant received the request for waiver of service. For purposes of computing any time prescribed or allowed by these rules, service of process shall be deemed effected 20 days before the time required to respond to the complaint.

(5) When the plaintiff files a waiver of service with the court, the action shall proceed, except as provided in subdivision (4) above, as if a summons and complaint had been served at the time of filing the waiver, and no further proof of service shall be required.

(j) Summons; Time Limit. If service of the initial process and initial pleading is not made upon a defendant within 120 days after filing of the initial pleading directed to that defendant the court, on its own initiative after notice or on motion, shall direct that service be effected within a specified time or shall dismiss the action without prejudice or drop that defendant as a party; provided that if the plaintiff shows good cause or excusable neglect for the failure, the court shall extend the time for service for an appropriate period. When a motion for leave to amend with the attached proposed amended complaint is filed, the 120-day period for service of amended complaints on the new party or parties shall begin upon the entry of an order granting leave to amend. A dismissal under this subdivision shall not be considered a voluntary dismissal or operate as an adjudication on the merits under rule 1.420(a)(1).

Committee Notes

1971 Amendment. Subdivisions (f), (g), and (h) of the existing rule are combined because they deal with the same subject matter. The "notice of suit" is changed to "notice of action" to comply with the statutory change in 1967. Subdivision (g) is new and provides for substitution of a certified or verified copy of a court order that must be served. The original is to be filed with the clerk and not removed. Subdivision (i) is relettered to (h).

1972 Amendment. Subdivision (a) is amended to require the officer issuing the process to sign it and place the court seal on it. This was required by former section 47.04, Florida Statutes, and is essential to the validity of process. When the statute was repealed these procedural requirements were omitted and inadvertently not included in the rule. Subdivision (b) is changed to eliminate the predicate for court appointment of a person to make service of process. This makes the rule more flexible and permits the court to appoint someone to make service at any appropriate time.

1980 Amendment. Subdivision (i) is added to eliminate pleading evidentiary facts for "long arm" service of process. It is based on the longstanding principle in service by publication that pleading the basis for service is sufficient if it is done in the language of the statute. See *McDaniel v. McElvy*, 91 Fla. 770, 108 So. 820 (1926). Confusion has been generated in the decisions under the "long arm" statute. See *Wm. E. Strasser Construction Corp. v. Linn*, 97 So. 2d 458 (Fla. 1957); *Hartman Agency, Inc. v. Indiana Farmers Mutual Insurance Co.*, 353 So. 2d 665 (Fla. 2d DCA 1978); and Drake v.

Scharlau, 353 So. 2d 961 (Fla. 2d DCA 1978). The amendment is not intended to change the distinction between pleading and proof as enunciated in *Elmex Corp. v. Atlantic Federal Savings & Loan Association of Fort Lauderdale*, 325 So. 2d 58 (Fla. 4th DCA 1976). It is intended to eliminate the necessity of pleading evidentiary facts as well as those of pecuniary benefit that were used in the Elmex case. The amendment is limited to pleading. If the statutory allegations are attacked by motion, the pleader must then prove the evidentiary facts to support the statutory requirements. If denied in a pleading, the allegations must be proved at trial. Otherwise, the allegations will be admitted under rule 1.110(e).

1988 Amendment. Subdivision (j) has been added to require plaintiffs to cause service of original summons within 120 days of filing the complaint absent good cause for further delay.

1992 Amendment. Subdivision (d) is repealed because the reason for the rule ceased when process was permitted to run beyond county boundaries. The amendment to subdivision (j) (redesignated as (i)) is intended to clarify that a dismissal under this subdivision is not to be considered as an adjudication on the merits under rule 1.420(a)(1) of these rules.

1996 Amendment. Subdivision (i) is added to provide some formality to the practice of requesting waiver of service of process by a sheriff or person appointed to serve papers or by publication. The committee intends that only the manner of service will be waived by this procedure. By accepting service pursuant to this rule, the defendant will not waive any objection to venue or jurisdiction over the person or admit to the sufficiency of the pleadings or to allegations with regard to long-arm or personal jurisdiction. For example, service of process would be void should a motion to dismiss be granted because the complaint did not allege the basis for long-arm jurisdiction over a nonresident defendant. *City Contract Bus Service, Inc. v. H.E. Woody*, 515 So. 2d 1354 (Fla. 1st DCA 1987). Under such circumstances, the defendant must be served pursuant to law or again waive service pursuant to this rule. Subdivision (i)(2)(F) allows the defendant 20 days from receipt (or 30 days if the defendant is outside of the United States) to return the waiver. Accordingly, the committee intends that the waiver be received by the plaintiff or the plaintiff's attorney by the twentieth day (or the thirtieth day if the defendant is outside of the United States). The former subdivision (i) has been redesignated as subdivision (j). Form 1.902 may be used to give notice of an action and request waiver of process pursuant to this rule.

2003 Amendment. Subdivision (j) is amended in accordance with *Totura & Co., Inc. v. Williams*, 754 So. 2d 671 (Fla. 2000). See the amendment to rule 1.190(a).

RULE 1.071 CONSTITUTIONAL CHALLENGE TO STATE STATUTE OR COUNTY OR MUNICIPAL CHARTER, ORDINANCE, OR FRANCHISE; NOTICE BY PARTY

A party that files a pleading, written motion, or other paper drawing into question the constitutionality of a state statute or a county or municipal charter, ordinance, or franchise must promptly

(a) file a notice of constitutional question stating the question and identifying the paper that raises it; and

(b) serve the notice and the pleading, written motion, or other paper drawing into question the constitutionality of a state statute or a county or municipal charter, ordinance, or franchise on the Attorney General or the state attorney of the judicial circuit in which the action is pending, by either certified or registered mail.

Service of the notice and pleading, written motion, or other paper does not require joinder of the Attorney General or the state attorney as a party to the action.

Committee Notes

2010 Adoption. This rule clarifies that, with respect to challenges to a state statute or municipal charter, ordinance, or franchise, service of the notice does not require joinder of the Attorney General or the state attorney as a party to the action; however, consistent with section 86.091, Florida Statutes, the Florida Attorney General has the discretion to participate and be heard on matters affecting the constitutionality of a statute. See, *e.g.*, *Mayo v. National Truck Brokers, Inc.*, 220 So. 2d 11 (Fla. 1969); *State ex rel. Shevin v. Kerwin*, 279 So. 2d 836 (Fla. 1973) (Attorney General may choose to participate in appeal even though he was not required to be a party at the trial court). The rule imposes a new requirement that the party challenging the statute, charter, ordinance, or franchise file verification with the court of compliance with section 86.091, Florida Statutes. See form 1.975.

RULE 1.080. SERVICE OF PLEADINGS AND PAPERS

(a) Service; When Required. Unless the court otherwise orders, every pleading subsequent to the initial pleading and every other paper filed in the action, except applications for witness subpoena, shall be served on each party. No service need be made on parties against whom a default has been entered, except that pleadings asserting new or additional claims against them shall be served in the manner provided for service of summons.

(b) Service; How Made. When service is required or permitted to be made upon a party represented by an attorney, service shall be made upon the attorney unless service upon the party is ordered by the court. Service on the attorney or party shall be made by delivering a copy or mailing it to the attorney or the party at the last known address or, if no address is known, by leaving it with the clerk of the court. Service by mail shall be complete upon mailing. Delivery of a copy within this rule shall be complete upon: (1) handing it to the attorney or to the party, (2) leaving it at the attorney's or party's office with a clerk or other person in charge thereof, (3) if there is no one in charge, leaving it in a conspicuous place therein, (4) if the office is closed or the person to be served has no office, leaving it at the person's usual place of abode with some person of his or her family above 15 years of age and informing such person of the contents, or (5) transmitting it by facsimile to the attorney's or party's office with a cover sheet containing the sender's name, firm, address, telephone number, and facsimile number, and the number of pages transmitted. When service is made by facsimile, a copy shall also be served by any other method permitted by this rule. Facsimile service occurs when transmission is complete. Service by delivery shall be deemed complete on the date of the delivery.

(c) Service; Numerous Defendants. In actions when the parties are unusually numerous, the court may regulate the service contemplated by these rules on motion or on its initiative in such manner as may be found to be just and reasonable.

(d) Filing. All original papers shall be filed with the court either before service or immediately thereafter, unless otherwise provided for by general law or other rules. If the original of any bond or other paper is not placed in the court file, a certified copy shall be so placed by the clerk.

(e) Filing Defined. The filing of papers with the court as required by these rules shall be made by filing them with the clerk, except that the judge may permit papers to be filed with the judge, in which event the judge shall note the filing date before him or her on the papers and transmit them to the clerk. The date of filing is that shown on the face of the paper by the judge's notation or the clerk's time stamp, whichever is earlier.

(f) Certificate of Service. When any attorney shall certify in substance:

"I certify that a copy hereof has been furnished to (here insert name or names) by (delivery) (mail) (fax) on .....(date)......

_____
Attorney"

the certificate shall be taken as prima facie proof of such service in compliance with these rules.

(g) Service by Clerk. If a party who is not represented by an attorney files a paper that does not show service of a copy on other parties, the clerk shall serve a copy of it on other parties as provided in subdivision (b).

(h) Service of Orders.

(1) A copy of all orders or judgments shall be transmitted by the court or under its direction to all parties at the time of entry of the order or judgment. No service need be made on parties against whom a default has been entered except orders setting an action for trial as prescribed in rule 1.440(c) and final judgments that shall be prepared and served as provided in subdivision (h)(2). The court may require that orders or judgments be prepared by a party, may require the party to furnish the court with stamped, addressed envelopes for service of the order or judgment, and may require that proposed orders and judgments be furnished to all parties before entry by the court of the order or judgment.

(2) When a final judgment is entered against a party in default, the court shall mail a conformed copy of it to the party. The party in whose favor the judgment is entered shall furnish the court with a copy of the judgment, unless it is prepared by the court, and the address of the party to be served. If the address is unknown, the copy need not be furnished.

(3) This subdivision is directory and a failure to comply with it does not affect the order or judgment or its finality or any proceedings arising in the action.

Committee Notes

1971 Amendment. Subdivision (g) is added to cover the situation when a party responds by a letter to the clerk and the letter may constitute the party's answer. The clerk is then required to furnish copies to parties who have appeared in the action and who are not shown to have received copies. It is not intended to apply to those litigious persons appearing in proper person who are familiar with the requirements of the rules. Subdivision (h) is added and the first part regulates the service of copies of orders. When a party is charged with preparation of an order, it requires service of the proposed form on other parties and delivery of sufficient copies to the court to be conformed and furnished to all parties after entry. The second part is intended to notify defendant whose address is known of the determination of the action by the court. Failure to comply with either part of subdivision (h) does not affect the order or judgment in any manner.

1972 Amendment. Subdivision (h) is amended because confusion has resulted in its application. Use of the term "party" has been misconstrued. It must be read in conjunction with subdivision (b) of the rule. When service can be made on an attorney, it should be made on the attorney. The term "party" is used throughout the rules because subdivision (b) makes the necessary substitution of the party's attorney throughout the rules. No certificate of service is required. The notation with the names of the persons served with a proposed form is not to be signed. The committee intended for the court to know who had been served only. Otherwise, the committee would have used the form of certificate of service in subdivision (f). Submission of copies and mailing of them by the court has proved cumbersome in practice and so it is deleted. The purpose of the rule was to ensure that all parties had an opportunity to see the proposed form before entry by the court.

1976 Amendment. The amendment made to this rule on July 26, 1972, was intended according to the committee notes "[t]o assure that all parties had an opportunity to see the proposed form before entry by the Court." This change followed on the heels of the 1971 amendment, which the committee felt had been confusing.

Two changes have been made to subdivision (h)(1), which have resulted in a wholesale redrafting of the rule. First, the provision requiring the submission of proposed orders to all counsel prior to entry by the court has been deleted, any inaccuracies in an order submitted to the court being remediable either by the court's own vigilance or later application by an interested party. Secondly, the rule now requires that conformed copies of any order entered by the court must be mailed to all parties of record in all instances (and to defaulted parties in 2 specified instances), for purposes of advising them of the date of the court's action as well as the substance of such action. Nothing in this new rule is meant to limit the power of the court to delegate the ministerial function of preparing orders.

1992 Amendment. Subdivisions (b) and (f) are amended to allow service pursuant to this rule to be made by facsimile. "Facsimile" or "fax" is a copy of a paper transmitted by electronic means to a printer receiving the transmission at a designated telephone number. When service is made by facsimile or fax, a second copy must be served by any other method permitted by this rule to ensure that a legible copy is received.

Court Commentary

1984 Amendment. The committee is recommending an amendment to rule 1.530(b) to cure the confusion created by *Casto v. Casto*, 404 So. 2d 1046 (Fla. 4th DCA 1980). That recommendation requires an amendment to rule 1.080(e) specifying that the date of filing is that shown on the face of the paper.

RULE 1.090. TIME

(a) **Computation.** In computing any period of time prescribed or allowed by these rules, by order of court, or by any applicable statute, the day of the act, event, or default from which the designated period of time begins to run shall not be included. The last day of the period so computed shall be included unless it is a Saturday, Sunday, or legal holiday, in which event the period shall run until the end of the next day which is neither a Saturday, Sunday, or legal holiday. When the period of time prescribed or allowed is less than 7 days, intermediate Saturdays, Sundays, and legal holidays shall be excluded in the computation.

(b) **Enlargement.** When an act is required or allowed to be done at or within a specified time by order of court, by these rules, or by notice given thereunder, for cause shown the court at any time in its discretion (1) with or without notice, may order the period enlarged if request therefor is made before the expiration of the period originally prescribed or as extended by a previous order, or (2) upon motion made and notice after the expiration of the specified period, may permit the act to be done when failure to act was the result of excusable neglect, but it may not extend the time for making a motion for new trial, for rehearing, or to alter or amend a judgment; making a motion for relief from a judgment under rule 1.540(b); taking an appeal or filing a petition for certiorari; or making a motion for a directed verdict.

(c) **Unaffected by Expiration of Term.** The period of time provided for the doing of any act or the taking of any proceeding shall not be affected or limited by the continued existence or expiration of a term of court. The continued existence or expiration of a term of court in no way affects the power of a court to do any act or take any proceeding in any action which is or has been pending before it.

(d) **For Motions.** A copy of any written motion which may not be heard ex parte and a copy of the notice of the hearing thereof shall be served a reasonable time before the time specified for the hearing.

(e) **Additional Time after Service by Mail.** When a party has the right or is required to do some act or take some proceeding within a prescribed period after the service of a notice or other paper upon that party and the notice or paper is served upon that party by mail, 5 days shall be added to the prescribed period.

RULE 1.100. PLEADINGS AND MOTIONS

(a) **Pleadings.** There shall be a complaint or, when so designated by a statute or rule, a petition, and an answer to it; an answer to a counterclaim denominated as such; an answer to a crossclaim if the answer contains a crossclaim; a third-party complaint if a person who was not an original party is summoned as a third-party defendant; and a third-party answer if a third-party complaint is served. If an answer or third-party answer contains an affirmative defense and the opposing party seeks to avoid it, the opposing party shall file a reply containing the avoidance. No other pleadings shall be allowed.

(b) **Motions.** An application to the court for an order shall be by motion which shall be made in writing unless made during a hearing or trial, shall state with particularity the grounds therefor, and shall set forth the relief or order sought. The requirement of writing is fulfilled if the motion is stated in a written notice of the hearing of the motion. All notices of hearing shall specify each motion or other matter to be heard.

(c) Caption.

(1) Every pleading, motion, order, judgment, or other paper shall have a caption containing the name of the court, the file number, and except for in rem proceedings, including forfeiture proceedings, the name of the first party on each side with an appropriate indication of other parties, and a designation identifying the party filing it and its nature or the nature of the order, as the case may be. In any in rem proceeding, every pleading, motion, order, judgment, or other paper shall have a caption containing the name of the court, the file number, the style "In re" (followed by the name or general description of the property), and a designation of the person or entity filing it and its nature or the nature of the order, as the case may be. In an in rem forfeiture proceeding, the style shall be "In re forfeiture of" (followed by the name or general description of the property). All papers filed in the action shall be styled in such a manner as to indicate clearly the subject matter of the paper and the party requesting or obtaining relief.

(2) A civil cover sheet (form 1.997) shall be completed and filed with the clerk at the time an initial complaint or petition is filed by the party initiating the action. If the cover sheet is not filed, the clerk shall accept the complaint or petition for filing; but all proceedings in the action shall be abated until a properly executed cover sheet is completed and filed. The clerk shall complete the civil cover sheet for a party appearing pro se.

(3) A final disposition form (form 1.998) shall be filed with the clerk by the prevailing party at the time of the filing of the order or judgment which disposes of the action. If the action is settled without a court order or judgment being entered, or dismissed by the parties, the plaintiff or petitioner immediately shall file a final disposition form (form 1.998) with the clerk. The clerk shall complete the final disposition form for a party appearing pro se, or when the action is dismissed by court order for lack of prosecution pursuant to rule 1.420(e).

(d) Motion in Lieu of Scire Facias. Any relief available by scire facias may be granted on motion after notice without the issuance of a writ of scire facias.

Committee Notes

1971 Amendment. The change requires a more complete designation of the document that is filed so that it may be more rapidly identified. It also specifies the applicability of the subdivision to all of the various documents that can be filed. For example, a motion to dismiss should now be entitled "defendant's motion to dismiss the complaint" rather than merely "motion" or "motion to dismiss."

1972 Amendment. Subdivision (a) is amended to make a reply mandatory when a party seeks to avoid an affirmative defense in an answer or third-party answer. It is intended to eliminate thereby the problems exemplified by *Tuggle v. Maddox*, 60 So. 2d 158 (Fla. 1952), and *Dickerson v. Orange State Oil Co.*, 123 So. 2d 562 (Fla. 2d DCA 1960).

1992 Amendment. Subdivision (b) is amended to require all notices of hearing to specify the motions or other matters to be heard.

2010 Amendment. Subdivision (c) is amended to address separately the caption for in rem proceedings, including in rem forfeiture proceedings.

RULE 1.110. GENERAL RULES OF PLEADING

(a) Forms of Pleadings. Forms of action and technical forms for seeking relief and of pleas, pleadings, or motions are abolished.

(b) Claims for Relief. A pleading which sets forth a claim for relief, whether an original claim, counterclaim, crossclaim, or third-party claim, must state a cause of action and shall contain (1) a short and plain statement of the grounds upon which the court's jurisdiction depends, unless the court already has jurisdiction and the claim needs no new grounds of jurisdiction to support it, (2) a short and plain statement of the ultimate facts showing that the pleader is entitled to relief, and (3) a demand for judgment for the relief to which the pleader deems himself or herself entitled. Relief in the alternative

Florida Rules of Civil Procedure 2012

or of several different types may be demanded. Every complaint shall be considered to demand general relief.

When filing an action for foreclosure of a mortgage on residential real property the complaint shall be verified. When verification of a document is required, the document filed shall include an oath, affirmation, or the following statement:

"Under penalty of perjury, I declare that I have read the foregoing, and the facts alleged therein are true and correct to the best of my knowledge and belief."

(c) The Answer. In the answer a pleader shall state in short and plain terms the pleader's defenses to each claim asserted and shall admit or deny the averments on which the adverse party relies. If the defendant is without knowledge, the defendant shall so state and such statement shall operate as a denial. Denial shall fairly meet the substance of the averments denied. When a pleader intends in good faith to deny only a part of an averment, the pleader shall specify so much of it as is true and shall deny the remainder. Unless the pleader intends in good faith to controvert all of the averments of the preceding pleading, the pleader may make denials as specific denials of designated averments or may generally deny all of the averments except such designated averments as the pleader expressly admits, but when the pleader does so intend to controvert all of its averments, including averments of the grounds upon which the court's jurisdiction depends, the pleader may do so by general denial.

(d) Affirmative Defenses. In pleading to a preceding pleading a party shall set forth affirmatively accord and satisfaction, arbitration and award, assumption of risk, contributory negligence, discharge in bankruptcy, duress, estoppel, failure of consideration, fraud, illegality, injury by fellow servant, laches, license, payment, release, res judicata, statute of frauds, statute of limitations, waiver, and any other matter constituting an avoidance or affirmative defense. When a party has mistakenly designated a defense as a counterclaim or a counterclaim as a defense, the court, on terms if justice so requires, shall treat the pleading as if there had been a proper designation. Affirmative defenses appearing on the face of a prior pleading may be asserted as grounds for a motion or defense under rule 1.140(b); provided this shall not limit amendments under rule 1.190 even if such ground is sustained.

(e) Effect of Failure to Deny. Averments in a pleading to which a responsive pleading is required, other than those as to the amount of damages, are admitted when not denied in the responsive pleading. Averments in a pleading to which no responsive pleading is required or permitted shall be taken as denied or avoided.

(f) Separate Statements. All averments of claim or defense shall be made in consecutively numbered paragraphs, the contents of each of which shall be limited as far as practicable to a statement of a single set of circumstances, and a paragraph may be referred to by number in all subsequent pleadings. Each claim founded upon a separate transaction or occurrence and each defense other than denials shall be stated in a separate count or defense when a separation facilitates the clear presentation of the matter set forth.

(g) Joinder of Causes of Action; Consistency. A pleader may set up in the same action as many claims or causes of action or defenses in the same right as the pleader has, and claims for relief may be stated in the alternative if separate items make up the cause of action, or if 2 or more causes of action are joined. A party may also set forth 2 or more statements of a claim or defense alternatively, either in 1 count or defense or in separate counts or defenses. When 2 or more statements are made in the alternative and 1 of them, if made independently, would be sufficient, the pleading is not made insufficient by the insufficiency of 1 or more of the alternative statements. A party may also state as many separate claims or defenses as that party has, regardless of consistency and whether based on legal or equitable grounds or both. All pleadings shall be construed so as to do substantial justice.

(h) Subsequent Pleadings. When the nature of an action permits pleadings subsequent to final judgment and the jurisdiction of the court over the parties has not terminated, the initial pleading subsequent to final judgment shall be designated a supplemental complaint or petition. The action shall then proceed in the same manner and time as though the supplemental complaint or petition were the

11

initial pleading in the action, including the issuance of any needed process. This subdivision shall not apply to proceedings that may be initiated by motion under these rules.

Committee Notes

1971 Amendment. Subdivision (h) is added to cover a situation usually arising in divorce judgment modifications, supplemental declaratory relief actions, or trust supervision. When any subsequent proceeding results in a pleading in the strict technical sense under rule 1.100(a), response by opposing parties will follow the same course as though the new pleading were the initial pleading in the action. The time for answering and authority for defenses under rule 1.140 will apply. The last sentence exempts post judgment motions under rules 1.480(c), 1.530, and 1.540, and similar proceedings from its purview.

RULE 1.120. PLEADING SPECIAL MATTERS

(a) Capacity. It is not necessary to aver the capacity of a party to sue or be sued, the authority of a party to sue or be sued in a representative capacity, or the legal existence of an organized association of persons that is made a party, except to the extent required to show the jurisdiction of the court. The initial pleading served on behalf of a minor party shall specifically aver the age of the minor party. When a party desires to raise an issue as to the legal existence of any party, the capacity of any party to sue or be sued, or the authority of a party to sue or be sued in a representative capacity, that party shall do so by specific negative averment which shall include such supporting particulars as are peculiarly within the pleader's knowledge.

(b) Fraud, Mistake, Condition of the Mind. In all averments of fraud or mistake, the circumstances constituting fraud or mistake shall be stated with such particularity as the circumstances may permit. Malice, intent, knowledge, mental attitude, and other condition of mind of a person may be averred generally.

(c) Conditions Precedent. In pleading the performance or occurrence of conditions precedent, it is sufficient to aver generally that all conditions precedent have been performed or have occurred. A denial of performance or occurrence shall be made specifically and with particularity.

(d) Official Document or Act. In pleading an official document or official act it is sufficient to aver that the document was issued or the act done in compliance with law.

(e) Judgment or Decree. In pleading a judgment or decree of a domestic or foreign court, a judicial or quasi-judicial tribunal, or a board or officer, it is sufficient to aver the judgment or decree without setting forth matter showing jurisdiction to render it.

(f) Time and Place. For the purpose of testing the sufficiency of a pleading, averments of time and place are material and shall be considered like all other averments of material matter.

(g) Special Damage. When items of special damage are claimed, they shall be specifically stated.

RULE 1.130. ATTACHING COPY OF CAUSE OF ACTION AND EXHIBITS

(a) Instruments Attached. All bonds, notes, bills of exchange, contracts, accounts, or documents upon which action may be brought or defense made, or a copy thereof or a copy of the portions thereof material to the pleadings, shall be incorporated in or attached to the pleading. No papers shall be unnecessarily annexed as exhibits. The pleadings shall contain no unnecessary recitals of deeds, documents, contracts, or other instruments.

(b) Part for All Purposes. Any exhibit attached to a pleading shall be considered a part thereof for all purposes. Statements in a pleading may be adopted by reference in a different part of the same pleading, in another pleading, or in any motion.

RULE 1.140. DEFENSES

(a) **When Presented.**

(1) Unless a different time is prescribed in a statute of Florida, a defendant shall serve an answer within 20 days after service of original process and the initial pleading on the defendant, or not later than the date fixed in a notice by publication. A party served with a pleading stating a crossclaim against that party shall serve an answer to it within 20 days after service on that party. The plaintiff shall serve an answer to a counterclaim within 20 days after service of the counterclaim. If a reply is required, the reply shall be served within 20 days after service of the answer.

(2) (A) Except when sued pursuant to section 768.28, Florida Statutes, the state of Florida, an agency of the state, or an officer or employee of the state sued in an official capacity shall serve an answer to the complaint or crossclaim, or a reply to a counterclaim, within 40 days after service.

(B) When sued pursuant to section 768.28, Florida Statutes, the Department of Financial Services or the defendant state agency shall have 30 days from the date of service within which to serve an answer to the complaint or crossclaim or a reply to a counterclaim.

(3) The service of a motion under this rule, except a motion for judgment on the pleadings or a motion to strike under subdivision (f), alters these periods of time so that if the court denies the motion or postpones its disposition until the trial on the merits, the responsive pleadings shall be served within 10 days after notice of the court's action or, if the court grants a motion for a more definite statement, the responsive pleadings shall be served within 10 days after service of the more definite statement unless a different time is fixed by the court in either case.

(4) If the court permits or requires an amended or responsive pleading or a more definite statement, the pleading or statement shall be served within 10 days after notice of the court's action. Responses to the pleadings or statements shall be served within 10 days of service of the pleadings or statements.

(b) **How Presented.** Every defense in law or fact to a claim for relief in a pleading shall be asserted in the responsive pleading, if one is required, but the following defenses may be made by motion at the option of the pleader: (1) lack of jurisdiction over the subject matter, (2) lack of jurisdiction over the person, (3) improper venue, (4) insufficiency of process, (5) insufficiency of service of process, (6) failure to state a cause of action, and (7) failure to join indispensable parties. A motion making any of these defenses shall be made before pleading if a further pleading is permitted. The grounds on which any of the enumerated defenses are based and the substantial matters of law intended to be argued shall be stated specifically and with particularity in the responsive pleading or motion. Any ground not stated shall be deemed to be waived except any ground showing that the court lacks jurisdiction of the subject matter may be made at any time. No defense or objection is waived by being joined with other defenses or objections in a responsive pleading or motion. If a pleading sets forth a claim for relief to which the adverse party is not required to serve a responsive pleading, the adverse party may assert any defense in law or fact to that claim for relief at the trial, except that the objection of failure to state a legal defense in an answer or reply shall be asserted by motion to strike the defense within 20 days after service of the answer or reply.

(c) **Motion for Judgment on the Pleadings.** After the pleadings are closed, but within such time as not to delay the trial, any party may move for judgment on the pleadings.

(d) **Preliminary Hearings.** The defenses 1 to 7 in subdivision (b) of this rule, whether made in a pleading or by motion, and the motion for judgment in subdivision (c) of this rule shall be heard and determined before trial on application of any party unless the court orders that the hearing and determination shall be deferred until the trial.

(e) **Motion for More Definite Statement.** If a pleading to which a responsive pleading is permitted is so vague or ambiguous that a party cannot reasonably be required to frame a responsive pleading, that party may move for a more definite statement before interposing a responsive pleading. The motion shall point out the defects complained of and the details desired. If the motion is granted and the order of the court is not obeyed within 10 days after notice of the order or such other time as the court may fix, the court may strike the pleading to which the motion was directed or make such order as it deems just.

(f) Motion to Strike. A party may move to strike or the court may strike redundant, immaterial, impertinent, or scandalous matter from any pleading at any time.

(g) Consolidation of Defenses. A party who makes a motion under this rule may join with it the other motions herein provided for and then available to that party. If a party makes a motion under this rule but omits from it any defenses or objections then available to that party that this rule permits to be raised by motion, that party shall not thereafter make a motion based on any of the defenses or objections omitted, except as provided in subdivision (h)(2) of this rule.

(h) Waiver of Defenses.

(1) A party waives all defenses and objections that the party does not present either by motion under subdivisions (b), (e), or (f) of this rule or, if the party has made no motion, in a responsive pleading except as provided in subdivision (h)(2).

(2) The defenses of failure to state a cause of action or a legal defense or to join an indispensable party may be raised by motion for judgment on the pleadings or at the trial on the merits in addition to being raised either in a motion under subdivision (b) or in the answer or reply. The defense of lack of jurisdiction of the subject matter may be raised at any time.

Committee Notes

1972 Amendment. Subdivision (a) is amended to eliminate the unnecessary statement of the return date when service is made by publication, and to accommodate the change proposed in rule 1.100(a) making a reply mandatory under certain circumstances. Motions to strike under subdivision (f) are divided into 2 categories, so subdivision (a) is also amended to accommodate this change by eliminating motions to strike under the new subdivision (f) as motions that toll the running of time. A motion to strike an insufficient legal defense will now be available under subdivision (b) and continue to toll the time for responsive pleading. Subdivision (b) is amended to include the defense of failure to state a sufficient legal defense. The proper method of attack for failure to state a legal defense remains a motion to strike. Subdivision (f) is changed to accommodate the 2 types of motions to strike. The motion to strike an insufficient legal defense is now in subdivision (b). The motion to strike under subdivision (f) does not toll the time for responsive pleading and can be made at any time, and the matter can be stricken by the court on its initiative at any time. Subdivision (g) follows the terminology of Federal Rule of Civil Procedure 12(g). Much difficulty has been experienced in the application of this and the succeeding subdivision with the result that the same defenses are being raised several times in an action. The intent of the rule is to permit the defenses to be raised one time, either by motion or by the responsive pleading, and thereafter only by motion for judgment on the pleadings or at the trial. Subdivision (h) also reflects this philosophy. It is based on federal rule 12(h) but more clearly states the purpose of the rule.

1988 Amendment. The amendment to subdivision (a) is to fix a time within which amended pleadings, responsive pleadings, or more definite statements required by the court and responses to those pleadings or statements must be served when no time limit is fixed by the court in its order. The court's authority to alter these time periods is contained in rule 1.090(b).

2007 Amendment. Subdivision (a) is amended to conform rule 1.140 to the statutory requirements of sections 48.111, 48.121, and 768.28, Florida Statutes. The rule is similar to Federal Rule of Civil Procedure 12(a).

RULE 1.150. SHAM PLEADINGS

(a) Motion to Strike. If a party deems any pleading or part thereof filed by another party to be a sham, that party may move to strike the pleading or part thereof before the cause is set for trial and the court shall hear the motion, taking evidence of the respective parties, and if the motion is sustained, the pleading to which the motion is directed shall be stricken. Default and summary judgment on the merits may be entered in the discretion of the court or the court may permit additional pleadings to be filed for good cause shown.

(b) **Contents of Motion.** The motion to strike shall be verified and shall set forth fully the facts on which the movant relies and may be supported by affidavit. No traverse of the motion shall be required.

RULE 1.160. MOTIONS

All motions and applications in the clerk's office for the issuance of mesne process and final process to enforce and execute judgments, for entering defaults, and for such other proceedings in the clerk's office as do not require an order of court shall be deemed motions and applications grantable as of course by the clerk. The clerk's action may be suspended or altered or rescinded by the court upon cause shown.

RULE 1.170. COUNTERCLAIMS AND CROSSCLAIMS

(a) **Compulsory Counterclaims.** A pleading shall state as a counterclaim any claim which at the time of serving the pleading the pleader has against any opposing party, provided it arises out of the transaction or occurrence that is the subject matter of the opposing party's claim and does not require for its adjudication the presence of third parties over whom the court cannot acquire jurisdiction. But the pleader need not state a claim if (1) at the time the action was commenced the claim was the subject of another pending action, or (2) the opposing party brought suit upon that party's claim by attachment or other process by which the court did not acquire jurisdiction to render a personal judgment on the claim and the pleader is not stating a counterclaim under this rule.

(b) **Permissive Counterclaim.** A pleading may state as a counterclaim any claim against an opposing party not arising out of the transaction or occurrence that is the subject matter of the opposing party's claim.

(c) **Counterclaim** Exceeding Opposing Claim. A counterclaim may or may not diminish or defeat the recovery sought by the opposing party. It may claim relief exceeding in amount or different in kind from that sought in the pleading of the opposing party.

(d) **Counterclaim against the State.** These rules shall not be construed to enlarge beyond the limits established by law the right to assert counterclaims or to claim credits against the state or any of its subdivisions or other governmental organizations thereof subject to suit or against a municipal corporation or against an officer, agency, or administrative board of the state.

(e) **Counterclaim Maturing or Acquired after Pleading.** A claim which matured or was acquired by the pleader after serving the pleading may be presented as a counterclaim by supplemental pleading with the permission of the court.

(f) **Omitted Counterclaim or Crossclaim.** When a pleader fails to set up a counterclaim or crossclaim through oversight, inadvertence, or excusable neglect, or when justice requires, the pleader may set up the counterclaim or crossclaim by amendment with leave of the court.

(g) **Crossclaim against Co-Party.** A pleading may state as a crossclaim any claim by one party against a co-party arising out of the transaction or occurrence that is the subject matter of either the original action or a counterclaim therein, or relating to any property that is the subject matter of the original action. The crossclaim may include a claim that the party against whom it is asserted is or may be liable to the crossclaimant for all or part of a claim asserted in the action against the crossclaimant. Service of a crossclaim on a party who has appeared in the action shall be made pursuant to rule 1.080(b). Service of a crossclaim against a party who has not appeared in the action shall be made in the manner provided for service of summons.

(h) **Additional Parties May Be Brought In.** When the presence of parties other than those to the original action is required to grant complete relief in the determination of a counterclaim or crossclaim, they shall be named in the counterclaim or crossclaim and be served with process and shall be parties to the action thereafter if jurisdiction of them can be obtained and their joinder will not deprive the court of jurisdiction of the action. Rules 1.250(b) and (c) apply to parties brought in under this subdivision.

(i) **Separate Trials; Separate Judgment.** If the court orders separate trials as provided in rule 1.270(b), judgment on a counterclaim or crossclaim may be rendered when the court has jurisdiction to do so even if a claim of the opposing party has been dismissed or otherwise disposed of.

(j) **Demand Exceeding Jurisdiction; Transfer of Action.** If the demand of any counterclaim or crossclaim exceeds the jurisdiction of the court in which the action is pending, the action shall be transferred forthwith to the court of the same county having jurisdiction of the demand in the counterclaim or crossclaim with only such alterations in the pleadings as are essential. The court shall order the transfer of the action and the transmittal of all papers in it to the proper court if the party asserting the demand exceeding the jurisdiction deposits with the court having jurisdiction a sum sufficient to pay the clerk's service charge in the court to which the action is transferred at the time of filing the counterclaim or crossclaim. Thereupon the original papers and deposit shall be transmitted and filed with a certified copy of the order. The court to which the action is transferred shall have full power and jurisdiction over the demands of all parties. Failure to make the service charge deposit at the time the counterclaim or crossclaim is filed, or within such further time as the court may allow, shall reduce a claim for damages to an amount within the jurisdiction of the court where the action is pending and waive the claim in other cases.

Committee Notes

1972 Amendment. Subdivision (h) is amended to conform with the philosophy of the 1968 amendment to rule 1.250(c). No justification exists to require more restrictive joinder provisions for counterclaims and crossclaims than is required for the initial pleading. The only safeguard required is that joinder does not deprive the court of jurisdiction. Subdivision (j) is amended to require deposit of the service charge for transfer when a counterclaim or crossclaim exceeding the jurisdiction of the court in which the action is pending is filed. This cures a practical problem when the defendant files a counterclaim or crossclaim exceeding the jurisdiction but neglects to pay the service charge to the court to which the action is transferred. The matter then remains in limbo and causes procedural difficulties in progressing the action.

1988 Amendment. The last 2 sentences were added to subdivision (g) to counter the construction of these rules and section 48.031(1), Florida Statutes, by an appellate court in *Fundaro v. Canadiana Corp.*, 409 So. 2d 1099 (Fla. 4th DCA 1982), to require service of all crossclaims with summons pursuant to rule 1.070. The purpose of this amendment is to make it clear that crossclaims must be served as initial pleadings only against a party who has not previously entered an appearance in the action.

RULE 1.180. THIRD-PARTY PRACTICE

(a) **When Available.** At any time after commencement of the action a defendant may have a summons and complaint served on a person not a party to the action who is or may be liable to the defendant for all or part of the plaintiff's claim against the defendant, and may also assert any other claim that arises out of the transaction or occurrence that is the subject matter of the plaintiff's claim. The defendant need not obtain leave of court if the defendant files the third-party complaint not later than 20 days after the defendant serves the original answer. Otherwise, the defendant must obtain leave on motion and notice to all parties to the action. The person served with the summons and third-party complaint, herein called the third-party defendant, shall make defenses to the defendant's claim as provided in rules 1.110 and 1.140 and counterclaims against the defendant and crossclaims against other third-party defendants as provided in rule 1.170. The third-party defendant may assert against the plaintiff any defenses that the defendant has to the plaintiff's claim. The third-party defendant may also assert any claim against the plaintiff arising out of the transaction or occurrence that is the subject matter of the plaintiff's claim against the defendant. The plaintiff may assert any claim against the third-party defendant arising out of the transaction or occurrence that is the subject matter of the plaintiff's claim against the defendant, and the third-party defendant thereupon shall assert a defense as provided in rules 1.110 and 1.140 and counterclaims and crossclaims as provided in rule 1.170. Any party may move to strike the third-party claim or for its severance or separate trial. A third-party defendant may proceed under this rule against any person not a party to the action who is or may be liable to the third-party defendant for all or part of the claim made in the action against the third-party defendant.

(b) When Plaintiff May Bring in Third Party. When a counterclaim is asserted against the plaintiff, the plaintiff may bring in a third party under circumstances which would entitle a defendant to do so under this rule.

Court Commentary

1984 Amendment. Subdivision (a) is amended to permit the defendant to have the same right to assert claims arising out of the transaction or occurrence that all of the other parties to the action have. It overrules the decisions in *Miramar Construction, Inc. v. El Conquistador Condominium*, 303 So. 2d 81 (Fla. 3d DCA 1974), and *Richard's Paint Mfg. Co. v. Onyx Paints, Inc.*, 363 So. 2d 596 (Fla. 4th DCA 1978), to that extent. The term defendant is used throughout instead of third-party plaintiff for clarity and brevity reasons and refers to the defendant serving the summons and third-party complaint on a third-party defendant or, when applicable, to the similar summons and fourth party.

RULE 1.190. AMENDED AND SUPPLEMENTAL PLEADINGS

(a) Amendments. A party may amend a pleading once as a matter of course at any time before a responsive pleading is served or, if the pleading is one to which no responsive pleading is permitted and the action has not been placed on the trial calendar, may so amend it at any time within 20 days after it is served. Otherwise a party may amend a pleading only by leave of court or by written consent of the adverse party. If a party files a motion to amend a pleading, the party shall attach the proposed amended pleading to the motion. Leave of court shall be given freely when justice so requires. A party shall plead in response to an amended pleading within 10 days after service of the amended pleading unless the court otherwise orders.

(b) Amendments to Conform with the Evidence. When issues not raised by the pleadings are tried by express or implied consent of the parties, they shall be treated in all respects as if they had been raised in the pleadings. Such amendment of the pleadings as may be necessary to cause them to conform to the evidence and to raise these issues may be made upon motion of any party at any time, even after judgment, but failure so to amend shall not affect the result of the trial of these issues. If the evidence is objected to at the trial on the ground that it is not within the issues made by the pleadings, the court may allow the pleadings to be amended to conform with the evidence and shall do so freely when the merits of the cause are more effectually presented thereby and the objecting party fails to satisfy the court that the admission of such evidence will prejudice the objecting party in maintaining an action or defense upon the merits.

(c) Relation Back of Amendments. When the claim or defense asserted in the amended pleading arose out of the conduct, transaction, or occurrence set forth or attempted to be set forth in the original pleading, the amendment shall relate back to the date of the original pleading.

(d) Supplemental Pleadings. Upon motion of a party the court may permit that party, upon reasonable notice and upon such terms as are just, to serve a supplemental pleading setting forth transactions or occurrences or events which have happened since the date of the pleading sought to be supplemented. If the court deems it advisable that the adverse party plead thereto, it shall so order, specifying the time therefor.

(e) Amendments Generally. At any time in furtherance of justice, upon such terms as may be just, the court may permit any process, proceeding, pleading, or record to be amended or material supplemental matter to be set forth in an amended or supplemental pleading. At every stage of the action the court must disregard any error or defect in the proceedings which does not affect the substantial rights of the parties.

(f) Claims for Punitive Damages. A motion for leave to amend a pleading to assert a claim for punitive damages shall make a reasonable showing, by evidence in the record or evidence to be proffered by the claimant, that provides a reasonable basis for recovery of such damages. The motion to amend can be filed separately and before the supporting evidence or proffer, but each shall be served on all parties at least 20 days before the hearing.

Committee Notes

1980 Amendment. The last clause of subdivision (a) is deleted to restore the decision in *Scarfone v. Denby*, 156 So. 2d 694 (Fla. 2d DCA 1963). The adoption of rule 1.500 requiring notice of an application for default after filing or serving of any paper eliminates the need for the clause. This will permit reinstatement of the procedure in federal practice and earlier Florida practice requiring a response to each amended pleading, thus simplifying the court file under the doctrine of *Dee v. Southern Brewing Co.*, 146 Fla. 588, 1 So. 2d 562 (1941).

2003 Amendment. Subdivision (a) is amended in accordance with *Totura & Co., Inc. v. Williams*, 754 So. 2d 671 (Fla. 2000). See the amendment to rule 1.070(j). Subdivision (f) is added to state the requirements for a party moving for leave of court to amend a pleading to assert a claim for punitive damages. See *Beverly Health & Rehabilitation Services, Inc. v. Meeks*, 778 So. 2d 322 (Fla. 2d DCA 2000).

RULE 1.200. PRETRIAL PROCEDURE

(a) Case Management Conference. At any time after responsive pleadings or motions are due, the court may order, or a party, by serving a notice, may convene, a case management conference. The matter to be considered shall be specified in the order or notice setting the conference. At such a conference the court may:

(1) schedule or reschedule the service of motions, pleadings, and other papers;

(2) set or reset the time of trials, subject to rule 1.440(c);

(3) coordinate the progress of the action if the complex litigation factors contained in rule 1.201(a)(2)(A)–(a)(2)(H) are present;

(4) limit, schedule, order, or expedite discovery;

(5) schedule disclosure of expert witnesses and the discovery of facts known and opinions held by such experts;

(6) schedule or hear motions in limine;

(7) pursue the possibilities of settlement;

(8) require filing of preliminary stipulations if issues can be narrowed;

(9) consider referring issues to a magistrate for findings of fact; and

(10) schedule other conferences or determine other matters that may aid in the disposition of the action.

(b) Pretrial Conference. After the action is at issue the court itself may or shall on the timely motion of any party require the parties to appear for a conference to consider and determine:

(1) the simplification of the issues;

(2) the necessity or desirability of amendments to the pleadings;

(3) the possibility of obtaining admissions of fact and of documents that will avoid unnecessary proof;

(4) the limitation of the number of expert witnesses;

(5) the potential use of juror notebooks; and

(6) any matters permitted under subdivision (a) of this rule.

(c) Notice. Reasonable notice shall be given for a case management conference, and 20 days' notice shall be given for a pretrial conference. On failure of a party to attend a conference, the court may dismiss the action, strike the pleadings, limit proof or witnesses, or take any other appropriate action. Any documents that the court requires for any conference shall be specified in the order. Orders setting pretrial conferences shall be uniform throughout the territorial jurisdiction of the court.

(d) Pretrial Order. The court shall make an order reciting the action taken at a conference and any stipulations made. The order shall control the subsequent course of the action unless modified to prevent injustice.

Committee Notes

1971 Amendment. The 3 paragraphs of the rule are lettered and given subtitles. The present last paragraph is placed second as subdivision (b) because the proceeding required under it is taken before that in the present second paragraph. The time for implementation is changed from settling the issues because the language is erroneous, the purpose of the conference being to settle some and prepare for the trial of other issues. The last 2 sentences of subdivision (b) are added to require uniformity by all judges of the court and to require specification of the documentary requirements for the conference. The last sentence of subdivision (c) is deleted since it is covered by the local rule provisions of rule 1.020(d). The reference to the parties in substitution for attorneys and counsel is one of style because the rules generally impose obligations on the parties except when the attorneys are specifically intended. It should be understood that those parties represented by attorneys will have the attorneys perform for them in the usual manner.

1972 Amendment. Subdivision (a) is amended to require the motion for a pretrial by a party to be timely. This is done to avoid motions for pretrial conferences made a short time before trial and requests for a continuance of the trial as a result of the pretrial conference order. The subdivision is also amended to require the clerk to send to the judge a copy of the motion by a party for the pretrial conference.

1988 Amendment. The purpose of adding subdivision (a)(5) is to spell out clearly for the bench and bar that case management conferences may be used for scheduling the disclosure of expert witnesses and the discovery of the opinion and factual information held by those experts. Subdivision (5) is not intended to expand discovery.

1992 Amendment. Subdivision (a) is amended to allow a party to set a case management conference in the same manner as a party may set a hearing on a motion. Subdivision (c) is amended to remove the mandatory language and make the notice requirement for a case management conference the same as that for a hearing on a motion; *i.e.*, reasonable notice.

Court Commentary

1984 Amendment. This is a substantial rewording of rule 1.200. Subdivision (a) is added to authorize case management conferences in an effort to give the court more control over the progress of the action. All of the matters that the court can do under the case management conference can be done at the present time under other rules or because of the court's authority otherwise. The new subdivision merely emphasizes the court's authority and arranges an orderly method for the exercise of that authority. Subdivisions (a), (b), and (c) of the existing rule are relettered accordingly. Subdivision (a) of the existing rule is also amended to delete the reference to requiring the attorneys to appear at a pretrial conference by referring to the parties for that purpose. This is consistent with the language used throughout the rules and does not contemplate a change in present procedure. Subdivisions (a)(5) and (a)(6) of the existing rule are deleted since they are now covered adequately under the new subdivision (a). Subdivisions (b) and (c) of the existing rule are amended to accommodate the 2 types of conferences that are now authorized by the rules.

RULE 1.201. COMPLEX LITIGATION

(a) **Complex Litigation Defined.** At any time after all defendants have been served, and an appearance has been entered in response to the complaint by each party or a default entered, any party, or the court on its own motion, may move to declare an action complex. However, any party may move to designate an action complex before all defendants have been served subject to a showing to the court why service has not been made on all defendants. The court shall convene a hearing to determine whether the action requires the use of complex litigation procedures and enter an order within 10 days of the conclusion of the hearing.

(1) A "complex action" is one that is likely to involve complicated legal or case management issues and that may require extensive judicial management to expedite the action, keep costs reasonable, or promote judicial efficiency.

(2) In deciding whether an action is complex, the court must consider whether the action is likely to involve:

(A) numerous pretrial motions raising difficult or novel legal issues or legal issues that are inextricably intertwined that will be timeconsuming to resolve;

(B) management of a large number of separately represented parties;

(C) coordination with related actions pending in one or more courts in other counties, states, or countries, or in a federal court;

(D) pretrial management of a large number of witnesses or a substantial amount of documentary evidence;

(E) substantial time required to complete the trial;

(F) management at trial of a large number of experts, witnesses, attorneys, or exhibits;

(G) substantial postjudgment judicial supervision; and

(H) any other analytical factors identified by the court or a party that tend to complicate comparable actions and which are likely to arise in the context of the instant action.

(3) If all of the parties, pro se or through counsel, sign and file with the clerk of the court a written stipulation to the fact that an action is complex and identifying the factors in (2)(A) through (2)(H) above that apply, the court shall enter an order designating the action as complex without a hearing.

(b) **Initial Case Management Report and Conference.** The court shall hold an initial case management conference within 60 days from the date of the order declaring the action complex.

(1) At least 20 days prior to the date of the initial case management conference, attorneys for the parties as well as any parties appearing pro se shall confer and prepare a joint statement, which shall be filed with the clerk of the court no later than 14 days before the conference, outlining a discovery plan and stating:

(A) a brief factual statement of the action, which includes the claims and defenses;

(B) a brief statement on the theory of damages by any party seeking affirmative relief;

(C) the likelihood of settlement;

(D) the likelihood of appearance in the action of additional parties and identification of any nonparties to whom any of the parties will seek to allocate fault;

(E) the proposed limits on the time: (i) to join other parties and to amend the pleadings, (ii) to file and hear motions, (iii) to identify any nonparties whose identity is known, or otherwise describe as specifically as practicable any nonparties whose identity is not known, (iv) to disclose expert witnesses, and (v) to complete discovery;

(F) the names of the attorneys responsible for handling the action;

(G) the necessity for a protective order to facilitate discovery;

(H) proposals for the formulation and simplification of issues, including the elimination of frivolous claims or defenses, and the number and timing of motions for summary judgment or partial summary judgment;

(I) the possibility of obtaining admissions of fact and voluntary exchange of documents and electronically stored information, stipulations regarding authenticity of documents, electronically stored information, and the need for advance rulings from the court on admissibility of evidence;

(J) suggestions on the advisability and timing of referring matters to a magistrate, master, other neutral, or mediation;

(K) a preliminary estimate of the time required for trial;

(L) requested date or dates for conferences before trial, a final pretrial conference, and trial;

(M) a description of pertinent documents and a list of fact witnesses the parties believe to be relevant;

(N) number of experts and fields of expertise; and

(O) any other information that might be helpful to the court in setting further conferences and the trial date.

(2) Lead trial counsel and a client representative shall attend the initial case management conference.

(3) Notwithstanding rule 1.440, at the initial case management conference, the court will set the trial date or dates no sooner than 6 months and no later than 24 months from the date of the conference unless good cause is shown for an earlier or later setting. The trial date or dates shall be on a docket having sufficient time within which to try the action and, when feasible, for a date or dates certain. The trial date shall be set after consultation with counsel and in the presence of all clients or authorized client representatives. The court shall, no later than 2 months prior to the date scheduled for jury selection, arrange for a sufficient number of available jurors. Continuance of the trial of a complex action should rarely be granted and then only upon good cause shown.

(c) The Case Management Order. The case management order shall address each matter set forth under rule 1.200(a) and set the action for a pretrial conference and trial. The case management order also shall specify the following:

(1) Dates by which all parties shall name their expert witnesses and provide the expert information required by rule 1.280(b)(4). If a party has named an expert witness in a field in which any other parties have not identified experts, the other parties may name experts in that field within 30 days thereafter. No additional experts may be named unless good cause is shown.

(2) Not more than 10 days after the date set for naming experts, the parties shall meet and schedule dates for deposition of experts and all other witnesses not yet deposed. At the time of the meeting each party is responsible for having secured three confirmed dates for its expert witnesses. In the event the parties cannot agree on a discovery deposition schedule, the court, upon motion, shall set the schedule. Any party may file the completed discovery deposition schedule agreed upon or entered

by the court. Once filed, the deposition dates in the schedule shall not be altered without consent of all parties or upon order of the court. Failure to comply with the discovery schedule may result in sanctions in accordance with rule 1.380.

(3) Dates by which all parties are to complete all other discovery.

(4) The court shall schedule periodic case management conferences and hearings on lengthy motions at reasonable intervals based on the particular needs of the action. The attorneys for the parties as well as any parties appearing pro se shall confer no later than 15 days prior to each case management conference or hearing. They shall notify the court at least 10 days prior to any case management conference or hearing if the parties stipulate that a case management conference or hearing time is unnecessary. Failure to timely notify the court that a case management conference or hearing time is unnecessary may result in sanctions.

(5) The case management order may include a briefing schedule setting forth a time period within which to file briefs or memoranda, responses, and reply briefs or memoranda, prior to the court considering such matters.

(6) A deadline for conducting alternative dispute resolution.

(d) Final Case Management Conference. The court shall schedule a final case management conference not less than 90 days prior to the date the case is set for trial. At least 10 days prior to the final case management conference the parties shall confer to prepare a case status report, which shall be filed with the clerk of the court either prior to or at the time of the final case management conference. The status report shall contain in separately numbered paragraphs:

(1) A list of all pending motions requiring action by the court and the date those motions are set for hearing.

(2) Any change regarding the estimated trial time.

(3) The names of the attorneys who will try the case.

(4) A list of the names and addresses of all nonexpert witnesses (including impeachment and rebuttal witnesses) intended to be called at trial. However, impeachment or rebuttal witnesses not identified in the case status report may be allowed to testify if the need for their testimony could not have been reasonably foreseen at the time the case status report was prepared.

(5) A list of all exhibits intended to be offered at trial.

(6) Certification that copies of witness and exhibit lists will be filed with the clerk of the court at least 48 hours prior to the date and time of the final case management conference.

(7) A deadline for the filing of amended lists of witnesses and exhibits, which amendments shall be allowed only upon motion and for good cause shown.

(8) Any other matters which could impact the timely and effective trial of the action.

RULE 1.210. PARTIES

(a) Parties Generally. Every action may be prosecuted in the name of the real party in interest, but a personal representative, administrator, guardian, trustee of an express trust, a party with whom or in whose name a contract has been made for the benefit of another, or a party expressly authorized by statute may sue in that person's own name without joining the party for whose benefit the action is brought. All persons having an interest in the subject of the action and in obtaining the relief demanded may join as plaintiffs and any person may be made a defendant who has or claims an interest adverse to the plaintiff. Any person may at any time be made a party if that person's presence is necessary or proper to a complete determination of the cause. Persons having a united interest may be joined on the same side as plaintiffs or defendants, and anyone who refuses to join may for such reason be made a defendant.

(b) Minors or Incompetent Persons. When a minor or incompetent person has a representative, such as a guardian or other like fiduciary, the representative may sue or defend on behalf of the minor or incompetent person. A minor or incompetent person who does not have a duly appointed representative may sue by next friend or by a guardian ad litem. The court shall appoint a guardian ad litem for a minor or incompetent person not otherwise represented in an action or shall make such other order as it deems proper for the protection of the minor or incompetent person.

Committee Notes

1980 Amendment. Subdivisions (c) and (d) are deleted. Both are obsolete. They were continued in effect earlier because the committee was uncertain about the need for them at the time. Subdivision (c) has been supplanted by section 737.402(2)(z), Florida Statutes (1979), that gives trustees the power to prosecute and defend actions, regardless of the conditions specified in the subdivision. The adoption of section 733.212, Florida Statutes (1979), eliminates the need for subdivision (d) because it provides an easier and less expensive method of eliminating the interests of an heir at law who is not a beneficiary under the will. To the extent that an heir at law is an indispensable party to a proceeding concerning a testamentary trust, due process requires notice and an opportunity to defend, so the rule would be unconstitutionally applied.

2003 Amendment. In subdivision (a), "an executor" is changed to "a personal representative" to conform to statutory language. See § 731.201(25), Fla. Stat. (2002).

RULE 1.220. CLASS ACTIONS

(a) Prerequisites to Class Representation. Before any claim or defense may be maintained on behalf of a class by one party or more suing or being sued as the representative of all the members of a class, the court shall first conclude that (1) the members of the class are so numerous that separate joinder of each member is impracticable, (2) the claim or defense of the representative party raises questions of law or fact common to the questions of law or fact raised by the claim or defense of each member of the class, (3) the claim or defense of the representative party is typical of the claim or defense of each member of the class, and (4) the representative party can fairly and adequately protect and represent the interests of each member of the class.

(b) Claims and Defenses Maintainable. A claim or defense may be maintained on behalf of a class if the court concludes that the prerequisites of subdivision (a) are satisfied, and that:

(1) the prosecution of separate claims or defenses by or against individual members of the class would create a risk of either:

(A) inconsistent or varying adjudications concerning individual members of the class which would establish incompatible standards of conduct for the party opposing the class; or

(B) adjudications concerning individual members of the class which would, as a practical matter, be dispositive of the interests of other members of the class who are not parties to the adjudications, or substantially impair or impede the ability of other members of the class who are not parties to the adjudications to protect their interests; or

(2) the party opposing the class has acted or refused to act on grounds generally applicable to all the members of the class, thereby making final injunctive relief or declaratory relief concerning the class as a whole appropriate; or

(3) the claim or defense is not maintainable under either subdivision (b)(1) or (b)(2), but the questions of law or fact common to the claim or defense of the representative party and the claim or defense of each member of the class predominate over any question of law or fact affecting only individual members of the class, and class representation is superior to other available methods for the fair and efficient adjudication of the controversy. The conclusions shall be derived from consideration of all relevant facts and circumstances, including (A) the respective interests of each member of the class in individually controlling the prosecution of separate claims or defenses, (B) the nature and extent of any pending litigation to which any member of the class is a party and in which any question of law or fact controverted in the subject action is to be adjudicated, (C) the desirability or

undesirability of concentrating the litigation in the forum where the subject action is instituted, and (D) the difficulties likely to be encountered in the management of the claim or defense on behalf of a class.

(c) **Pleading Requirements.** Any pleading, counterclaim, or crossclaim alleging the existence of a class shall contain the following:

(1) Next to its caption the designation: "Class Representation."

(2) Under a separate heading, designated as "Class Representation Allegations," specific recitation of:

(A) the particular provision of subdivision (b) under which it is claimed that the claim or defense is maintainable on behalf of a class;

(B) the questions of law or fact that are common to the claim or defense of the representative party and the claim or defense of each member of the class;

(C) the particular facts and circumstances that show the claim or defense advanced by the representative party is typical of the claim or defense of each member of the class;

(D) (i) the approximate number of class members, (ii) a definition of the alleged class, and (iii) the particular facts and circumstances that show the representative party will fairly and adequately protect and represent the interests of each member of the class; and

(E) the particular facts and circumstances that support the conclusions required of the court in determining that the action may be maintained as a class action pursuant to the particular provision of subdivision (b) under which it is claimed that the claim or defense is maintainable on behalf of a class.

(d) **Determination of Class Representation; Notice; Judgment: Claim or Defense Maintained Partly on Behalf of a Class.**

(1) As soon as practicable after service of any pleading alleging the existence of a class under this rule and before service of an order for pretrial conference or a notice for trial, after hearing the court shall enter an order determining whether the claim or defense is maintainable on behalf of a class on the application of any party or on the court's initiative. Irrespective of whether the court determines that the claim or defense is maintainable on behalf of a class, the order shall separately state the findings of fact and conclusions of law upon which the determination is based. In making the determination the court (A) may allow the claim or defense to be so maintained, and, if so, shall state under which subsection of subdivision (b) the claim or defense is to be maintained, (B) may disallow the class representation and strike the class representation allegations, or (C) may order postponement of the determination pending the completion of discovery concerning whether the claim or defense is maintainable on behalf of a class. If the court rules that the claim or defense shall be maintained on behalf of a class under subdivision (b)(3), the order shall also provide for the notice required by subdivision (d)(2). If the court rules that the claim or defense shall be maintained on behalf of a class under subdivision (b)(1) or subdivision (b)(2), the order shall also provide for the notice required by subdivision (d)(2), except when a showing is made that the notice is not required, the court may provide for another kind of notice to the class as is appropriate. When the court orders postponement of its determination, the court shall also establish a date, if possible, for further consideration and final disposition of the motion. An order under this subsection may be conditional and may be altered or amended before entry of a judgment on the merits of the action.

(2) As soon as is practicable after the court determines that a claim or defense is maintainable on behalf of a class, notice of the pendency of the claim or defense shall be given by the party asserting the existence of the class to all the members of the class. The notice shall be given to each member of the class who can be identified and located through reasonable effort and shall be given to the other members of the class in the manner determined by the court to be most practicable under the circumstances. Unless otherwise ordered by the court, the party asserting the existence of the class shall initially pay for the cost of giving notice. The notice shall inform each member of the class that (A) any member of the class who files a statement with the court by the date specified in the notice

asking to be excluded shall be excluded from the class, (B) the judgment, whether favorable or not, will include all members who do not request exclusion, and (C) any member who does not request exclusion may make a separate appearance within the time specified in the notice.

(3) The judgment determining a claim or defense maintained on behalf of a class under subdivision (b)(1) or (b)(2), whether or not favorable to the class, shall include and describe those persons whom the court finds to be members of the class. The judgment determining a claim or defense maintained on behalf of a class under subdivision (b)(3), whether or not favorable to the class, shall include and identify those to whom the notice provided in subdivision (d)(2) was directed, who have not requested exclusion and whom the court finds to be members of the class.

(4) When appropriate, (A) a claim or defense may be brought or maintained on behalf of a class concerning particular issues, or (B) class representation may be divided into subclasses, and each subclass may be treated as a separate and distinct class and the provisions of this rule shall be applied accordingly.

(e) **Dismissal or Compromise.** After a claim or defense is determined to be maintainable on behalf of a class under subdivision (d), the claim or defense shall not be voluntarily withdrawn, dismissed, or compromised without approval of the court after notice and hearing. Notice of any proposed voluntary withdrawal, dismissal, or compromise shall be given to all members of the class as the court directs.

Committee Notes

1980 Amendment. The class action rule has been completely revised to bring it in line with modern practice. The rule is based on Federal Rule of Civil Procedure 23, but a number of changes have been made to eliminate problems in the federal rule through court decisions. Generally, the rule provides for the prerequisites to class representation, an early determination about whether the claim or defense is maintainable on behalf of a class, notice to all members of the class, provisions for the members of the class to exclude themselves, the form of judgment, and the procedure governing dismissal or compromise of a claim or defense maintained on behalf of a class. The prerequisites of subdivision (a) are changed from those in federal rule 23 only to the extent necessary to incorporate the criteria enunciated in *Port Royal v. Conboy*, 154 So. 2d 734 (Fla. 2d DCA 1963). The notice requirements have been made more explicit and stringent than those in the federal rule.

RULE 1.221. HOMEOWNERS' ASSOCIATIONS AND CONDOMINIUM ASSOCIATIONS

A homeowners' or condominium association, after control of such association is obtained by homeowners or unit owners other than the developer, may institute, maintain, settle, or appeal actions or hearings in its name on behalf of all association members concerning matters of common interest to the members, including, but not limited to: (1) the common property, area, or elements; (2) the roof or structural components of a building, or other improvements (in the case of homeowners' associations, being specifically limited to those improvements for which the association is responsible); (3) mechanical, electrical, or plumbing elements serving a property or an improvement or building (in the case of homeowners' associations, being specifically limited to those elements for which the association is responsible); (4) representations of the developer pertaining to any existing or proposed commonly used facility; (5) protests of ad valorem taxes on commonly used facilities; and, in the case of homeowners' associations, (6) defense of actions in eminent domain or prosecution of inverse condemnation actions. If an association has the authority to maintain a class action under this rule, the association may be joined in an action as representative of that class with reference to litigation and disputes involving the matters for which the association could bring a class action under this rule. Nothing herein limits any statutory or common law right of any individual homeowner or unit owner, or class of such owners, to bring any action that may otherwise be available. An action under this rule shall not be subject to the requirements of rule 1.220.

Committee Notes

1980 Adoption. The present rule relating to condominium associations [1.220(b)] is left intact but renumbered as rule 1.221.

2007 Amendment. Consistent with amendments to section 720.303(1), Florida Statutes, homeowners' associations have been added to the rule.

RULE 1.222. MOBILE HOMEOWNERS' ASSOCIATIONS

A mobile homeowners' association may institute, maintain, settle, or appeal actions or hearings in its name on behalf of all homeowners concerning matters of common interest, including, but not limited to: the common property; structural components of a building or other improvements; mechanical, electrical, and plumbing elements serving the park property; and protests of ad valorem taxes on commonly used facilities. If the association has the authority to maintain a class action under this rule, the association may be joined in an action as representative of that class with reference to litigation and disputes involving the matters for which the association could bring a class action under this rule. Nothing herein limits any statutory or common law right of any individual homeowner or class of homeowners to bring any action which may otherwise be available. An action under this rule shall not be subject to the requirements of rule 1.220.

1988 Editor's Note: Rule 1.222 was adopted in Lanca Homeowners, Inc. v. Lantana Cascade of Palm Beach, Ltd., *541 So.2d 1121 (Fla. 1988).*

RULE 1.230. INTERVENTIONS

Anyone claiming an interest in pending litigation may at any time be permitted to assert a right by intervention, but the intervention shall be in subordination to, and in recognition of, the propriety of the main proceeding, unless otherwise ordered by the court in its discretion.

RULE 1.240. INTERPLEADER

Persons having claims against the plaintiff may be joined as defendants and required to interplead when their claims are such that the plaintiff is or may be exposed to double or multiple liability. It is not ground for objection to the joinder that the claim of the several claimants or the titles on which their claims depend do not have a common origin or are not identical but are adverse to and independent of one another, or that the plaintiff avers that the plaintiff is not liable in whole or in part to any or all of the claimants. A defendant exposed to similar liability may obtain such interpleader by way of crossclaim or counterclaim. The provisions of this rule supplement and do not in any way limit the joinder of parties otherwise permitted.

RULE 1.250. MISJOINDER AND NONJOINDER OF PARTIES

(a) Misjoinder. Misjoinder of parties is not a ground for dismissal of an action. Any claim against a party may be severed and proceeded with separately.

(b) Dropping Parties. Parties may be dropped by an adverse party in the manner provided for voluntary dismissal in rule 1.420(a)(1) subject to the exception stated in that rule. If notice of lis pendens has been filed in the action against a party so dropped, the notice of dismissal shall be recorded and cancels the notice of lis pendens without the necessity of a court order. Parties may be dropped by order of court on its own initiative or the motion of any party at any stage of the action on such terms as are just.

(c) Adding Parties. Parties may be added once as a matter of course within the same time that pleadings can be so amended under rule 1.190(a). If amendment by leave of court or stipulation of the parties is permitted, parties may be added in the amended pleading without further order of court. Parties may be added by order of court on its own initiative or on motion of any party at any stage of the action and on such terms as are just.

Committee Notes

1972 Amendment. Subdivision (c) is amended to permit the addition of parties when the pleadings are amended by stipulation. This conforms the subdivision to all of the permissive types of amendment under rule 1.190(a). It was an inadvertent omission by the committee when the rule in its present form was adopted in 1968 as can be seen by reference to the 1968 committee note.

RULE 1.260. SURVIVOR; SUBSTITUTION OF PARTIES

(a) Death.

(1) If a party dies and the claim is not thereby extinguished, the court may order substitution of the proper parties. The motion for substitution may be made by any party or by the successors or representatives of the deceased party and, together with the notice of hearing, shall be served on all parties as provided in rule 1.080 and upon persons not parties in the manner provided for the service of a summons. Unless the motion for substitution is made within 90 days after the death is suggested upon the record by service of a statement of the fact of the death in the manner provided for the service of the motion, the action shall be dismissed as to the deceased party.

(2) In the event of the death of one or more of the plaintiffs or of one or more of the defendants in an action in which the right sought to be enforced survives only to the surviving plaintiffs or only against the surviving defendants, the action shall not abate. The death shall be suggested upon the record and the action shall proceed in favor of or against the surviving parties.

(b) Incompetency. If a party becomes incompetent, the court, upon motion served as provided in subdivision (a) of this rule, may allow the action to be continued by or against that person's representative.

(c) Transfer of Interest. In case of any transfer of interest, the action may be continued by or against the original party, unless the court upon motion directs the person to whom the interest is transferred to be substituted in the action or joined with the original party. Service of the motion shall be made as provided in subdivision (a) of this rule.

(d) Public Officers; Death or Separation from Office.

(1) When a public officer is a party to an action in an official capacity and during its pendency dies, resigns, or otherwise ceases to hold office, the action does not abate and the officer's successor is automatically substituted as a party. Proceedings following the substitution shall be in the name of the substituted party, but any misnomer not affecting the substantial rights of the parties shall be disregarded. An order of substitution may be entered at any time, but the omission to enter such an order shall not affect the substitution.

(2) When a public officer sues or is sued in an official capacity, the officer may be described as a party by the official title rather than by name but the court may require the officer's name to be added.

RULE 1.270. CONSOLIDATION; SEPARATE TRIALS

(a) Consolidation. When actions involving a common question of law or fact are pending before the court, it may order a joint hearing or trial of any or all the matters in issue in the actions; it may order all the actions consolidated; and it may make such orders concerning proceedings therein as may tend to avoid unnecessary costs or delay.

(b) Separate Trials. The court in furtherance of convenience or to avoid prejudice may order a separate trial of any claim, crossclaim, counterclaim, or third-party claim or of any separate issue or of any number of claims, crossclaims, counterclaims, third-party claims, or issues.

RULE 1.280. GENERAL PROVISIONS GOVERNING DISCOVERY

(a) Discovery Methods. Parties may obtain discovery by one or more of the following methods: depositions upon oral examination or written questions; written interrogatories; production of documents or things or permission to enter upon land or other property for inspection and other purposes; physical and mental examinations; and requests for admission. Unless the court orders otherwise and under subdivision (c) of this rule, the frequency of use of these methods is not limited, except as provided in rules 1.200, 1.340, and 1.370.

(b) Scope of Discovery. Unless otherwise limited by order of the court in accordance with these rules, the scope of discovery is as follows:

(1) In General. Parties may obtain discovery regarding any matter, not privileged, that is relevant to the subject matter of the pending action, whether it relates to the claim or defense of the party seeking discovery or the claim or defense of any other party, including the existence, description, nature, custody, condition, and location of any books, documents, or other tangible things and the identity and location of persons having knowledge of any discoverable matter. It is not ground for objection that the information sought will be inadmissible at the trial if the information sought appears reasonably calculated to lead to the discovery of admissible evidence.

(2) Indemnity Agreements. A party may obtain discovery of the existence and contents of any agreement under which any person may be liable to satisfy part or all of a judgment that may be entered in the action or to indemnify or to reimburse a party for payments made to satisfy the judgment. Information concerning the agreement is not admissible in evidence at trial by reason of disclosure.

(3) Trial Preparation: Materials. Subject to the provisions of subdivision (b)(4) of this rule, a party may obtain discovery of documents and tangible things otherwise discoverable under subdivision (b)(1) of this rule and prepared in anticipation of litigation or for trial by or for another party or by or for that party's representative, including that party's attorney, consultant, surety, indemnitor, insurer, or agent, only upon a showing that the party seeking discovery has need of the materials in the preparation of the case and is unable without undue hardship to obtain the substantial equivalent of the materials by other means. In ordering discovery of the materials when the required showing has been made, the court shall protect against disclosure of the mental impressions, conclusions, opinions, or legal theories of an attorney or other representative of a party concerning the litigation. Without the required showing a party may obtain a copy of a statement concerning the action or its subject matter previously made by that party. Upon request without the required showing a person not a party may obtain a copy of a statement concerning the action or its subject matter previously made by that person. If the request is refused, the person may move for an order to obtain a copy. The provisions of rule 1.380(a)(4) apply to the award of expenses incurred as a result of making the motion. For purposes of this paragraph, a statement previously made is a written statement signed or otherwise adopted or approved by the person making it, or a stenographic, mechanical, electrical, or other recording or transcription of it that is a substantially verbatim recital of an oral statement by the person making it and contemporaneously recorded.

(4) Trial Preparation: Experts. Discovery of facts known and opinions held by experts, otherwise discoverable under the provisions of subdivision (b)(1) of this rule and acquired or developed in anticipation of litigation or for trial, may be obtained only as follows:

(A)　(i) By interrogatories a party may require any other party to identify each person whom the other party expects to call as an expert witness at trial and to state the subject matter on which the expert is expected to testify, and to state the substance of the facts and opinions to which the expert is expected to testify and a summary of the grounds for each opinion.

(ii) Any person disclosed by interrogatories or otherwise as a person expected to be called as an expert witness at trial may be deposed in accordance with rule 1.390 without motion or order of court.

(iii) A party may obtain the following discovery regarding any person disclosed by interrogatories or otherwise as a person expected to be called as an expert witness at trial:

1. The scope of employment in the pending case and the compensation for such service.

2. The expert's general litigation experience, including the percentage of work performed for plaintiffs and defendants.

3. The identity of other cases, within a reasonable time period, in which the expert has testified by deposition or at trial.

4. An approximation of the portion of the expert's involvement as an expert witness, which may be based on the number of hours, percentage of hours, or percentage of earned income derived from serving as an expert witness; however, the expert shall not be required to disclose his or her earnings as an expert witness or income derived from other services.

An expert may be required to produce financial and business records only under the most unusual or compelling circumstances and may not be compelled to compile or produce nonexistent documents. Upon motion, the court may order further discovery by other means, subject to such restrictions as to scope and other provisions pursuant to subdivision (b)(4)(C) of this rule concerning fees and expenses as the court may deem appropriate.

(B) A party may discover facts known or opinions held by an expert who has been retained or specially employed by another party in anticipation of litigation or preparation for trial and who is not expected to be called as a witness at trial, only as provided in rule 1.360(b) or upon a showing of exceptional circumstances under which it is impracticable for the party seeking discovery to obtain facts or opinions on the same subject by other means.

(C) Unless manifest injustice would result, the court shall require that the party seeking discovery pay the expert a reasonable fee for time spent in responding to discovery under subdivisions (b)(4)(A) and (b)(4)(B) of this rule; and concerning discovery from an expert obtained under subdivision (b)(4)(A) of this rule the court may require, and concerning discovery obtained under subdivision (b)(4)(B) of this rule shall require, the party seeking discovery to pay the other party a fair part of the fees and expenses reasonably incurred by the latter party in obtaining facts and opinions from the expert.

(D) As used in these rules an expert shall be an expert witness as defined in rule 1.390(a).

(5) Claims of Privilege or Protection of Trial Preparation Materials. When a party withholds information otherwise discoverable under these rules by claiming that it is privileged or subject to protection as trial preparation material, the party shall make the claim expressly and shall describe the nature of the documents, communications, or things not produced or disclosed in a manner that, without revealing information itself privileged or protected, will enable other parties to assess the applicability of the privilege or protection.

(c) **Protective Orders.** Upon motion by a party or by the person from whom discovery is sought, and for good cause shown, the court in which the action is pending may make any order to protect a party or person from annoyance, embarrassment, oppression, or undue burden or expense that justice requires, including one or more of the following: (1) that the discovery not be had; (2) that the discovery may be had only on specified terms and conditions, including a designation of the time or place; (3) that the discovery may be had only by a method of discovery other than that selected by the party seeking discovery; (4) that certain matters not be inquired into, or that the scope of the discovery be limited to certain matters; (5) that discovery be conducted with no one present except persons designated by the court; (6) that a deposition after being sealed be opened only by order of the court; (7) that a trade secret or other confidential research, development, or commercial information not be disclosed or be disclosed only in a designated way; and (8) that the parties simultaneously file specified documents or information enclosed in sealed envelopes to be opened as directed by the court. If the motion for a protective order is denied in whole or in part, the court may, on such terms and conditions as are just, order that any party or person provide or permit discovery. The provisions of rule 1.380(a)(4) apply to the award of expenses incurred in relation to the motion.

(d) **Sequence and Timing of Discovery.** Except as provided in subdivision (b)(4) or unless the court upon motion for the convenience of parties and witnesses and in the interest of justice orders otherwise, methods of discovery may be used in any sequence, and the fact that a party is conducting discovery, whether by deposition or otherwise, shall not delay any other party's discovery.

(e) **Supplementing of Responses.** A party who has responded to a request for discovery with a response that was complete when made is under no duty to supplement the response to include information thereafter acquired.

29

(f) Court Filing of Documents and Discovery. Information obtained during discovery shall not be filed with the court until such time as it is filed for good cause. The requirement of good cause is satisfied only where the filing of the information is allowed or required by another applicable rule of procedure or by court order. All filings of discovery documents shall comply with Florida Rule of Judicial Administration 2.425. The court shall have authority to impose sanctions for violation of this rule.

Committee Notes

1972 Amendment. The rule is derived from Federal Rule of Civil Procedure 26 as amended in 1970. Subdivisions (a), (b)(2), and (b)(3) are new. Subdivision (c) contains material from former rule 1.310(b). Subdivisions (d) and (e) are new, but the latter is similar to former rule 1.340(d). Significant changes are made in discovery from experts. The general rearrangement of the discovery rule is more logical and is the result of 35 years of experience under the federal rules.

1988 Amendment. Subdivision (b)(2) has been added to enable discovery of the existence and contents of indemnity agreements and is the result of the enactment of sections 627.7262 and 627.7264, Florida Statutes, proscribing the joinder of insurers but providing for disclosure. This rule is derived from Federal Rule of Civil Procedure 26(b)(2). Subdivisions (b)(2) and (b)(3) have been redesignated as (b)(3) and (b)(4) respectively.

The purpose of the amendment to subdivision (b)(3)(A) (renumbered (b)(4)(A)) is to allow, without leave of court, the depositions of experts who have been disclosed as expected to be used at trial. The purpose of subdivision (b)(4)(D) is to define the term "expert" as used in these rules.

1996 Amendment. The amendments to subdivision (b)(4)(A) are derived from the Supreme Court's decision in *Elkins v. Syken*, 672 So. 2d 517 (Fla. 1996). They are intended to avoid annoyance, embarrassment, and undue expense while still permitting the adverse party to obtain relevant information regarding the potential bias or interest of the expert witness.

Subdivision (b)(5) is added and is derived from Federal Rule of Civil Procedure 26(b)(5) (1993).

2011 Amendment. Subdivision (f) is added to ensure that information obtained during discovery is not filed with the court unless there is good cause for the documents to be filed, and that information obtained during discovery that includes certain private information shall not be filed with the court unless the private information is redacted as required by Florida Rule of Judicial Administration 2.425.

Court Commentary

2000 Amendment. *Allstate Insurance Co. v. Boecher*, 733 So. 2d 993, 999 (Fla. 1999), clarifies that subdivision (b)(4)(A)(iii) is not intended "to place a blanket bar on discovery from parties about information they have in their possession about an expert, including the party's financial relationship with the expert."

RULE 1.285. INADVERTENT DISCLOSURE OF PRIVILEGED MATERIALS

(a) Assertion of Privilege as to Inadvertently Disclosed Materials. Any party, person, or entity, after inadvertent disclosure of any materials pursuant to these rules, may thereafter assert any privilege recognized by law as to those materials. This right exists without regard to whether the disclosure was made pursuant to formal demand or informal request. In order to assert the privilege, the party, person, or entity, shall, within 10 days of actually discovering the inadvertent disclosure, serve written notice of the assertion of privilege on the party to whom the materials were disclosed. The notice shall specify with particularity the materials as to which the privilege is asserted, the nature of the privilege asserted, and the date on which the inadvertent disclosure was actually discovered.

(b) Duty of the Party Receiving Notice of an Assertion of Privilege. A party receiving notice of an assertion of privilege under subdivision (a) shall promptly return, sequester, or destroy the materials specified in the notice, as well as any copies of the material. The party receiving the notice shall also promptly notify any other party, person, or entity to whom it has disclosed the materials of the fact that the notice has been served and of the effect of this rule. That party shall also take reasonable steps to retrieve the materials disclosed. Nothing herein affects any obligation pursuant to R. Regulating Fla. Bar 4-4.4(b).

(c) **Right to Challenge Assertion of Privilege.** Any party receiving a notice made under subdivision (a) has the right to challenge the assertion of privilege. The grounds for the challenge may include, but are not limited to, the following:

(1) The materials in question are not privileged.

(2) The disclosing party, person, or entity lacks standing to assert the privilege.

(3) The disclosing party, person, or entity has failed to serve timely notice under this rule.

(4) The circumstances surrounding the production or disclosure of the materials warrant a finding that the disclosing party, person, or entity has waived its assertion that the material is protected by a privilege.

Any party seeking to challenge the assertion of privilege shall do so by serving notice of its challenge on the party, person, or entity asserting the privilege. Notice of the challenge shall be served within 20 days of service of the original notice given by the disclosing party, person, or entity. The notice of the recipient's challenge shall specify the grounds for the challenge. Failure to serve timely notice of challenge is a waiver of the right to challenge.

(d) **Effect of Determination that Privilege Applies.** When an order is entered determining that materials are privileged or that the right to challenge the privilege has been waived, the court shall direct what shall be done with the materials and any copies so as to preserve all rights of appellate review. The recipient of the materials shall also give prompt notice of the court's determination to any other party, person, or entity to whom it had disclosed the materials.

RULE 1.290. DEPOSITIONS BEFORE ACTION OR PENDING APPEAL

(a) **Before Action.**

(1) **Petition.** A person who desires to perpetuate that person's own testimony or that of another person regarding any matter that may be cognizable in any court of this state may file a verified petition in the circuit court in the county of the residence of any expected adverse party. The petition shall be entitled in the name of the petitioner and shall show: (1) that the petitioner expects to be a party to an action cognizable in a court of Florida, but is presently unable to bring it or cause it to be brought, (2) the subject matter of the expected action and the petitioner's interest therein, (3) the facts which the petitioner desires to establish by the proposed testimony and the petitioner's reasons for desiring to perpetuate it, (4) the names or a description of the persons the petitioner expects will be adverse parties and their addresses so far as known, and (5) the names and addresses of the persons to be examined and the substance of the testimony which the petitioner expects to elicit from each; and shall ask for an order authorizing the petitioner to take the deposition of the persons to be examined named in the petition for the purpose of perpetuating their testimony.

(2) **Notice and Service.** The petitioner shall thereafter serve a notice upon each person named in the petition as an expected adverse party, together with a copy of the petition, stating that the petitioner will apply to the court at a time and place named therein for an order described in the petition. At least 20 days before the date of hearing the notice shall be served either within or without the county in the manner provided by law for service of summons, but if such service cannot with due diligence be made upon any expected adverse party named in the petition, the court may make an order for service by publication or otherwise, and shall appoint an attorney for persons not served in the manner provided by law for service of summons who shall represent them, and if they are not otherwise represented, shall cross-examine the deponent.

(3) **Order and Examination.** If the court is satisfied that the perpetuation of the testimony may prevent a failure or delay of justice, it shall make an order designating or describing the persons whose depositions may be taken and specifying the subject matter of the examination and

whether the deposition shall be taken upon oral examination or written interrogatories. The deposition may then be taken in accordance with these rules and the court may make orders in accordance with the requirements of these rules. For the purpose of applying these rules to depositions for perpetuating testimony, each reference therein to the court in which the action is pending shall be deemed to refer to the court in which the petition for such deposition was filed.

(4) **Use of Deposition.** A deposition taken under this rule may be used in any action involving the same subject matter subsequently brought in any court in accordance with rule 1.330.

(b) **Pending Appeal.** If an appeal has been taken from a judgment of any court or before the taking of an appeal if the time therefor has not expired, the court in which the judgment was rendered may allow the taking of the depositions of witnesses to perpetuate their testimony for use in the event of further proceedings in the court. In such case the party who desires to perpetuate the testimony may make a motion for leave to take the deposition upon the same notice and service as if the action was pending in the court. The motion shall show (1) the names and addresses of persons to be examined and the substance of the testimony which the movant expects to elicit from each, and (2) the reason for perpetuating their testimony. If the court finds that the perpetuation of the testimony is proper to avoid a failure or delay in justice, it may make an order allowing the deposition to be taken and may make orders of the character provided for by these rules, and thereupon the deposition may be taken and used in the same manner and under the same conditions as are prescribed in these rules for depositions taken in actions pending in the court.

(c) **Perpetuation by Action.** This rule does not limit the power of a court to entertain an action to perpetuate testimony.

Committee Notes

1980 Amendment. Subdivision (d) is repealed because depositions de bene esse are obsolete. Rules 1.280 and 1.310 with the remainder of this rule cover all needed deposition circumstances and do so better. Subdivision (d) was taken from former chapter 63, Florida Statutes, and is not a complete procedure without reference to the parts of the statute not carried forward in the rule.

RULE 1.300. PERSONS BEFORE WHOM DEPOSITIONS MAY BE TAKEN

(a) **Persons Authorized.** Depositions may be taken before any notary public or judicial officer or before any officer authorized by the statutes of Florida to take acknowledgments or proof of executions of deeds or by any person appointed by the court in which the action is pending.

(b) **In Foreign Countries.** In a foreign country depositions may be taken (1) on notice before a person authorized to administer oaths in the place in which the examination is held, either by the law thereof or by the law of Florida or of the United States, (2) before a person commissioned by the court, and a person so commissioned shall have the power by virtue of the commission to administer any necessary oath and take testimony, or (3) pursuant to a letter rogatory. A commission or a letter rogatory shall be issued on application and notice and on terms that are just and appropriate. It is not requisite to the issuance of a commission or a letter rogatory that the taking of the deposition in any other manner is impracticable or inconvenient, and both a commission and a letter rogatory may be issued in proper cases. A notice or commission may designate the person before whom the deposition is to be taken either by name or descriptive title. A letter rogatory may be addressed "To the Appropriate Authority in .....(name of country)......" Evidence obtained in response to a letter rogatory need not be excluded merely for the reason that it is not a verbatim transcript or that the testimony was not taken under oath or any similar departure from the requirements for depositions taken within Florida under these rules.

(c) **Selection by Stipulation.** If the parties so stipulate in writing, depositions may be taken before any person at any time or place upon any notice and in any manner and when so taken may be used like other depositions.

(d) **Persons Disqualified.** Unless so stipulated by the parties, no deposition shall be taken before a person who is a relative, employee, attorney, or counsel of any of the parties, is a relative or employee of any of the parties' attorney or counsel, or is financially interested in the action.

RULE 1.310. DEPOSITIONS UPON ORAL EXAMINATION

(a) **When Depositions May Be Taken.** After commencement of the action any party may take the testimony of any person, including a party, by deposition upon oral examination. Leave of court, granted with or without notice, must be obtained only if the plaintiff seeks to take a deposition within 30 days after service of the process and initial pleading upon any defendant, except that leave is not required (1) if a defendant has served a notice of taking deposition or otherwise sought discovery, or (2) if special notice is given as provided in subdivision (b)(2) of this rule. The attendance of witnesses may be compelled by subpoena as provided in rule 1.410. The deposition of a person confined in prison may be taken only by leave of court on such terms as the court prescribes.

(b) **Notice; Method of Taking; Production at Deposition.**

(1) A party desiring to take the deposition of any person upon oral examination shall give reasonable notice in writing to every other party to the action. The notice shall state the time and place for taking the deposition and the name and address of each person to be examined, if known, and, if the name is not known, a general description sufficient to identify the person or the particular class or group to which the person belongs. If a subpoena duces tecum is to be served on the person to be examined, the designation of the materials to be produced under the subpoena shall be attached to or included in the notice.

(2) Leave of court is not required for the taking of a deposition by plaintiff if the notice states that the person to be examined is about to go out of the state and will be unavailable for examination unless a deposition is taken before expiration of the 30-day period under subdivision (a). If a party shows that when served with notice under this subdivision that party was unable through the exercise of diligence to obtain counsel to represent the party at the taking of the deposition, the deposition may not be used against that party.

(3) For cause shown the court may enlarge or shorten the time for taking the deposition.

(4) Any deposition may be recorded by videotape without leave of the court or stipulation of the parties, provided the deposition is taken in accordance with this subdivision.

(A) Notice. A party intending to videotape a deposition shall state in the notice that the deposition is to be videotaped and shall give the name and address of the operator. Any subpoena served on the person to be examined shall state the method or methods for recording the testimony.

(B) Stenographer. Videotaped depositions shall also be recorded stenographically, unless all parties agree otherwise.

(C) Procedure. At the beginning of the deposition, the officer before whom it is taken shall, on camera: (i) identify the style of the action, (ii) state the date, and (iii) swear the witness.

(D) Custody of Tape and Copies. The attorney for the party requesting the videotaping of the deposition shall take custody of and be responsible for the safeguarding of the videotape, shall permit the viewing of it by the opposing party, and, if requested, shall provide a copy of the videotape at the expense of the party requesting the copy.

(E) Cost of Videotaped Depositions. The party requesting the videotaping shall bear the initial cost of videotaping.

(5) The notice to a party deponent may be accompanied by a request made in compliance with rule 1.350 for the production of documents and tangible things at the taking of the deposition. The procedure of rule 1.350 shall apply to the request. Rule 1.351 provides the exclusive procedure for obtaining documents or things by subpoena from nonparties without deposing the custodian or other person in possession of the documents.

(6) In the notice a party may name as the deponent a public or private corporation, a partnership or association, or a governmental agency, and designate with reasonable particularity the matters on which examination is requested. The organization so named shall designate one or more

officers, directors, or managing agents, or other persons who consent to do so, to testify on its behalf and may state the matters on which each person designated will testify. The persons so designated shall testify about matters known or reasonably available to the organization. This subdivision does not preclude taking a deposition by any other procedure authorized in these rules.

(7) On motion the court may order that the testimony at a deposition be taken by telephone. The order may prescribe the manner in which the deposition will be taken. A party may also arrange for a stenographic transcription at that party's own initial expense.

(8) Any minor subpoenaed for testimony shall have the right to be accompanied by a parent or guardian at all times during the taking of testimony notwithstanding the invocation of the rule of sequestration of section 90.616, Florida Statutes, except upon a showing that the presence of a parent or guardian is likely to have a material, negative impact on the credibility or accuracy of the minor's testimony, or that the interests of the parent or guardian are in actual or potential conflict with the interests of the minor.

(c) Examination and Cross-Examination; Record of Examination; Oath; Objections. Examination and cross-examination of witnesses may proceed as permitted at the trial. The officer before whom the deposition is to be taken shall put the witness on oath and shall personally, or by someone acting under the officer's direction and in the officer's presence, record the testimony of the witness, except that when a deposition is being taken by telephone, the witness shall be sworn by a person present with the witness who is qualified to administer an oath in that location. The testimony shall be taken stenographically or recorded by any other means ordered in accordance with subdivision (b)(4) of this rule. If requested by one of the parties, the testimony shall be transcribed at the initial cost of the requesting party and prompt notice of the request shall be given to all other parties. All objections made at time of the examination to the qualifications of the officer taking the deposition, the manner of taking it, the evidence presented, or the conduct of any party, and any other objection to the proceedings shall be noted by the officer upon the deposition. Any objection during a deposition shall be stated concisely and in a nonargumentative and nonsuggestive manner. A party may instruct a deponent not to answer only when necessary to preserve a privilege, to enforce a limitation on evidence directed by the court, or to present a motion under subdivision (d). Otherwise, evidence objected to shall be taken subject to the objections. Instead of participating in the oral examination, parties may serve written questions in a sealed envelope on the party taking the deposition and that party shall transmit them to the officer, who shall propound them to the witness and record the answers verbatim.

(d) Motion to Terminate or Limit Examination. At any time during the taking of the deposition, on motion of a party or of the deponent and upon a showing that the examination is being conducted in bad faith or in such manner as unreasonably to annoy, embarrass, or oppress the deponent or party, or that objection and instruction to a deponent not to answer are being made in violation of rule 1.310(c), the court in which the action is pending or the circuit court where the deposition is being taken may order the officer conducting the examination to cease forthwith from taking the deposition or may limit the scope and manner of the taking of the deposition under rule 1.280(c). If the order terminates the examination, it shall be resumed thereafter only upon the order of the court in which the action is pending. Upon demand of any party or the deponent, the taking of the deposition shall be suspended for the time necessary to make a motion for an order. The provisions of rule 1.380(a) apply to the award of expenses incurred in relation to the motion.

(e) Witness Review. If the testimony is transcribed, the transcript shall be furnished to the witness for examination and shall be read to or by the witness unless the examination and reading are waived by the witness and by the parties. Any changes in form or substance that the witness wants to make shall be listed in writing by the officer with a statement of the reasons given by the witness for making the changes. The changes shall be attached to the transcript. It shall then be signed by the witness unless the parties waived the signing or the witness is ill, cannot be found, or refuses to sign. If the transcript is not signed by the witness within a reasonable time after it is furnished to the witness, the officer shall sign the transcript and state on the transcript the waiver, illness, absence of the witness, or refusal to sign with any reasons given therefor. The deposition may then be used as fully as though signed unless the court holds that the reasons given for the refusal to sign require rejection of the deposition wholly or partly, on motion under rule 1.330(d)(4).

34

(f) Filing; Exhibits.

(1) If the deposition is transcribed, the officer shall certify on each copy of the deposition that the witness was duly sworn by the officer and that the deposition is a true record of the testimony given by the witness. Documents and things produced for inspection during the examination of the witness shall be marked for identification and annexed to and returned with the deposition upon the request of a party, and may be inspected and copied by any party, except that the person producing the materials may substitute copies to be marked for identification if that person affords to all parties fair opportunity to verify the copies by comparison with the originals. If the person producing the materials requests their return, the officer shall mark them, give each party an opportunity to inspect and copy them, and return them to the person producing them and the materials may then be used in the same manner as if annexed to and returned with the deposition.

(2) Upon payment of reasonable charges therefor the officer shall furnish a copy of the deposition to any party or to the deponent.

(3) A copy of a deposition may be filed only under the following circumstances:

(A) It may be filed in compliance with Florida Rule of Judicial Administration 2.425 and rule 1.280(f) by a party or the witness when the contents of the deposition must be considered by the court on any matter pending before the court. Prompt notice of the filing of the deposition shall be given to all parties unless notice is waived. A party filing the deposition shall furnish a copy of the deposition or the part being filed to other parties unless the party already has a copy.

(B) If the court determines that a deposition previously taken is necessary for the decision of a matter pending before the court, the court may order that a copy be filed by any party at the initial cost of the party, and the filing party shall comply with rules 2.425 and 1.280(f).

(g) Obtaining Copies. A party or witness who does not have a copy of the deposition may obtain it from the officer taking the deposition unless the court orders otherwise. If the deposition is obtained from a person other than the officer, the reasonable cost of reproducing the copies shall be paid to the person by the requesting party or witness.

(h) Failure to Attend or to Serve Subpoena; Expenses.

(1) If the party giving the notice of the taking of a deposition fails to attend and proceed therewith and another party attends in person or by attorney pursuant to the notice, the court may order the party giving the notice to pay to the other party the reasonable expenses incurred by the other party and the other party's attorney in attending, including reasonable attorneys' fees.

(2) If the party giving the notice of the taking of a deposition of a witness fails to serve a subpoena upon the witness and the witness because of the failure does not attend and if another party attends in person or by attorney because that other party expects the deposition of that witness to be taken, the court may order the party giving the notice to pay to the other party the reasonable expenses incurred by that other party and that other party's attorney in attending, including reasonable attorneys' fees.

Committee Notes

1972 Amendment. Derived from Federal Rule of Civil Procedure 30 as amended in 1970. Subdivision (a) is derived from rule 1.280(a); subdivision (b) from rule 1.310(a) with additional matter added; the first sentence of subdivision (c) has been added and clarifying language added throughout the remainder of the rule.

1976 Amendment. Subdivision (b)(4) has been amended to allow the taking of a videotaped deposition as a matter of right. Provisions for the taxation of costs and the entry of a standard order are included as well. This new amendment allows the contemporaneous stenographic transcription of a videotaped deposition.

35

1988 Amendment. The amendments to subdivision (b)(4) are to provide for depositions by videotape as a matter of right.

The notice provision is to ensure that specific notice is given that the deposition will be videotaped and to disclose the identity of the operator. It was decided not to make special provision for a number of days' notice.

The requirement that a stenographer be present (who is also the person likely to be swearing the deponent) is to ensure the availability of a transcript (although not required). The transcript would be a tool to ensure the accuracy of the videotape and thus eliminate the need to establish other procedures aimed at the same objective (like time clocks in the picture and the like). This does not mean that a transcript must be made. As at ordinary depositions, this would be up to the litigants.

Technical videotaping procedures were not included. It is anticipated that technical problems may be addressed by the court on motions to quash or motions for protective orders.

Subdivision (c) has been amended to accommodate the taking of depositions by telephone. The amendment requires the deponent to be sworn by a person authorized to administer oaths in the deponent's location and who is present with the deponent.

1992 Amendment. Subdivision (b)(4)(D) is amended to clarify an ambiguity in whether the cost of the videotape copy is to be borne by the party requesting the videotaping or by the party requesting the copy. The amendment requires the party requesting the copy to bear the cost of the copy.

1996 Amendment. Subdivision (c) is amended to state the existing law, which authorizes attorneys to instruct deponents not to answer questions only in specific situations. This amendment is derived from Federal Rule of Civil Procedure 30(d) as amended in 1993.

2010 Amendment. Subdivision (b)(5) is amended to clarify that the procedure set forth in rule 1.351 must be followed when requesting or receiving documents or things without testimony, from nonparties pursuant to a subpoena. The amendment is intended to prevent the use of rules 1.310 and 1.410 to request documents from nonparties pursuant to a subpoena without giving the opposing party the opportunity to object to the subpoena before it is served on the nonparty as required by rule 1.351.

2011 Amendment. A reference to Florida Rule of Judicial Administration 2.425 and rule 1.280(f) is added to require persons filing discovery materials with the court to make sure that good cause exists prior to filing discovery materials and that certain specific personal information is redacted.

Court Commentary

1984 Amendment. Subdivision (b)(7) is added to authorize deposition by telephone, with provision for any party to have a stenographic transcription at that party's own initial expense.

Subdivision (d) is changed to permit any party to terminate the deposition, not just the objecting party.

Subdivision (e) is changed to eliminate the confusing requirement that a transcript be submitted to the witness. The term has been construed as requiring the court reporter to travel, if necessary, to the witness, and creates a problem when a witness is deposed in Florida and thereafter leaves the state before signing. The change is intended to permit the parties and the court reporter to handle such situations on an ad hoc basis as is most appropriate.

Subdivision (f) is the committee's action in response to the petition seeking amendment to rule 1.310(f) filed in the Supreme Court Case No. 62,699. Subdivision (f) is changed to clarify the need for furnishing copies when a deposition, or part of it, is properly filed, to authorize the court to require a deposition to be both transcribed and filed, and to specify that a party who does not obtain a copy of the deposition may get it from the court reporter unless ordered otherwise by the court. This eliminates the present requirement of furnishing a copy of the deposition, or material part of it, to a person who already has a copy in subdivision (f)(3)(A).

Subdivision (f)(3)(B) broadens the authority of the court to require the filing of a deposition that has been taken, but not transcribed.

Subdivision (g) requires a party to obtain a copy of the deposition from the court reporter unless the court orders otherwise. Generally, the court should not order a party who has a copy of the deposition to furnish it to someone who has neglected to obtain it when the deposition was transcribed. The person should obtain it from the court reporter unless there is a good reason why it cannot be obtained from the reporter.

RULE 1.320. DEPOSITIONS UPON WRITTEN QUESTIONS

(a) **Serving Questions; Notice.** After commencement of the action any party may take the testimony of any person, including a party, by deposition upon written questions. The attendance of witnesses may be compelled by the use of subpoena as provided in rule 1.410. The deposition of a person confined in prison may be taken only by leave of court on such terms as the court prescribes. A party desiring to take a deposition upon written questions shall serve them with a notice stating (1) the name and address of the person who is to answer them, if known, and, if the name is not known, a general description sufficient to identify the person or the particular class or group to which that person belongs, and (2) the name or descriptive title and address of the officer before whom the deposition is to be taken. A deposition upon written questions may be taken of a public or private corporation, a partnership or association, or a governmental agency in accordance with rule 1.310(b)(6). Within 30 days after the notice and written questions are served, a party may serve cross questions upon all other parties. Within 10 days after being served with cross questions, a party may serve redirect questions upon all other parties. Within 10 days after being served with redirect questions, a party may serve recross questions upon all other parties. The court may for cause shown enlarge or shorten the time.

(b) **Officer to Take Responses and Prepare Record.** A copy of the notice and copies of all questions served shall be delivered by the party taking the depositions to the officer designated in the notice, who shall proceed promptly to take the testimony of the witness in the manner provided by rules 1.310(c), (e), and (f) in response to the questions and to prepare the deposition, attaching the copy of the notice and the questions received by the officer. The questions shall not be filed separately from the deposition unless a party seeks to have the court consider the questions before the questions are submitted to the witness.

Committee Notes

1972 Amendment. Derived from Federal Rule of Civil Procedure 31 as amended in 1970. The name of interrogatories has been changed to questions to avoid confusion with interrogatories to parties under rule 1.340. Language changes resulting from the rearrangement of the discovery rules have been inserted and subdivision (d) deleted.

RULE 1.330. USE OF DEPOSITIONS IN COURT PROCEEDINGS

(a) **Use of Depositions.** At the trial or upon the hearing of a motion or an interlocutory proceeding, any part or all of a deposition may be used against any party who was present or represented at the taking of the deposition or who had reasonable notice of it so far as admissible under the rules of evidence applied as though the witness were then present and testifying in accordance with any of the following provisions:

(1) Any deposition may be used by any party for the purpose of contradicting or impeaching the testimony of the deponent as a witness or for any purpose permitted by the Florida Evidence Code.

(2) The deposition of a party or of anyone who at the time of taking the deposition was an officer, director, or managing agent or a person designated under rule 1.310(b)(6) or 1.320(a) to testify on behalf of a public or private corporation, a partnership or association, or a governmental agency that is a party may be used by an adverse party for any purpose.

(3) The deposition of a witness, whether or not a party, may be used by any party for any purpose if the court finds: (A) that the witness is dead; (B) that the witness is at a greater distance than

100 miles from the place of trial or hearing, or is out of the state, unless it appears that the absence of the witness was procured by the party offering the deposition; (C) that the witness is unable to attend or testify because of age, illness, infirmity, or imprisonment; (D) that the party offering the deposition has been unable to procure the attendance of the witness by subpoena; (E) upon application and notice, that such exceptional circumstances exist as to make it desirable, in the interest of justice and with due regard to the importance of presenting the testimony of witnesses orally in open court, to allow the deposition to be used; or (F) the witness is an expert or skilled witness.

(4) If only part of a deposition is offered in evidence by a party, an adverse party may require the party to introduce any other part that in fairness ought to be considered with the part introduced, and any party may introduce any other parts.

(5) Substitution of parties pursuant to rule 1.260 does not affect the right to use depositions previously taken and, when an action in any court of the United States or of any state has been dismissed and another action involving the same subject matter is afterward brought between the same parties or their representatives or successors in interest, all depositions lawfully taken and duly filed in the former action may be used in the latter as if originally taken for it.

(6) If a civil action is afterward brought, all depositions lawfully taken in a medical liability mediation proceeding may be used in the civil action as if originally taken for it.

(b) Objections to Admissibility. Subject to the provisions of rule 1.300(b) and subdivision (d)(3) of this rule, objection may be made at the trial or hearing to receiving in evidence any deposition or part of it for any reason that would require the exclusion of the evidence if the witness were then present and testifying.

(c) Effect of Taking or Using Depositions. A party does not make a person the party's own witness for any purpose by taking the person's deposition. The introduction in evidence of the deposition or any part of it for any purpose other than that of contradicting or impeaching the deponent makes the deponent the witness of the party introducing the deposition, but this shall not apply to the use by an adverse party of a deposition under subdivision (a)(2) of this rule. At the trial or hearing any party may rebut any relevant evidence contained in a deposition whether introduced by that party or by any other party.

(d) Effect of Errors and Irregularities.

(1) As to Notice. All errors and irregularities in the notice for taking a deposition are waived unless written objection is promptly served upon the party giving the notice.

(2) As to Disqualification of Officer. Objection to taking a deposition because of disqualification of the officer before whom it is to be taken is waived unless made before the taking of the deposition begins or as soon thereafter as the disqualification becomes known or could be discovered with reasonable diligence.

(3) As to Taking of Deposition.

(A) Objections to the competency of a witness or to the competency, relevancy, or materiality of testimony are not waived by failure to make them before or during the taking of the deposition unless the ground of the objection is one that might have been obviated or removed if presented at that time.

(B) Errors and irregularities occurring at the oral examination in the manner of taking the deposition, in the form of the questions or answers, in the oath or affirmation, or in the conduct of parties and errors of any kind that might be obviated, removed, or cured if promptly presented are waived unless timely objection to them is made at the taking of the deposition.

(C) Objections to the form of written questions submitted under rule 1.320 are waived unless served in writing upon the party propounding them within the time allowed for serving the succeeding cross or other questions and within 10 days after service of the last questions authorized.

(4) As to Completion and Return. Errors and irregularities in the manner in which the testimony is transcribed or the deposition is prepared, signed, certified, or otherwise dealt with by the officer under rules 1.310 and 1.320 are waived unless a motion to suppress the deposition or some part of it is made with reasonable promptness after the defect is, or with due diligence might have been, discovered.

Committee Notes

1972 Amendment. Derived from Federal Rule of Civil Procedure 32 as amended in 1970. Subdivisions (a), (b), and (c) are former rules 1.280(d), (f), and (g) respectively. Subdivision (d) is derived from the entire former rule 1.330.

1998 Amendment. Subdivision (a)(1) was amended to clarify that, in addition to the uses of depositions prescribed by these rules, depositions may be used for any purpose permitted by the Florida Evidence Code (chapter 90, Fla. Stat.). This amendment is consistent with the 1980 amendment to Rule 32 of the Federal Rules of Civil Procedure.

RULE 1.340. INTERROGATORIES TO PARTIES

(a) Procedure for Use. Without leave of court, any party may serve upon any other party written interrogatories to be answered (1) by the party to whom the interrogatories are directed, or (2) if that party is a public or private corporation or partnership or association or governmental agency, by any officer or agent, who shall furnish the information available to that party. Interrogatories may be served on the plaintiff after commencement of the action and on any other party with or after service of the process and initial pleading upon that party. The interrogatories shall not exceed 30, including all subparts, unless the court permits a larger number on motion and notice and for good cause. If the supreme court has approved a form of interrogatories for the type of action, the initial interrogatories on a subject included therein shall be from the form approved by the court. A party may serve fewer than all of the approved interrogatories within a form. Other interrogatories may be added to the approved forms without leave of court, so long as the total of approved and additional interrogatories does not exceed 30. Each interrogatory shall be answered separately and fully in writing under oath unless it is objected to, in which event the grounds for objection shall be stated and signed by the attorney making it. The party to whom the interrogatories are directed shall serve the answers and any objections within 30 days after the service of the interrogatories, except that a defendant may serve answers or objections within 45 days after service of the process and initial pleading upon that defendant. The court may allow a shorter or longer time. The party submitting the interrogatories may move for an order under rule 1.380(a) on any objection to or other failure to answer an interrogatory.

(b) Scope; Use at Trial. Interrogatories may relate to any matters that can be inquired into under rule 1.280(b), and the answers may be used to the extent permitted by the rules of evidence except as otherwise provided in this subdivision. An interrogatory otherwise proper is not objectionable merely because an answer to the interrogatory involves an opinion or contention that relates to fact or calls for a conclusion or asks for information not within the personal knowledge of the party. A party shall respond to such an interrogatory by giving the information the party has and the source on which the information is based. Such a qualified answer may not be used as direct evidence for or impeachment against the party giving the answer unless the court finds it otherwise admissible under the rules of evidence. If a party introduces an answer to an interrogatory, any other party may require that party to introduce any other interrogatory and answer that in fairness ought to be considered with it.

(c) Option to Produce Records. When the answer to an interrogatory may be derived or ascertained from the records of the party to whom the interrogatory is directed or from an examination, audit, or inspection of the records or from a compilation, abstract, or summary based on the records and the burden of deriving or ascertaining the answer is substantially the same for the party serving the interrogatory as for the party to whom it is directed, an answer to the interrogatory specifying the records from which the answer may be derived or ascertained and offering to give the party serving the interrogatory a reasonable opportunity to examine, audit, or inspect the records and to make copies, compilations, abstracts, or summaries is a sufficient answer. An answer shall be in sufficient detail to permit the interrogating party to locate and to identify, as readily as can the party interrogated, the records from which the answer may be derived or ascertained, or shall identify a person or persons representing the interrogated party who will be available to assist the interrogating party in locating and identifying the records at the time they are produced.

(d) Effect on Co-Party. Answers made by a party shall not be binding on a co-party.

(e) Service and Filing. Interrogatories shall be arranged so that a blank space is provided after each separately numbered interrogatory. The space shall be reasonably sufficient to enable the answering party to insert the answer within the space. If sufficient space is not provided, the answering party may attach additional papers with answers and refer to them in the space provided in the interrogatories. The interrogatories shall be served on the party to whom the interrogatories are directed and copies shall be served on all other parties. A certificate of service of the interrogatories shall be filed, giving the date of service and the name of the party to whom they were directed. The answers to the interrogatories shall be served upon the party originally propounding the interrogatories and a copy shall be served on all other parties by the answering party. The original or any copy of the answers to interrogatories may be filed in compliance with Florida Rule of Judicial Administration 2.425 and rule 1.280(f) by any party when the court should consider the answers to interrogatories in determining any matter pending before the court. The court may order a copy of the answers to interrogatories filed at any time when the court determines that examination of the answers to interrogatories is necessary to determine any matter pending before the court.

Committee Notes

1972 Amendment. Subdivisions (a), (b), and (c) are derived from Federal Rule of Civil Procedure 33 as amended in 1970. Changes from the existing rule expand the time for answering, permit interrogatories to be served with the initial pleading or at any time thereafter, and eliminate the requirement of a hearing on objections. If objections are made, the interrogating party has the responsibility of setting a hearing if that party wants an answer. If the interrogatories are not sufficiently important, the interrogating party may let the matter drop. Subdivision (b) covers the same matter as the present rule 1.340(b) except those parts that have been transferred to rule 1.280. It also eliminates the confusion between facts and opinions or contentions by requiring that all be given. Subdivision (c) gives the interrogated party an option to produce business records from which the interrogating party can derive the answers to questions. Subdivision (d) is former subdivision (c) without change. Former subdivision (d) is repealed because it is covered in rule 1.280(e). Subdivision (e) is derived from the New Jersey rules and is intended to place both the interrogatories and the answers to them in a convenient place in the court file so that they can be referred to with less confusion.

The requirement for filing a copy before the answers are received is necessary in the event of a dispute concerning what was done or the appropriate times involved.

1988 Amendment. The word "initial" in the 1984 amendment to subdivision (a) resulted in some confusion, so it has been deleted. Also the total number of interrogatories which may be propounded without leave of court is enlarged to 30 from 25. Form interrogatories which have been approved by the supreme court must be used; and those so used, with their subparts, are included in the total number permitted. The amendments are not intended to change any other requirement of the rule.

2011 Amendment. A reference to Florida Rule of Judicial Administration 2.425 and rule 1.280(f) is added to require persons filing discovery materials with the court to make sure that good cause exists prior to filing discovery materials and that certain specific personal information is redacted.

Court Commentary

1984 Amendment. Subdivision (a) is amended by adding the reference to approved forms of interrogatories. The intent is to eliminate the burden of unnecessary interrogatories.

Subdivision (c) is amended to add the requirement of detail in identifying records when they are produced as an alternative to answering the interrogatory or to designate the persons who will locate the records.

Subdivision (e) is changed to eliminate the requirement of serving an original and a copy of the interrogatories and of the answers in light of the 1981 amendment that no longer permits filing except in special circumstances.

Subdivision (f) is deleted since the Medical Liability Mediation Proceedings have been eliminated.

RULE 1.350. PRODUCTION OF DOCUMENTS AND THINGS AND ENTRY UPON LAND FOR INSPECTION AND OTHER PURPOSES

(a) **Request; Scope.** Any party may request any other party (1) to produce and permit the party making the request, or someone acting in the requesting party's behalf, to inspect and copy any designated documents, including writings, drawings, graphs, charts, photographs, phono-records, and other data compilations from which information can be obtained, translated, if necessary, by the party to whom the request is directed through detection devices into reasonably usable form, that constitute or contain matters within the scope of rule 1.280(b) and that are in the possession, custody, or control of the party to whom the request is directed; (2) to inspect and copy, test, or sample any tangible things that constitute or contain matters within the scope of rule 1.280(b) and that are in the possession, custody, or control of the party to whom the request is directed; or (3) to permit entry upon designated land or other property in the possession or control of the party upon whom the request is served for the purpose of inspection and measuring, surveying, photographing, testing, or sampling the property or any designated object or operation on it within the scope of rule 1.280(b).

(b) **Procedure.** Without leave of court the request may be served on the plaintiff after commencement of the action and on any other party with or after service of the process and initial pleading on that party. The request shall set forth the items to be inspected, either by individual item or category, and describe each item and category with reasonable particularity. The request shall specify a reasonable time, place, and manner of making the inspection or performing the related acts. The party to whom the request is directed shall serve a written response within 30 days after service of the request, except that a defendant may serve a response within 45 days after service of the process and initial pleading on that defendant. The court may allow a shorter or longer time. For each item or category the response shall state that inspection and related activities will be permitted as requested unless the request is objected to, in which event the reasons for the objection shall be stated. If an objection is made to part of an item or category, the part shall be specified. When producing documents, the producing party shall either produce them as they are kept in the usual course of business or shall identify them to correspond with the categories in the request. The party submitting the request may move for an order under rule 1.380 concerning any objection, failure to respond to the request, or any part of it, or failure to permit inspection as requested.

(c) **Persons Not Parties.** This rule does not preclude an independent action against a person not a party for production of documents and things and permission to enter upon land.

(d) **Filing of Documents.** Unless required by the court, a party shall not file any of the documents or things produced with the response. Documents or things may be filed in compliance with Florida Rule of Judicial Administration 2.425 and rule 1.280(f) when they should be considered by the court in determining a matter pending before the court.

Committee Notes

1972 Amendment. Derived from Federal Rule of Civil Procedure 34 as amended in 1970. The new rule eliminates the good cause requirement of the former rule, changes the time for making the request and responding to it, and changes the procedure for the response. If no objection to the discovery is made, inspection is had without a court order. While the good cause requirement has been eliminated, the change is not intended to overrule cases limiting discovery under this rule to the scope of ordinary discovery, nor is it intended to overrule cases limiting unreasonable requests such as those reviewed in *Van Devere v. Holmes*, 156 So. 2d 899 (Fla. 3d DCA 1963); *IBM v. Elder*, 187 So. 2d 82 (Fla. 3d DCA 1966); and *Miami v. Florida Public Service Commission*, 226 So. 2d 217 (Fla. 1969). It is intended that the court review each objection and weigh the need for discovery and the likely results of it against the right of privacy of the party or witness or custodian.

1980 Amendment. Subdivision (b) is amended to require production of documents as they are kept in the usual course of business or in accordance with the categories in the request.

2011 Amendment. A reference to Florida Rule of Judicial Administration 2.425 and rule 1.280(f) is added to require persons filing discovery materials with the court to make sure that good cause exists prior to filing discovery materials and that certain specific personal information is redacted.

RULE 1.351. PRODUCTION OF DOCUMENTS AND THINGS WITHOUT DEPOSITION

(a) **Request; Scope.** A party may seek inspection and copying of any documents or things within the scope of rule 1.350(a) from a person who is not a party by issuance of a subpoena directing the production of the documents or things when the requesting party does not seek to depose the custodian or other person in possession of the documents or things. This rule provides the exclusive procedure for obtaining documents or things by subpoena from nonparties without deposing the custodian or other person in possession of the documents or things pursuant to rule 1.310.

(b) **Procedure.** A party desiring production under this rule shall serve notice on every other party of the intent to serve a subpoena under this rule at least 10 days before the subpoena is issued if service is by delivery and 15 days before the subpoena is issued if the service is by mail. The proposed subpoena shall be attached to the notice and shall state the time, place, and method for production of the documents or things, and the name and address of the person who is to produce the documents or things, if known, and if not known, a general description sufficient to identify the person or the particular class or group to which the person belongs; shall include a designation of the items to be produced; and shall state that the person who will be asked to produce the documents or things has the right to object to the production under this rule and that the person will not be required to surrender the documents or things. A copy of the notice and proposed subpoena shall not be furnished to the person upon whom the subpoena is to be served. If any party serves an objection to production under this rule within 10 days of service of the notice, the documents or things shall not be produced pending resolution of the objection in accordance with subdivision (d).

(c) **Subpoena.** If no objection is made by a party under subdivision (b), an attorney of record in the action may issue a subpoena or the party desiring production shall deliver to the clerk for issuance a subpoena together with a certificate of counsel or pro se party that no timely objection has been received from any party, and the clerk shall issue the subpoena and deliver it to the party desiring production. Service within the state of Florida of a nonparty subpoena shall be deemed sufficient if it complies with rule 1.410(d) or if (1) service is accomplished by mail or hand delivery by a commercial delivery service, and (2) written confirmation of delivery, with the date of service and the name and signature of the person accepting the subpoena, is obtained and filed by the party seeking production. The subpoena shall be identical to the copy attached to the notice and shall specify that no testimony may be taken and shall require only production of the documents or things specified in it. The subpoena may give the recipient an option to deliver or mail legible copies of the documents or things to the party serving the subpoena. The person upon whom the subpoena is served may condition the preparation of copies on the payment in advance of the reasonable costs of preparing the copies. The subpoena shall require production only in the county of the residence of the custodian or other person in possession of the documents or things or in the county where the documents or things are located or where the custodian or person in possession usually conducts business. If the person upon whom the subpoena is served objects at any time before the production of the documents or things, the documents or things shall not be produced under this rule, and relief may be obtained pursuant to rule 1.310.

(d) **Ruling on Objection.** If an objection is made by a party under subdivision (b), the party desiring production may file a motion with the court seeking a ruling on the objection or may proceed pursuant to rule 1.310.

(e) **Copies Furnished.** If the subpoena is complied with by delivery or mailing of copies as provided in subdivision (c), the party receiving the copies shall furnish a legible copy of each item furnished to any other party who requests it upon the payment of the reasonable cost of preparing the copies.

(f) Independent Action. This rule does not affect the right of any party to bring an independent action for production of documents and things or permission to enter upon land.

Committee Notes

1980 Adoption. This rule is designed to eliminate the need of taking a deposition of a records custodian when the person seeking discovery wants copies of the records only. It authorizes objections by any other party as well as the custodian of the records. If any person objects, recourse must be had to rule 1.310.

1996 Amendment. This rule was amended to avoid premature production of documents by nonparties, to clarify the clerk's role in the process, and to further clarify that any objection to the use of this rule does not contemplate a hearing before the court but directs the party to rule 1.310 to obtain the desired production. This amendment is not intended to preclude all communication between parties and nonparties. It is intended only to prohibit a party from prematurely sending to a nonparty a copy of the required notice or the proposed subpoena. This rule was also amended along with rule 1.410 to allow attorneys to issue subpoenas. See Committee Note for rule 1.410.

2007 Amendment. Subdivisions (b) and (d) were amended to permit a party seeking nonparty discovery to have other parties' objections resolved by the court.

2010 Amendment. Subdivision (a) is amended to clarify that the procedure set forth in rule 1.351, not rule 1.310, shall be followed when requesting or receiving documents or things, without testimony, from nonparties pursuant to a subpoena.

RULE 1.360. EXAMINATION OF PERSONS

(a) Request; Scope.

(1) A party may request any other party to submit to, or to produce a person in that other party's custody or legal control for, examination by a qualified expert when the condition that is the subject of the requested examination is in controversy.

(A) When the physical condition of a party or other person under subdivision (a)(1) is in controversy, the request may be served on the plaintiff without leave of court after commencement of the action, and on any other person with or after service of the process and initial pleading on that party. The request shall specify a reasonable time, place, manner, conditions, and scope of the examination and the person or persons by whom the examination is to be made. The party to whom the request is directed shall serve a response within 30 days after service of the request, except that a defendant need not serve a response until 45 days after service of the process and initial pleading on that defendant. The court may allow a shorter or longer time. The response shall state that the examination will be permitted as requested unless the request is objected to, in which event the reasons for the objection shall be stated. If the examination is to be recorded or observed by others, the request or response shall also include the number of people attending, their role, and the method or methods of recording.

(B) In cases where the condition in controversy is not physical, a party may move for an examination by a qualified expert as in subdivision (a)(1). The order for examination shall be made only after notice to the person to be examined and to all parties, and shall specify the time, place, manner, conditions, and scope of the examination and the person or persons by whom it is to be made.

(C) Any minor required to submit to examination pursuant to this rule shall have the right to be accompanied by a parent or guardian at all times during the examination, except upon a showing that the presence of a parent or guardian is likely to have a material, negative impact on the minor's examination.

(2) An examination under this rule is authorized only when the party submitting the request has good cause for the examination. At any hearing the party submitting the request shall have the burden of showing good cause.

(3) Upon request of either the party requesting the examination or the party or person to be examined, the court may establish protective rules governing such examination.

(b) Report of Examiner.

(1) If requested by the party to whom a request for examination or against whom an order is made under subdivision (a)(1)(A) or (a)(1)(B) or by the person examined, the party requesting the examination to be made shall deliver to the other party a copy of a detailed written report of the examiner setting out the examiner's findings, including results of all tests made, diagnosis, and conclusions, with similar reports of all earlier examinations of the same condition. After delivery of the detailed written report, the party requesting the examination to be made shall be entitled upon request to receive from the party to whom the request for examination or against whom the order is made a similar report of any examination of the same condition previously or thereafter made, unless in the case of a report of examination of a person not a party the party shows the inability to obtain it. On motion, the court may order delivery of a report on such terms as are just; and if an examiner fails or refuses to make a report, the court may exclude the examiner's testimony if offered at the trial.

(2) By requesting and obtaining a report of the examination so ordered or requested or by taking the deposition of the examiner, the party examined waives any privilege that party may have in that action or any other involving the same controversy regarding the testimony of every other person who has examined or may thereafter examine that party concerning the same condition.

(3) This subdivision applies to examinations made by agreement of the parties unless the agreement provides otherwise. This subdivision does not preclude discovery of a report of an examiner or taking the deposition of the examiner in accordance with any other rule.

(c) Examiner as Witness. The examiner may be called as a witness by any party to the action, but shall not be identified as appointed by the court.

Committee Notes

1972 Amendment. Derived from Federal Rule of Civil Procedure 35 as amended in 1970. The good cause requirement under this rule has been retained so that the requirements of *Schlagenhauf v. Holder*, 379 U.S. 104, 85 S. Ct. 234, 13 L. Ed. 2d 152 (1964), have not been affected. Subdivision (b) is changed to make it clear that reports can be obtained whether an order for the examination has been entered or not and that all earlier reports of the same condition can also be obtained.

1988 Amendment. This amendment to subdivision (a) is intended to broaden the scope of rule 1.360 to accommodate the examination of a person by experts other than physicians.

RULE 1.370. REQUESTS FOR ADMISSION

(a) Request for Admission. A party may serve upon any other party a written request for the admission of the truth of any matters within the scope of rule 1.280(b) set forth in the request that relate to statements or opinions of fact or of the application of law to fact, including the genuineness of any documents described in the request. Copies of documents shall be served with the request unless they have been or are otherwise furnished or made available for inspection and copying. Without leave of court the request may be served upon the plaintiff after commencement of the action and upon any other party with or after service of the process and initial pleading upon that party. The request for admission shall not exceed 30 requests, including all subparts, unless the court permits a larger number on motion and notice and for good cause, or the parties propounding and responding to the requests stipulate to a larger number. Each matter of which an admission is requested shall be separately set forth. The matter is admitted unless the party to whom the request is directed serves upon the party requesting the admission a written answer or objection addressed to the matter within 30 days after service of the request or such shorter or longer time as the court may allow but, unless the court shortens the time, a defendant shall not be required to serve answers or objections before the expiration of 45 days after service of the process and initial pleading upon the defendant. If objection is made, the reasons shall be stated. The answer shall specifically deny the matter or set forth in detail the reasons why the answering party cannot truthfully admit or deny the matter. A denial shall fairly meet the substance of the requested admission, and when good faith requires that a party qualify an answer or deny only a part of the matter of which an admission is requested, the party shall specify so much of it as is true and qualify or deny the remainder. An answering party may not give lack of information or knowledge as a reason for failure to admit or deny unless that party states that that party has made reasonable inquiry and that the information known or readily obtainable by that party is insufficient to enable that party to admit or deny. A party who considers that a matter of which an admission has been requested presents a genuine issue for trial may not object to the request on that ground alone; the party may deny the matter or set forth reasons why the party cannot admit or deny it, subject to rule 1.380(c). The party who has requested the admissions may move to determine the sufficiency of the answers or objections. Unless the court determines that an objection is justified, it shall order that an answer be served. If the court determines that an answer does not comply with the requirements of this rule, it may order either that the matter is admitted or that an amended answer be served. Instead of these orders the court may determine that final disposition of the request be made at a pretrial conference or at a designated time before trial. The provisions of rule 1.380(a)(4) apply to the award of expenses incurred in relation to the motion.

(b) **Effect of Admission.** Any matter admitted under this rule is conclusively established unless the court on motion permits withdrawal or amendment of the admission. Subject to rule 1.200 governing amendment of a pretrial order, the court may permit withdrawal or amendment when the presentation of the merits of the action will be subserved by it and the party who obtained the admission fails to satisfy the court that withdrawal or amendment will prejudice that party in maintaining an action or defense on the merits. Any admission made by a party under this rule is for the purpose of the pending action only and is not an admission for any other purpose nor may it be used against that party in any other proceeding.

Committee Notes

1972 Amendment. Derived from Federal Rule of Civil Procedure 36 as amended in 1970. The rule is changed to eliminate distinctions between questions of opinion, fact, and mixed questions. The time sequences are changed in accordance with the other discovery rules, and case law is incorporated by providing for amendment and withdrawal of the answers and for judicial scrutiny to determine the sufficiency of the answers.

2003 Amendment. The total number of requests for admission that may be served without leave of court is limited to 30, including all subparts.

RULE 1.380. FAILURE TO MAKE DISCOVERY; SANCTIONS

(a) **Motion for Order Compelling Discovery.** Upon reasonable notice to other parties and all persons affected, a party may apply for an order compelling discovery as follows:

(1) **Appropriate Court.** An application for an order to a party may be made to the court in which the action is pending or in accordance with rule 1.310(d). An application for an order to a deponent who is not a party shall be made to the circuit court where the deposition is being taken.

(2) **Motion.** If a deponent fails to answer a question propounded or submitted under rule 1.310 or 1.320, or a corporation or other entity fails to make a designation under rule 1.310(b)(6) or 1.320(a), or a party fails to answer an interrogatory submitted under rule 1.340, or if a party in response to a request for inspection submitted under rule 1.350 fails to respond that inspection will be permitted as requested or fails to permit inspection as requested, or if a party in response to a request for examination of a person submitted under rule 1.360(a) objects to the examination, fails to respond that the examination will be permitted as requested, or fails to submit to or to produce a person in that party's custody or legal control for examination, the discovering party may move for an order compelling an answer, or a designation or an order compelling inspection, or an order compelling an examination in accordance with the request. The motion must include a certification that the movant, in good faith, has conferred or attempted to confer with the person or party failing to make the discovery in an effort to secure the information or material without court action. When taking a deposition on oral examination, the proponent of the question may complete or adjourn the examination before applying for an order. If the court denies the motion in whole or in part, it may make such protective order as it would have been empowered to make on a motion made pursuant to rule 1.280(c).

(3) Evasive or Incomplete Answer. For purposes of this subdivision an evasive or incomplete answer shall be treated as a failure to answer.

(4) Award of Expenses of Motion. If the motion is granted and after opportunity for hearing, the court shall require the party or deponent whose conduct necessitated the motion or the party or counsel advising the conduct to pay to the moving party the reasonable expenses incurred in obtaining the order that may include attorneys' fees, unless the court finds that the movant failed to certify in the motion that a good faith effort was made to obtain the discovery without court action, that the opposition to the motion was justified, or that other circumstances make an award of expenses unjust. If the motion is denied and after opportunity for hearing, the court shall require the moving party to pay to the party or deponent who opposed the motion the reasonable expenses incurred in opposing the motion that may include attorneys' fees, unless the court finds that the making of the motion was substantially justified or that other circumstances make an award of expenses unjust. If the motion is granted in part and denied in part, the court may apportion the reasonable expenses incurred as a result of making the motion among the parties and persons.

(b) Failure to Comply with Order.

(1) If a deponent fails to be sworn or to answer a question after being directed to do so by the court, the failure may be considered a contempt of the court.

(2) If a party or an officer, director, or managing agent of a party or a person designated under rule 1.310(b)(6) or 1.320(a) to testify on behalf of a party fails to obey an order to provide or permit discovery, including an order made under subdivision (a) of this rule or rule 1.360, the court in which the action is pending may make any of the following orders:

(A) An order that the matters regarding which the questions were asked or any other designated facts shall be taken to be established for the purposes of the action in accordance with the claim of the party obtaining the order.

(B) An order refusing to allow the disobedient party to support or oppose designated claims or defenses, or prohibiting that party from introducing designated matters in evidence.

(C) An order striking out pleadings or parts of them or staying further proceedings until the order is obeyed, or dismissing the action or proceeding or any part of it, or rendering a judgment by default against the disobedient party.

(D) Instead of any of the foregoing orders or in addition to them, an order treating as a contempt of court the failure to obey any orders except an order to submit to an examination made pursuant to rule 1.360(a)(1)(B) or subdivision (a)(2) of this rule.

(E) When a party has failed to comply with an order under rule 1.360(a)(1)(B) requiring that party to produce another for examination, the orders listed in paragraphs (A), (B), and (C) of this subdivision, unless the party failing to comply shows the inability to produce the person for examination. Instead of any of the foregoing orders or in addition to them, the court shall require the party failing to obey the order to pay the reasonable expenses caused by the failure, which may include attorneys' fees, unless the court finds that the failure was justified or that other circumstances make an award of expenses unjust.

(c) Expenses on Failure to Admit. If a party fails to admit the genuineness of any document or the truth of any matter as requested under rule 1.370 and if the party requesting the admissions thereafter proves the genuineness of the document or the truth of the matter, the requesting party may file a motion for an order requiring the other party to pay the requesting party the reasonable expenses incurred in making that proof, which may include attorneys' fees. The court shall issue such an order at the time a party requesting the admissions proves the genuineness of the document or the truth of the matter, upon motion by the requesting party, unless it finds that (1) the request was held objectionable pursuant to rule 1.370(a), (2) the admission sought was of no substantial importance, or (3) there was other good reason for the failure to admit.

(d) Failure of Party to Attend at Own Deposition or Serve Answers to Interrogatories or Respond to Request for Inspection. If a party or an officer, director, or managing agent of a party or a person designated under rule 1.310(b)(6) or 1.320(a) to testify on behalf of a party fails (1) to appear before the officer who is to take the deposition after being served with a proper notice, (2) to serve answers or objections to interrogatories submitted under rule 1.340 after proper service of the interrogatories, or (3) to serve a written response to a request for inspection submitted under rule 1.350 after proper service of the request, the court in which the action is pending may take any action authorized under paragraphs (A), (B), and (C) of subdivision (b)(2) of this rule. Any motion specifying a failure under clause (2) or (3) of this subdivision shall include a certification that the movant, in good faith, has conferred or attempted to confer with the party failing to answer or respond in an effort to obtain such answer or response without court action. Instead of any order or in addition to it, the court shall require the party failing to act to pay the reasonable expenses caused by the failure, which may include attorneys' fees, unless the court finds that the failure was justified or that other circumstances make an award of expenses unjust. The failure to act described in this subdivision may not be excused on the ground that the discovery sought is objectionable unless the party failing to act has applied for a protective order as provided by rule 1.280(c).

Committee Notes

1972 Amendment. Derived from Federal Rule of Civil Procedure 37 as amended in 1970. Subdivision (a)(3) is new and makes it clear that an evasive or incomplete answer is a failure to answer under the rule. Other clarifying changes have been made within the general scope of the rule to ensure that complete coverage of all discovery failures is afforded.

2003 Amendment. Subdivision (c) is amended to require a court to make a ruling on a request for reimbursement at the time of the hearing on the requesting party's motion for entitlement to such relief. The court may, in its discretion, defer ruling on the amount of the costs or fees in order to hold an evidentiary hearing whenever convenient to the court and counsel.

2005 Amendment. Following the example of Federal Rule of Civil Procedure 37 as amended in 1993, language is included in subdivision (a)(2) that requires litigants to seek to resolve discovery disputes by informal means before filing a motion with the court. This requirement is based on successful experience with the federal rule as well as similar local rules of state trial courts. Subdivision (a)(4) is revised to provide that a party should not be awarded its expenses for filing a motion that might have been avoided by conferring with opposing counsel. Subdivision (d) is revised to require that, where a party failed to file any response to a rule 1.340 interrogatory or a rule 1.350 request, the discovering party should attempt to obtain such responses before filing a motion for sanctions.

RULE 1.390. DEPOSITIONS OF EXPERT WITNESSES

(a) Definition. The term "expert witness" as used herein applies exclusively to a person duly and regularly engaged in the practice of a profession who holds a professional degree from a university or college and has had special professional training and experience, or one possessed of special knowledge or skill about the subject upon which called to testify.

(b) Procedure. The testimony of an expert or skilled witness may be taken at any time before the trial in accordance with the rules for taking depositions and may be used at trial, regardless of the place of residence of the witness or whether the witness is within the distance prescribed by rule 1.330(a)(3). No special form of notice need be given that the deposition will be used for trial.

(c) Fee. An expert or skilled witness whose deposition is taken shall be allowed a witness fee in such reasonable amount as the court may determine. The court shall also determine a reasonable time within which payment must be made, if the deponent and party cannot agree. All parties and the deponent shall be served with notice of any hearing to determine the fee. Any reasonable fee paid to an expert or skilled witness may be taxed as costs.

(d) Applicability. Nothing in this rule shall prevent the taking of any deposition as otherwise provided by law.

Committee Notes

1972 Amendment. This rule has caused more difficulty in recent years than any other discovery rule. It was enacted as a statute originally to make the presentation of expert testimony less expensive and less onerous to the expert and to admit the expert's deposition at trial regardless of the expert's residence. In spite of its intent, courts seem determined to misconstrue the plain language of the rule and cause complications that the committee and the legislature did not envisage. See *Owca v. Zemzicki*, 137 So. 2d 876 (Fla. 2d DCA 1962); *Cook v. Lichtblau*, 176 So. 2d 523 (Fla. 2d DCA 1965); and *Bondy v. West*, 219 So. 2d 117 (Fla. 2d DCA 1969). The committee hopes the amendment to subdivision (b) will show that the intent of the rule is to permit a deposition taken of an expert in conformity with any rule for the taking of a deposition to be admitted, if otherwise admissible under the rules of evidence, regardless of the residence of the expert. In short, the rule eliminates the necessity of any of the requirements of rule 1.330(a)(3) when the deposition offered is that of an expert.

1988 Amendment. Subdivision (c) has been amended to clarify the procedure to be used in paying an expert witness for his or her appearance at a deposition.

RULE 1.410. SUBPOENA

(a) Subpoena Generally. Subpoenas for testimony before the court, subpoenas for production of tangible evidence, and subpoenas for taking depositions may be issued by the clerk of court or by any attorney of record in an action.

(b) Subpoena for Testimony before the Court.

(1) Every subpoena for testimony before the court shall be issued by an attorney of record in an action or by the clerk under the seal of the court and shall state the name of the court and the title of the action and shall command each person to whom it is directed to attend and give testimony at a time and place specified in it.

(2) On oral request of an attorney or party and without praecipe, the clerk shall issue a subpoena for testimony before the court or a subpoena for the production of documentary evidence before the court signed and sealed but otherwise in blank, both as to the title of the action and the name of the person to whom it is directed, and the subpoena shall be filled in before service by the attorney or party.

(c) For Production of Documentary Evidence. A subpoena may also command the person to whom it is directed to produce the books, papers, documents, or tangible things designated therein, but the court, upon motion made promptly and in any event at or before the time specified in the subpoena for compliance therewith, may (1) quash or modify the subpoena if it is unreasonable and oppressive, or (2) condition denial of the motion upon the advancement by the person in whose behalf the subpoena is issued of the reasonable cost of producing the books, papers, documents, or tangible things. A party seeking production of evidence at trial which would be subject to a subpoena may compel such production by serving a notice to produce such evidence on an adverse party as provided in rule 1.080(b). Such notice shall have the same effect and be subject to the same limitations as a subpoena served on the party.

(d) Service. A subpoena may be served by any person authorized by law to serve process or by any other person who is not a party and who is not less than 18 years of age. Service of a subpoena upon a person named therein shall be made as provided by law. Proof of such service shall be made by affidavit of the person making service except as applicable under rule 1.351(c) for the production of documents and things by a nonparty without deposition, if not served by an officer authorized by law to do so.

(e) Subpoena for Taking Depositions.

(1) Filing a notice to take a deposition as provided in rule 1.310(b) or 1.320(a) with a certificate of service on it showing service on all parties to the action constitutes an authorization for the issuance of subpoenas for the persons named or described in the notice by the clerk of the court in which the action is pending or by an attorney of record in the action. The subpoena shall state the

method for recording the testimony. The subpoena may command the person to whom it is directed to produce designated books, papers, documents, or tangible things that constitute or contain evidence relating to any of the matters within the scope of the examination permitted by rule 1.280(b), but in that event the subpoena will be subject to the provisions of rule 1.280(c) and subdivision (c) of this rule. Within 10 days after its service, or on or before the time specified in the subpoena for compliance if the time is less than 10 days after service, the person to whom the subpoena is directed may serve written objection to inspection or copying of any of the designated materials. If objection is made, the party serving the subpoena shall not be entitled to inspect and copy the materials except pursuant to an order of the court from which the subpoena was issued. If objection has been made, the party serving the subpoena may move for an order at any time before or during the taking of the deposition upon notice to the deponent.

(2) A person may be required to attend an examination only in the county wherein the person resides or is employed or transacts business in person or at such other convenient place as may be fixed by an order of court.

(f) **Contempt.** Failure by any person without adequate excuse to obey a subpoena served upon that person may be deemed a contempt of the court from which the subpoena issued.

(g) **Depositions before Commissioners Appointed in this State by Courts of Other States; Subpoena Powers; etc.** When any person authorized by the laws of Florida to administer oaths is appointed by a court of record of any other state, jurisdiction, or government as commissioner to take the testimony of any named witness within this state, that witness may be compelled to attend and testify before that commissioner by witness subpoena issued by the clerk of any circuit court at the instance of that commissioner or by other process or proceedings in the same manner as if that commissioner had been appointed by a court of this state; provided that no document or paper writing shall be compulsorily annexed as an exhibit to such deposition or otherwise permanently removed from the possession of the witness producing it, but in lieu thereof a photostatic copy may be annexed to and transmitted with such executed commission to the court of issuance.

(h) **Subpoena of Minor.** Any minor subpoenaed for testimony shall have the right to be accompanied by a parent or guardian at all times during the taking of testimony notwithstanding the invocation of the rule of sequestration of section 90.616, Florida Statutes, except upon a showing that the presence of a parent or guardian is likely to have a material, negative impact on the credibility or accuracy of the minor's testimony, or that the interests of the parent or guardian are in actual or potential conflict with the interests of the minor.

Committee Notes

1972 Amendment. Subdivisions (a) and (d) are amended to show the intent of the rule that subpoenas for deposition may not be issued in blank by the clerk, but only for trial. The reason for the distinction is valid. A subpoena for appearance before the court is not subject to abuse because the court can correct any attempt to abuse the use of blank subpoenas. Since a judge is not present at a deposition, additional protection for the parties and the deponent is required and subpoenas should not be issued in blank. Subdivision (d) is also modified to conform with the revised federal rule on subpoenas for depositions to permit an objection by the deponent to the production of material required by a subpoena to be produced.

1980 Amendment. Subdivision (c) is revised to conform with section 48.031, Florida Statutes (1979).

1996 Amendment. This rule is amended to allow an attorney (as referred to in Fla. R. Jud. Admin. 2.060(a)B(b)), as an officer of the court, and the clerk to issue subpoenas in the name of the court. This amendment is not intended to change any other requirement or precedent for the issuance or use of subpoenas. For example, a notice of taking the deposition must be filed and served before a subpoena for deposition may be issued.

RULE 1.420. DISMISSAL OF ACTIONS

(a) **Voluntary Dismissal.**

(1) **By Parties.** Except in actions in which property has been seized or is in the custody of the court, an action, a claim, or any part of an action or claim may be dismissed by plaintiff without order of court (A) before trial by serving, or during trial by stating on the record, a notice of dismissal at any time before a hearing on motion for summary judgment, or if none is served or if the motion is denied, before retirement of the jury in a case tried before a jury or before submission of a nonjury case to the court for decision, or (B) by filing a stipulation of dismissal signed by all current parties to the action. Unless otherwise stated in the notice or stipulation, the dismissal is without prejudice, except that a notice of dismissal operates as an adjudication on the merits when served by a plaintiff who has once dismissed in any court an action based on or including the same claim.

(2) **By Order of Court; If Counterclaim.** Except as provided in subdivision (a)(1) of this rule, an action shall not be dismissed at a party's instance except on order of the court and upon such terms and conditions as the court deems proper. If a counterclaim has been served by a defendant prior to the service upon the defendant of the plaintiff's notice of dismissal, the action shall not be dismissed against defendant's objections unless the counterclaim can remain pending for independent adjudication by the court. Unless otherwise specified in the order, a dismissal under this paragraph is without prejudice.

(b) **Involuntary Dismissal.** Any party may move for dismissal of an action or of any claim against that party for failure of an adverse party to comply with these rules or any order of court. Notice of hearing on the motion shall be served as required under rule 1.090(d). After a party seeking affirmative relief in an action tried by the court without a jury has completed the presentation of evidence, any other party may move for a dismissal on the ground that on the facts and the law the party seeking affirmative relief has shown no right to relief, without waiving the right to offer evidence if the motion is not granted. The court as trier of the facts may then determine them and render judgment against the party seeking affirmative relief or may decline to render judgment until the close of all the evidence. Unless the court in its order for dismissal otherwise specifies, a dismissal under this subdivision and any dismissal not provided for in this rule, other than a dismissal for lack of jurisdiction or for improper venue or for lack of an indispensable party, operates as an adjudication on the merits.

(c) **Dismissal of Counterclaim, Crossclaim, or Third-Party Claim.** The provisions of this rule apply to the dismissal of any counterclaim, crossclaim, or third-party claim.

(d) **Costs.** Costs in any action dismissed under this rule shall be assessed and judgment for costs entered in that action, once the action is concluded as to the party seeking taxation of costs. When one or more other claims remain pending following dismissal of any claim under this rule, taxable costs attributable solely to the dismissed claim may be assessed and judgment for costs in that claim entered in the action, but only when all claims are resolved at the trial court level as to the party seeking taxation of costs. If a party who has once dismissed a claim in any court of this state commences an action based upon or including the same claim against the same adverse party, the court shall make such order for the payment of costs of the claim previously dismissed as it may deem proper and shall stay the proceedings in the action until the party seeking affirmative relief has complied with the order.

(e) **Failure to Prosecute.** In all actions in which it appears on the face of the record that no activity by filing of pleadings, order of court, or otherwise has occurred for a period of 10 months, and no order staying the action has been issued nor stipulation for stay approved by the court, any interested person, whether a party to the action or not, the court, or the clerk of the court may serve notice to all parties that no such activity has occurred. If no such record activity has occurred within the 10 months immediately preceding the service of such notice, and no record activity occurs within the 60 days immediately following the service of such notice, and if no stay was issued or approved prior to the expiration of such 60-day period, the action shall be dismissed by the court on its own motion or on the motion of any interested person, whether a party to the action or not, after reasonable notice to the parties, unless a party shows good cause in writing at least 5 days before the hearing on the motion why the action should remain pending. Mere inaction for a period of less than 1 year shall not be sufficient cause for dismissal for failure to prosecute.

(f) Effect on Lis Pendens. If a notice of lis pendens has been filed in connection with a claim for affirmative relief that is dismissed under this rule, the notice of lis pendens connected with the dismissed claim is automatically dissolved at the same time. The notice, stipulation, or order shall be recorded.

Committee Notes

1976 Amendment. Subdivision (e) has been amended to prevent the dismissal of an action for inactivity alone unless 1 year has elapsed since the occurrence of activity of record. Nonrecord activity will not toll the 1-year time period.

1980 Amendment. Subdivision (e) has been amended to except from the requirement of record activity a stay that is ordered or approved by the court.

1992 Amendment. Subdivision (f) is amended to provide for automatic dissolution of lis pendens on claims that are settled even though the entire action may not have been dismissed.

2005 Amendment. Subdivision (e) has been amended to provide that an action may not be dismissed for lack of prosecution without prior notice to the claimant and adequate opportunity for the claimant to recommence prosecution of the action to avert dismissal.

Court Commentary

1984 Amendment. A perennial real property title problem occurs because of the failure to properly dispose of notices of lis pendens in the order of dismissal. Accordingly, the reference in subdivision (a)(1) to disposition of notices of lis pendens has been deleted and a separate subdivision created to automatically dissolve notices of lis pendens whenever an action is dismissed under this rule.

RULE 1.430. DEMAND FOR JURY TRIAL; WAIVER

(a) Right Preserved. The right of trial by jury as declared by the Constitution or by statute shall be preserved to the parties inviolate.

(b) Demand. Any party may demand a trial by jury of any issue triable of right by a jury by serving upon the other party a demand therefor in writing at any time after commencement of the action and not later than 10 days after the service of the last pleading directed to such issue. The demand may be indorsed upon a pleading of the party.

(c) Specification of Issues. In the demand a party may specify the issues that the party wishes so tried; otherwise, the party is deemed to demand trial by jury for all issues so triable. If a party has demanded trial by jury for only some of the issues, any other party may serve a demand for trial by jury of any other or all of the issues triable by jury 10 days after service of the demand or such lesser time as the court may order.

(d) Waiver. A party who fails to serve a demand as required by this rule waives trial by jury. If waived, a jury trial may not be granted without the consent of the parties, but the court may allow an amendment in the proceedings to demand a trial by jury or order a trial by jury on its own motion. A demand for trial by jury may not be withdrawn without the consent of the parties.

Committee Notes

1972 Amendment. Subdivision (d) is amended to conform to the decisions construing it. See *Wood v. Warriner*, 62 So. 2d 728 (Fla. 1953); *Bittner v. Walsh*, 132 So. 2d 799 (Fla. 1st DCA 1961); and *Shores v. Murphy*, 88 So. 2d 294 (Fla. 1956). It is not intended to overrule *Wertman v. Tipping*, 166 So. 2d 666 (Fla. 1st DCA 1964), that requires a moving party to show justice requires a jury.

RULE 1.431. TRIAL JURY

(a) **Questionnaire.**

(1) The circuit court may direct the authority charged by law with the selection of prospective jurors to furnish each prospective juror with a questionnaire in the form approved by the supreme court from time to time to assist the authority in selecting prospective jurors. The questionnaire shall be used after the names of jurors have been selected as provided by law but before certification and the placing of the names of prospective jurors in the jury box. The questionnaire shall be used to determine those who are not qualified to serve as jurors under any statutory ground of disqualification.

(2) To assist in voir dire examination at trial, any court may direct the clerk to furnish prospective jurors selected for service with a questionnaire in the form approved by the supreme court from time to time. The prospective jurors shall be asked to complete and return the forms. Completed forms may be inspected in the clerk's office and copies shall be available in court during the voir dire examination for use by parties and the court.

(b) **Examination by Parties.** The parties have the right to examine jurors orally on their voir dire. The order in which the parties may examine each juror shall be determined by the court. The court may ask such questions of the jurors as it deems necessary, but the right of the parties to conduct a reasonable examination of each juror orally shall be preserved.

(c) **Challenge for Cause.**

(1) On motion of any party, the court shall examine any prospective juror on oath to determine whether that person is related, within the third degree, to (i) any party, (ii) the attorney of any party, or (iii) any other person or entity against whom liability or blame is alleged in the pleadings, or is related to any person alleged to have been wronged or injured by the commission of the wrong for the trial of which the juror is called, or has any interest in the action, or has formed or expressed any opinion, or is sensible of any bias or prejudice concerning it, or is an employee or has been an employee of any party or any other person or entity against whom liability or blame is alleged in the pleadings, within 30 days before the trial. A party objecting to the juror may introduce any other competent evidence to support the objection. If it appears that the juror does not stand indifferent to the action or any of the foregoing grounds of objection exists or that the juror is otherwise incompetent, another shall be called in that juror's place.

(2) The fact that any person selected for jury duty from bystanders or the body of the county and not from a jury list lawfully selected has served as a juror in the court in which that person is called at any other time within 1 year is a ground of challenge for cause.

(3) When the nature of any civil action requires a knowledge of reading, writing, and arithmetic, or any of them, to enable a juror to understand the evidence to be offered, the fact that any prospective juror does not possess the qualifications is a ground of challenge for cause.

(d) **Peremptory Challenges.** Each party is entitled to 3 peremptory challenges of jurors, but when the number of parties on opposite sides is unequal, the opposing parties are entitled to the same aggregate number of peremptory challenges to be determined on the basis of 3 peremptory challenges to each party on the side with the greater number of parties. The additional peremptory challenges accruing to multiple parties on the opposing side shall be divided equally among them. Any additional peremptory challenges not capable of equal division shall be exercised separately or jointly as determined by the court.

(e) **Exercise of Challenges.** All challenges shall be addressed to the court outside the hearing of the jury in a manner selected by the court so that the jury panel is not aware of the nature of the challenge, the party making the challenge, or the basis of the court's ruling on the challenge, if for cause.

(f) **Swearing of Jurors.** No one shall be sworn as a juror until the jury has been accepted by the parties or until all challenges have been exhausted.

(g) Alternate Jurors.

(1) The court may direct that 1 or 2 jurors be impaneled to sit as alternate jurors in addition to the regular panel. Alternate jurors in the order in which they are called shall replace jurors who have become unable or disqualified to perform their duties before the jury retires to consider its verdict. Alternate jurors shall be drawn in the same manner, have the same qualifications, be subject to the same examination, take the same oath, and have the same functions, powers, facilities, and privileges as principal jurors. An alternate juror who does not replace a principal juror shall be discharged when the jury retires to consider the verdict.

(2) If alternate jurors are called, each party shall be entitled to one peremptory challenge in the selection of the alternate juror or jurors, but when the number of parties on opposite sides is unequal, the opposing parties shall be entitled to the same aggregate number of peremptory challenges to be determined on the basis of 1 peremptory challenge to each party on the side with the greater number of parties. The additional peremptory challenges allowed pursuant to this subdivision may be used only against the alternate jurors. The peremptory challenges allowed pursuant to subdivision (d) of this rule shall not be used against the alternate jurors.

(h) Interview of a Juror. A party who believes that grounds for legal challenge to a verdict exist may move for an order permitting an interview of a juror or jurors to determine whether the verdict is subject to the challenge. The motion shall be served within 10 days after rendition of the verdict unless good cause is shown for the failure to make the motion within that time. The motion shall state the name and address of each juror to be interviewed and the grounds for challenge that the party believes may exist. After notice and hearing, the trial judge shall enter an order denying the motion or permitting the interview. If the interview is permitted, the court may prescribe the place, manner, conditions, and scope of the interview.

Committee Notes

1971 Adoption. Subdivision (a) is new. It is intended to replace section 40.101, Florida Statutes, declared unconstitutional in *Smith v. Portante*, 212 So. 2d 298 (Fla. 1968), after supplying the deficiencies in the statute. It is intended to simplify the task of selecting prospective jurors, both for the venire and for the panel for trial in a particular action. The forms referred to in subdivision (a) are forms 1.983 and 1.984. Subdivisions (b)–(e) are sections 53.031, 53.021, 53.011, and 53.051, Florida Statutes, without substantial change.

1976 Amendment. Subdivision (e) has been added to establish a procedure for challenging jurors without members of the panel knowing the source of the challenge, to avoid prejudice. Subdivision (f) is a renumbering of the previously enacted rule regarding alternate jurors.

Subdivision (g) has been added to establish a procedure for interviewing jurors. See also Canons of Professional Responsibility DR 7-108.

1988 Amendment. Subdivision (f) has been added to ensure the right to "back-strike" prospective jurors until the entire panel has been accepted in civil cases. This right to back-strike until the jurors have been sworn has been long recognized in Florida. *Florida Rock Industries, Inc. v. United Building Systems, Inc.*, 408 So. 2d 630 (Fla. 5th DCA 1982). However, in the recent case of *Valdes v. State*, 443 So. 2d 223 (Fla. 1st DCA 1984), the court held that it was not error for a court to swear jurors one at a time as they were accepted and thereby prevent retrospective peremptory challenges. The purpose of this subdivision is to prevent the use of individual swearing of jurors in civil cases. Former subdivisions (f) and (g) have been redesignated as (g) and (h) respectively.

1992 Amendment. Subdivision (g)(2) is amended to minimize the inequity in numbers of peremptory challenges allowed in selecting alternate jurors in actions with multiple parties.

2005 Amendment. Subdivision (c)(1) is amended to ensure that prospective jurors may be challenged for cause based on bias in favor of or against nonparties against whom liability or blame may be alleged in accordance with the decisions in *Fabre v. Marin*, 623 So. 2d 1182 (Fla. 1993), or *Nash v. Wells Fargo Guard Services, Inc.*, 678 So. 2d 1262 (Fla. 1996).

53

RULE 1.440. SETTING ACTION FOR TRIAL

(a) **When at Issue.** An action is at issue after any motions directed to the last pleading served have been disposed of or, if no such motions are served, 20 days after service of the last pleading. The party entitled to serve motions directed to the last pleading may waive the right to do so by filing a notice for trial at any time after the last pleading is served. The existence of crossclaims among the parties shall not prevent the court from setting the action for trial on the issues raised by the complaint, answer, and any answer to a counterclaim.

(b) **Notice for Trial.** Thereafter any party may file and serve a notice that the action is at issue and ready to be set for trial. The notice shall include an estimate of the time required, whether the trial is to be by a jury or not, and whether the trial is on the original action or a subsequent proceeding. The clerk shall then submit the notice and the case file to the court.

(c) **Setting for Trial.** If the court finds the action ready to be set for trial, it shall enter an order fixing a date for trial. Trial shall be set not less than 30 days from the service of the notice for trial. By giving the same notice the court may set an action for trial. In actions in which the damages are not liquidated, the order setting an action for trial shall be served on parties who are in default in accordance with rule 1.080(a).

(d) **Applicability.** This rule does not apply to actions to which chapter 51, Florida Statutes (1967), applies or to cases designated as complex pursuant to rule 1.201.

Committee Notes

1972 Amendment. All references to the pretrial conference are deleted because these are covered in rule 1.200.

1980 Amendment. Subdivision (b) is amended to specify whether the trial will be on the original pleadings or subsequent pleadings under rule 1.110(h).

1988 Amendment. Subdivision (c) was amended to clarify a confusion regarding the notice for trial which resulted from a 1968 amendment.

Court Commentary

1984 Amendment. Subdivision (a) is amended by adding a sentence to emphasize the authority given in rule 1.270(b) for the severing of issues for trial.

Subdivision (c) is amended to delete the reference to law actions so that the rule will apply to all actions in which unliquidated damages are sought.

RULE 1.442. PROPOSALS FOR SETTLEMENT

(a) **Applicability.** This rule applies to all proposals for settlement authorized by Florida law, regardless of the terms used to refer to such offers, demands, or proposals, and supersedes all other provisions of the rules and statutes that may be inconsistent with this rule.

(b) **Service of Proposal.** A proposal to a defendant shall be served no earlier than 90 days after service of process on that defendant; a proposal to a plaintiff shall be served no earlier than 90 days after the action has been commenced. No proposal shall be served later than 45 days before the date set for trial or the first day of the docket on which the case is set for trial, whichever is earlier.

(c) **Form and Content of Proposal for Settlement.**

(1) A proposal shall be in writing and shall identify the applicable Florida law under which it is being made.

(2) A proposal shall:

(A) name the party or parties making the proposal and the party or parties to whom the proposal is being made;

(B) identify the claim or claims the proposal is attempting to resolve;

(C) state with particularity any relevant conditions;

(D) state the total amount of the proposal and state with particularity all nonmonetary terms of the proposal;

(E) state with particularity the amount proposed to settle a claim for punitive damages, if any;

(F) state whether the proposal includes attorneys' fees and whether attorneys' fees are part of the legal claim; and

(G) include a certificate of service in the form required by rule 1.080(f).

(3) A proposal may be made by or to any party or parties and by or to any combination of parties properly identified in the proposal. A joint proposal shall state the amount and terms attributable to each party.

(4) Notwithstanding subdivision (c)(3), when a party is alleged to be solely vicariously, constructively, derivatively, or technically liable, whether by operation of law or by contract, a joint proposal made by or served on such a party need not state the apportionment or contribution as to that party. Acceptance by any party shall be without prejudice to rights of contribution or indemnity.

(d) Service and Filing. A proposal shall be served on the party or parties to whom it is made but shall not be filed unless necessary to enforce the provisions of this rule.

(e) Withdrawal. A proposal may be withdrawn in writing provided the written withdrawal is delivered before a written acceptance is delivered. Once withdrawn, a proposal is void.

(f) Acceptance and Rejection.

(1) A proposal shall be deemed rejected unless accepted by delivery of a written notice of acceptance within 30 days after service of the proposal. The provisions of rule 1.090(e) do not apply to this subdivision. No oral communications shall constitute an acceptance, rejection, or counteroffer under the provisions of this rule.

(2) In any case in which the existence of a class is alleged, the time for acceptance of a proposal for settlement is extended to 30 days after the date the order granting or denying certification is filed.

(g) Sanctions. Any party seeking sanctions pursuant to applicable Florida law, based on the failure of the proposal's recipient to accept a proposal, shall do so by serving a motion in accordance with rule 1.525.

(h) Costs and Fees.

(1) If a party is entitled to costs and fees pursuant to applicable Florida law, the court may, in its discretion, determine that a proposal was not made in good faith. In such case, the court may disallow an award of costs and attorneys' fees.

(2) When determining the reasonableness of the amount of an award of attorneys' fees pursuant to this section, the court shall consider, along with all other relevant criteria, the following factors:

(A) The then-apparent merit or lack of merit in the claim.

(B) The number and nature of proposals made by the parties.

(C) The closeness of questions of fact and law at issue.

(D) Whether the party making the proposal had unreasonably refused to furnish information necessary to evaluate the reasonableness of the proposal.

(E) Whether the suit was in the nature of a test case presenting questions of far-reaching importance affecting nonparties.

(F) The amount of the additional delay cost and expense that the party making the proposal reasonably would be expected to incur if the litigation were to be prolonged.

(i) Evidence of Proposal. Evidence of a proposal or acceptance thereof is admissible only in proceedings to enforce an accepted proposal or to determine the imposition of sanctions.

(j) Effect of Mediation. Mediation shall have no effect on the dates during which parties are permitted to make or accept a proposal for settlement under the terms of the rule.

Committee Notes

1996 Amendment. This rule was amended to reconcile, where possible, sections 44.102(6) (formerly 44.102(5)(b)), 45.061, 73.032, and 768.79, Florida Statutes, and the decisions of the Florida Supreme Court in *Knealing v. Puleo*, 675 So. 2d 593 (Fla. 1996), *TGI Friday's, Inc. v. Dvorak*, 663 So. 2d 606 (Fla. 1995), and *Timmons v. Combs*, 608 So. 2d 1 (Fla. 1992). This rule replaces former rule 1.442, which was repealed by the Timmons decision, and supersedes those sections of the Florida Statutes and the prior decisions of the court, where reconciliation is impossible, in order to provide a workable structure for proposing settlements in civil actions. The provision which requires that a joint proposal state the amount and terms attributable to each party is in order to conform with *Fabre v. Marin*, 623 So. 2d 1182 (Fla. 1993).

2000 Amendment. Subdivision (f)(2) was added to establish the time for acceptance of proposals for settlement in class actions. "Filing" is defined in rule 1.080(e). Subdivision (g) is amended to conform with new rule 1.525.

RULE 1.450. EVIDENCE

(a) Record of Excluded Evidence. In an action tried by a jury if an objection to a question propounded to a witness is sustained by the court, the examining attorney may make a specific offer of what the attorney expects to prove by the answer of the witness. The court may require the offer to be made out of the hearing of the jury. The court may add such other or further statement as clearly shows the character of the evidence, the form in which it was offered, the objection made, and the ruling thereon. In actions tried without a jury the same procedure may be followed except that the court upon request shall take and report the evidence in full unless it clearly appears that the evidence is not admissible on any ground or that the witness is privileged.

(b) Filing. When documentary evidence is introduced in an action, the clerk or the judge shall endorse an identifying number or symbol on it and when proffered or admitted in evidence, it shall be filed by the clerk or judge and considered in the custody of the court and not withdrawn except with written leave of court.

Committee Notes

1971 Amendment. Subdivision (d) is amended to eliminate the necessity of a court order for disposal of exhibits. The clerk must retain the exhibits for 1 year unless the court permits removal earlier. If removal is not effected within the year, the clerk may destroy or dispose of the exhibits after giving the specified notice.

1996 Amendment. Former subdivision (a) entitled "Adverse Witness" is deleted because it is no longer needed or appropriate because the matters with which it deals are treated in the Florida Evidence Code.

Court Commentary

1984 Amendment. Subdivision (d) was repealed by the supreme court; see 403 So. 2d 926.

Subdivision (e): This rule was originally promulgated by the supreme court in *Carter v. Sparkman*, 335 So. 2d 802, 806 (Fla. 1976).

In *The Florida Bar, in re Rules of Civil Procedure*, 391 So. 2d 165 (Fla. 1980), the court requested the committee to consider the continued appropriateness of rule 1.450(e). In response, the committee recommended its deletion. After oral argument in *The Florida Bar: In re Rules of Civil Procedure*, 429 So. 2d 311, the court specifically declined to abolish the rule or to adopt a similar rule for other types of actions.

The committee again considered rule 1.450(e) in depth and at length and again recommends its deletion for the reason that no exception should be made in the rule to a particular type of action.

Subdivision (f): The West's Desk Copy Florida Rules of Court, at page 62, points out:

"The per curiam opinion of the Florida Supreme Court of June 21, 1979 (403 So.2d 926) provides: _On March 8, 1979, the Court proposed new Rule 1.450 of the Florida Rules of Civil Procedure which would provide for the disposal of exhibits and depositions in civil matters. Absent further action by the Court, the proposed rule was to become effective July 2, 1979. The Court has carefully considered the responses received regarding proposed Rule 1.450(f) and now feels that the July 2, 1979, effective date does not allow sufficient time for full reflection on matters raised in these responses. Therefore, the effective date for Rule 1.450(f) is, by this order, delayed until further order of the Court.'"

The retention of court records is the subject of Florida Rule of Judicial Administration 2.075.

RULE 1.452. QUESTIONS BY JURORS

(a) Questions Permitted. The court shall permit jurors to submit to the court written questions directed to witnesses or to the court. Such questions will be submitted after all counsel have concluded their questioning of a witness.

(b) Procedure. Any juror who has a question directed to the witness or the court shall prepare an unsigned, written question and give the question to the bailiff, who will give the question to the judge.

(c) Objections. Out of the presence of the jury, the judge will read the question to all counsel, allow counsel to see the written question, and give counsel an opportunity to object to the question.

RULE 1.455. JUROR NOTEBOOKS

In its discretion, the court may authorize documents and exhibits to be included in notebooks for use by the jurors during trial to aid them in performing their duties.

RULE 1.460. CONTINUANCES

A motion for continuance shall be in writing unless made at a trial and, except for good cause shown, shall be signed by the party requesting the continuance. The motion shall state all of the facts that the movant contends entitle the movant to a continuance. If a continuance is sought on the ground of nonavailability of a witness, the motion must show when it is believed the witness will be available.

Committee Notes

1980 Amendment. Subdivision (a), deleted by amendment, was initially adopted when trials were set at a docket sounding prescribed by statute. Even then, the rule was honored more in the breach than the observance. Trials are no longer uniformly set in that manner, and continuances are granted generally without reference to the rule. Under the revised rule, motions for continuance can be filed at any time that the need arises and need not be in writing if the parties are before the court.

1988 Amendment. The supreme court, by adopting Florida Rule of Judicial Administration 2.085(c), effective July 1, 1986, required all motions for continuance to be signed by the litigant requesting the continuance. The amendment conforms rule 1.460 to rule 2.085(c); but, by including an exception for good cause, it recognizes that circumstances justifying a continuance may excuse the signature of the party.

RULE 1.470. EXCEPTIONS UNNECESSARY; JURY INSTRUCTIONS

(a) Adverse Ruling. For appellate purposes no exception shall be necessary to any adverse ruling, order, instruction, or thing whatsoever said or done at the trial or prior thereto or after verdict, which was said or done after objection made and considered by the trial court and which affected the substantial rights of the party complaining and which is assigned as error.

(b) Instructions to Jury. The Florida Standard Jury Instructions appearing on the court's website at www.floridasupremecourt.org/jury_instructions/instructions.shtml shall be used by the trial judges of this state in instructing the jury in civil actions to the extent that the Standard Jury Instructions are applicable, unless the trial judge determines that an applicable Standard Jury Instruction is erroneous or inadequate. If the trial judge modifies a Standard Jury Instruction or gives such other instruction as the judge determines necessary to accurately and sufficiently instruct the jury, upon timely objection to the instruction, the trial judge shall state on the record or in a separate order the legal basis for varying from the Standard Jury Instruction. Similarly, in all circumstances in which the notes accompanying the Florida Standard Jury Instructions contain a recommendation that a certain type of instruction not be given, the trial judge shall follow the recommendation unless the judge determines that the giving of such an instruction is necessary to accurately and sufficiently instruct the jury, in which even the judge shall give such instruction as the judge deems appropriate and necessary. If the trial judge does not follow such a recommendation of the Florida Standard Jury Instructions, upon timely objection to the instruction, the trial judge shall state on the record or in a separate order the legal basis of the determination that such instruction is necessary. Not later than at the close of the evidence, the parties shall file written requests that the court instruct the jury on the law set forth in such requests. The court shall then require counsel to appear before it to settle the instructions to be given. At such conference, all objections shall be made and ruled upon and the court shall inform counsel of such instructions as it will give. No party may assign as error the giving of any instruction unless that party objects thereto at such time, or the failure to give any instruction unless that party requested the same. The court shall orally instruct the jury before or after the arguments of counsel and may provide appropriate instructions during the trial. If the instructions are given prior to final argument, the presiding judge shall give the jury final procedural instructions after final arguments are concluded and prior to deliberations. The court shall provide each juror with a written set of the instructions for his or her use in deliberations. The court shall file a copy of such instructions.

(c) Orders on New Trial, Directed Verdicts, etc. It shall not be necessary to object or except to any order granting or denying motions for new trials, directed verdicts, or judgments non obstante veredicto or in arrest of judgment to entitle the party against whom such ruling is made to have the same reviewed by an appellate court.

Committee Notes

1988 Amendment. The word "general" in the third sentence of subdivision (b) was deleted to require the court to specifically inform counsel of the charges it intends to give. The last sentence of that subdivision was amended to encourage judges to furnish written copies of their charges to juries.

2010 Amendment. Portions of form 1.985 were modified and moved to subdivision (b) of 1.470 to require the court to use published standard instructions where applicable and necessary, to permit the judge to vary from the published standard jury instructions, and notes only when necessary to accurately and sufficiently instruct the jury, and to require the parties to object to preserve error in variance from published standard jury instructions and notes.

RULE 1.480. MOTION FOR A DIRECTED VERDICT

(a) Effect. A party who moves for a directed verdict at the close of the evidence offered by the adverse party may offer evidence in the event the motion is denied without having reserved the right to do so and to the same extent as if the motion had not been made. The denial of a motion for a directed verdict shall not operate to discharge the jury. A motion for a directed verdict shall state the specific grounds therefor. The order directing a verdict is effective without any assent of the jury.

(b) Reservation of Decision on Motion. When a motion for a directed verdict is denied or for any reason is not granted, the court is deemed to have submitted the action to the jury subject to a later determination of the legal questions raised by the motion. Within 10 days after the return of a verdict, a party who has timely moved for a directed verdict may serve a motion to set aside the verdict and any judgment entered thereon and to enter judgment in accordance with the motion for a directed verdict. If a verdict was not returned, a party who has timely moved for a directed verdict may serve a motion for judgment in accordance with the motion for a directed verdict within 10 days after discharge of the jury.

(c) Joined with Motion for New Trial. A motion for a new trial may be joined with this motion or a new trial may be requested in the alternative. If a verdict was returned, the court may allow the judgment to stand or may reopen the judgment and either order a new trial or direct the entry of judgment as if the requested verdict had been directed. If no verdict was returned, the court may direct the entry of judgment as if the requested verdict had been directed or may order a new trial.

Committee Notes

1996 Amendment. Subdivision (b) is amended to clarify that the time limitations in this rule are based on service.

2010 Amendment. Subdivision (b) is amended to conform to 2006 changes to Federal Rule of Civil Procedure 50(b) eliminating the requirement for renewing at the close of all the evidence a motion for directed verdict already made at the close of an adverse party's evidence.

RULE 1.481. VERDICTS

In all actions when punitive damages are sought, the verdict shall state the amount of punitive damages separately from the amounts of other damages awarded.

RULE 1.490. MAGISTRATES

(a) General Magistrates. Judges of the circuit court may appoint as many general magistrates from among the members of the Bar in the circuit as the judges find necessary, and the general magistrates shall continue in office until removed by the court. The order making an appointment shall be recorded. Every person appointed as a general magistrate shall take the oath required of officers by the Constitution and the oath shall be recorded before the magistrate discharges any duties of that office.

(b) Special Magistrates. The court may appoint members of The Florida Bar as special magistrates for any particular service required by the court, and they shall be governed by all the provisions of law and rules relating to magistrates except they shall not be required to make oath or give bond unless specifically required by the order appointing them. Upon a showing that the appointment is advisable, a person other than a member of the Bar may be appointed.

(c) Reference. No reference shall be to a magistrate, either general or special, without the consent of the parties. When a reference is made to a magistrate, either party may set the action for hearing before the magistrate.

(d) General Powers and Duties. Every magistrate shall perform all of the duties that pertain to the office according to the practice in chancery and under the direction of the court. Process issued by a magistrate shall be directed as provided by law. Hearings before any magistrate, examiner, or commissioner shall be held in the county where the action is pending, but hearings may be held at any place by order of the court within or without the state to meet the convenience of the witnesses or the parties. All grounds of disqualification of a judge shall apply to magistrates.

(e) Bond. When not otherwise provided by law, the court may require magistrates who are appointed to dispose of real or personal property to give bond and surety conditioned for the proper payment of all moneys that may come into their hands and for the due performance of their duties as the court may direct. The bond shall be made payable to the State of Florida and shall be for the benefit of all persons aggrieved by any act of the magistrate.

(f) Hearings. The magistrate shall assign a time and place for proceedings as soon as reasonably possible after the reference is made and give notice to each of the parties. If any party fails to appear, the magistrate may proceed ex parte or may adjourn the proceeding to a future day, giving notice to the absent party of the adjournment. The magistrate shall proceed with reasonable diligence in every reference and with the least practicable delay. Any party may apply to the court for an order to the magistrate to speed the proceedings and to make the report and to certify to the court the reason for any delay. Unless otherwise ordered by the court, all hearings shall be held in the courthouse of the county where the action is pending. The evidence shall be taken in writing by the magistrate or by some other person under the magistrate's authority in the magistrate's presence and shall be filed with the magistrate's report. The magistrate shall have authority to examine the parties on oath upon all matters contained in the reference and to require production of all books, papers, writings, vouchers, and other documents applicable to it and to examine on oath orally all witnesses produced by the parties. The magistrate shall admit evidence by deposition or that is otherwise admissible in court. The magistrate may take all actions concerning evidence that can be taken by the court and in the same manner. All parties accounting before a magistrate shall bring in their accounts in the form of accounts payable and receivable, and any other parties who are not satisfied with the account may examine the accounting party orally or by interrogatories or deposition as the magistrate directs. All depositions and documents that have been taken or used previously in the action may be used before the magistrate.

(g) Magistrate's Report. In the reports made by the magistrate no part of any statement of facts, account, charge, deposition, examination, or answer used before the magistrate shall be recited. The matters shall be identified to inform the court what items were used.

(h) Filing Report; Notice; Exceptions. The magistrate shall file the report and serve copies on the parties. The parties may serve exceptions to the report within 10 days from the time it is served on them. If no exceptions are filed within that period, the court shall take appropriate action on the report. If exceptions are filed, they shall be heard on reasonable notice by either party.

Committee Notes

1971 Amendment. The entire rule has been revised. Obsolete language has been omitted and changes made to meet objections shown by the use of local rules in many circuits. Subdivisions (a) and (b) are not substantially changed. Subdivision (c) is shortened and eliminates the useless priority for setting the matter for hearing to permit either party to go forward. Subdivision (d) eliminates the right of the parties to stipulate to the place of hearing. Subdivision (e) is not substantially changed. Subdivisions (f), (g), (h), and (i) are combined. The right to use affidavits is eliminated because of the unavailability of cross-examination and possible constitutional questions. The vague general authority of the magistrate under subdivision (g) is made specific by limiting it to actions that the court could take. Subdivision (j) is repealed because it is covered in the new subdivision (f). Subdivision (g) is the same as former subdivision (k) after eliminating the reference to affidavits. Subdivision (h) is the same as former subdivision (l).

1980 Amendment. Subdivision (d) is amended to delete the specific reference to the direction of process so that process issued by the master will be governed by the law applicable to process generally.

Court Commentary

1984 Amendment. The consent of all parties is required for any reference to a special master. Special masters may be used as provided by statute even with the rule change. See *Slatcoff v. Dezen,* 74 So. 2d 59 (Fla. 1954).

RULE 1.500. DEFAULTS AND FINAL JUDGMENTS THEREON

(a) **By the Clerk.** When a party against whom affirmative relief is sought has failed to file or serve any paper in the action, the party seeking relief may have the clerk enter a default against the party failing to serve or file such paper.

(b) **By the Court.** When a party against whom affirmative relief is sought has failed to plead or otherwise defend as provided by these rules or any applicable statute or any order of court, the court may enter a default against such party; provided that if such party has filed or served any paper in the action, that party shall be served with notice of the application for default.

(c) **Right to Plead.** A party may plead or otherwise defend at any time before default is entered. If a party in default files any paper after the default is entered, the clerk shall notify the party of the entry of the default. The clerk shall make an entry on the progress docket showing the notification.

(d) **Setting aside Default.** The court may set aside a default, and if a final judgment consequent thereon has been entered, the court may set it aside in accordance with rule 1.540(b).

(e) **Final Judgment.** Final judgments after default may be entered by the court at any time, but no judgment may be entered against an infant or incompetent person unless represented in the action by a general guardian, committee, conservator, or other representative who has appeared in it or unless the court has made an order under rule 1.210(b) providing that no representative is necessary for the infant or incompetent. If it is necessary to take an account or to determine the amount of damages or to establish the truth of any averment by evidence or to make an investigation of any other matter to enable the court to enter judgment or to effectuate it, the court may receive affidavits, make references, or conduct hearings as it deems necessary and shall accord a right of trial by jury to the parties when required by the Constitution or any statute.

Court Commentary

1984 Amendment. Subdivision (c) is amended to change the method by which the clerk handles papers filed after a default is entered. Instead of returning the papers to the party in default, the clerk will now be required to file them and merely notify the party that a default has been entered. The party can then take whatever action the party believes is appropriate.

This is to enable the court to judge the effect, if any, of the filing of any paper upon the default and the propriety of entering final judgment without notice to the party against whom the default was entered.

RULE 1.510. SUMMARY JUDGMENT

(a) **For Claimant.** A party seeking to recover upon a claim, counterclaim, crossclaim, or third-party claim or to obtain a declaratory judgment may move for a summary judgment in that party's favor upon all or any part thereof with or without supporting affidavits at any time after the expiration of 20 days from the commencement of the action or after service of a motion for summary judgment by the adverse party.

(b) **For Defending Party.** A party against whom a claim, counterclaim, crossclaim, or third-party claim is asserted or a declaratory judgment is sought may move for a summary judgment in that party's favor as to all or any part thereof at any time with or without supporting affidavits.

(c) **Motion and Proceedings Thereon.** The motion shall state with particularity the grounds upon which it is based and the substantial matters of law to be argued and shall specifically identify any affidavits, answers to interrogatories, admissions, depositions, and other materials as would be admissible in evidence ("summary judgment evidence") on which the movant relies. The movant shall serve the motion at least 20 days before the time fixed for the hearing, and shall also serve at that time a copy of any summary judgment evidence on which the movant relies that has not already been filed with the court. The adverse party shall identify, by notice mailed to the movant's attorney at least 5 days prior to the day of the hearing, or delivered no later than 5:00 p.m. 2 business days prior to the day of the hearing, any summary judgment evidence on which the adverse party relies. To the extent that summary judgment evidence has not already been filed with the court, the adverse party shall serve a copy on the movant by mail at least 5 days prior to the day of the hearing, or by delivery to the movant's attorney no later than 5:00 p.m. 2 business days prior to the day of hearing. The judgment sought shall be rendered forthwith if the pleadings and summary judgment evidence on file show that there is no genuine issue as to any material fact and that the moving party is entitled to a judgment as a matter of law. A summary judgment, interlocutory in character, may be rendered on the issue of liability alone although there is a genuine issue as to the amount of damages.

(d) Case Not Fully Adjudicated on Motion. On motion under this rule if judgment is not rendered upon the whole case or for all the relief asked and a trial or the taking of testimony and a final hearing is necessary, the court at the hearing of the motion, by examining the pleadings and the evidence before it and by interrogating counsel, shall ascertain, if practicable, what material facts exist without substantial controversy and what material facts are actually and in good faith controverted. It shall thereupon make an order specifying the facts that appear without substantial controversy, including the extent to which the amount of damages or other relief is not in controversy, and directing such further proceedings in the action as are just. On the trial or final hearing of the action the facts so specified shall be deemed established, and the trial or final hearing shall be conducted accordingly.

(e) Form of Affidavits; Further Testimony. Supporting and opposing affidavits shall be made on personal knowledge, shall set forth such facts as would be admissible in evidence, and shall show affirmatively that the affiant is competent to testify to the matters stated therein. Sworn or certified copies of all papers or parts thereof referred to in an affidavit shall be attached thereto or served therewith. The court may permit affidavits to be supplemented or opposed by depositions, answers to interrogatories, or by further affidavits.

(f) When Affidavits Are Unavailable. If it appears from the affidavits of a party opposing the motion that the party cannot for reasons stated present by affidavit facts essential to justify opposition, the court may refuse the application for judgment or may order a continuance to permit affidavits to be obtained or depositions to be taken or discovery to be had or may make such other order as is just.

(g) Affidavits Made in Bad Faith. If it appears to the satisfaction of the court at any time that any of the affidavits presented pursuant to this rule are presented in bad faith or solely for the purpose of delay, the court shall forthwith order the party employing them to pay to the other party the amount of the reasonable expenses which the filing of the affidavits caused the other party to incur, including reasonable attorneys' fees, and any offending party or attorney may be adjudged guilty of contempt.

Committee Notes

1976 Amendment. Subdivision (c) has been amended to require a movant to state with particularity the grounds and legal authority which the movant will rely upon in seeking summary judgment. This amendment will eliminate surprise and bring the summary judgment rule into conformity with the identical provision in rule 1.140(b) with respect to motions to dismiss.

1992 Amendment. The amendment to subdivision (c) will require timely service of opposing affidavits, whether by mail or by delivery, prior to the day of the hearing on a motion for summary judgment.

2005 Amendment. Subdivision (c) has been amended to ensure that the moving party and the adverse party are each given advance notice of and, where appropriate, copies of the evidentiary material on which the other party relies in connection with a summary judgment motion.

RULE 1.520. VIEW

Upon motion of either party the jury may be taken to view the premises or place in question or any property, matter, or thing relating to the controversy between the parties when it appears that view is necessary to a just decision; but the party making the motion shall advance a sum sufficient to defray the expenses of the jury and the officer who attends them in taking the view, which expense shall be taxed as costs if the party who advanced it prevails.

RULE 1.525. MOTIONS FOR COSTS AND ATTORNEYS' FEES

Any party seeking a judgment taxing costs, attorneys' fees, or both shall serve a motion no later than 30 days after filing of the judgment, including a judgment of dismissal, or the service of a notice of voluntary dismissal, which judgment or notice concludes the action as to that party.

Committee Notes

2000 Adoption. This rule is intended to establish a time requirement to serve motions for costs and attorneys' fees.

Court Commentary

2000 Adoption. This rule only establishes time requirements for serving motions for costs, attorneys' fees, or both, and in no way affects or overrules the pleading requirements outlined by this Court in *Stockman v. Downs*, 573 So. 2d 835 (Fla. 1991).

RULE 1.530. MOTIONS FOR NEW TRIAL AND REHEARING; AMENDMENTS OF JUDGMENTS

(a) Jury and Non-Jury Actions. A new trial may be granted to all or any of the parties and on all or a part of the issues. On a motion for a rehearing of matters heard without a jury, including summary judgments, the court may open the judgment if one has been entered, take additional testimony, and enter a new judgment.

(b) Time for Motion. A motion for new trial or for rehearing shall be served not later than 10 days after the return of the verdict in a jury action or the date of filing of the judgment in a non-jury action. A timely motion may be amended to state new grounds in the discretion of the court at any time before the motion is determined.

(c) Time for Serving Affidavits. When a motion for a new trial is based on affidavits, the affidavits shall be served with the motion. The opposing party has 10 days after such service within which to serve opposing affidavits, which period may be extended for an additional period not exceeding 20 days either by the court for good cause shown or by the parties by written stipulation. The court may permit reply affidavits.

(d) On Initiative of Court. Not later than 10 days after entry of judgment or within the time of ruling on a timely motion for a rehearing or a new trial made by a party, the court of its own initiative may order a rehearing or a new trial for any reason for which it might have granted a rehearing or a new trial on motion of a party.

(e) When Motion Is Unnecessary; Non-Jury Case. When an action has been tried by the court without a jury, the sufficiency of the evidence to support the judgment may be raised on appeal whether or not the party raising the question has made any objection thereto in the trial court or made a motion for rehearing, for new trial, or to alter or amend the judgment.

(f) Order Granting to Specify Grounds. All orders granting a new trial shall specify the specific grounds therefor. If such an order is appealed and does not state the specific grounds, the appellate court shall relinquish its jurisdiction to the trial court for entry of an order specifying the grounds for granting the new trial.

(g) Motion to Alter or Amend a Judgment. A motion to alter or amend the judgment shall be served not later than 10 days after entry of the judgment, except that this rule does not affect the remedies in rule 1.540(b).

Committee Notes

1992 Amendment. In subdivision (e), the reference to assignments of error is eliminated to conform to amendments to the Florida Rules of Appellate Procedure.

Court Commentary

1984 Amendment. Subdivision (b): This clarifies the time in which a motion for rehearing may be served. It specifies that the date of filing as shown on the face of the judgment in a non-jury action is the date from which the time for serving a motion for rehearing is calculated.

There is no change in the time for serving a motion for new trial in a jury action, except the motion may be served before the rendition of the judgment.

RULE 1.540. RELIEF FROM JUDGMENT, DECREES, OR ORDERS

(a) **Clerical Mistakes.** Clerical mistakes in judgments, decrees, or other parts of the record and errors therein arising from oversight or omission may be corrected by the court at any time on its own initiative or on the motion of any party and after such notice, if any, as the court orders. During the pendency of an appeal such mistakes may be so corrected before the record on appeal is docketed in the appellate court, and thereafter while the appeal is pending may be so corrected with leave of the appellate court.

(b) **Mistakes; Inadvertence; Excusable Neglect; Newly Discovered Evidence; Fraud; etc.** On motion and upon such terms as are just, the court may relieve a party or a party's legal representative from a final judgment, decree, order, or proceeding for the following reasons: (1) mistake, inadvertence, surprise, or excusable neglect; (2) newly discovered evidence which by due diligence could not have been discovered in time to move for a new trial or rehearing; (3) fraud (whether heretofore denominated intrinsic or extrinsic), misrepresentation, or other misconduct of an adverse party; (4) that the judgment or decree is void; or (5) that the judgment or decree has been satisfied, released, or discharged, or a prior judgment or decree upon which it is based has been reversed or otherwise vacated, or it is no longer equitable that the judgment or decree should have prospective application. The motion shall be filed within a reasonable time, and for reasons (1), (2), and (3) not more than 1 year after the judgment, decree, order, or proceeding was entered or taken. A motion under this subdivision does not affect the finality of a judgment or decree or suspend its operation. This rule does not limit the power of a court to entertain an independent action to relieve a party from a judgment, decree, order, or proceeding or to set aside a judgment or decree for fraud upon the court.

Writs of coram nobis, coram vobis, audita querela, and bills of review and bills in the nature of a bill of review are abolished, and the procedure for obtaining any relief from a judgment or decree shall be by motion as prescribed in these rules or by an independent action.

Committee Notes

1992 Amendment. Subdivision (b) is amended to remove the 1-year limitation for a motion under this rule based on fraudulent financial affidavits in marital cases.

2003 Amendment. Subdivision (b) is amended to clarify that motions must be filed.

RULE 1.550. EXECUTIONS AND FINAL PROCESS

(a) **Issuance.** Executions on judgments shall issue during the life of the judgment on the oral request of the party entitled to it or that party's attorney without praecipe. No execution or other final process shall issue until the judgment on which it is based has been recorded nor within the time for serving a motion for new trial or rehearing, and if a motion for new trial or rehearing is timely served, until it is determined; provided execution or other final process may be issued on special order of the court at any time after judgment.

(b) Stay. The court before which an execution or other process based on a final judgment is returnable may stay such execution or other process and suspend proceedings thereon for good cause on motion and notice to all adverse parties.

RULE 1.560. DISCOVERY IN AID OF EXECUTION

(a) In General. In aid of a judgment, decree, or execution the judgment creditor or the successor in interest, when that interest appears of record, may obtain discovery from any person, including the judgment debtor, in the manner provided in these rules.

(b) Fact Information Sheet. In addition to any other discovery available to a judgment creditor under this rule, the court, at the request of the judgment creditor, shall order the judgment debtor or debtors to complete form 1.977, including all required attachments, within 45 days of the order or such other reasonable time as determined by the court. Failure to obey the order may be considered contempt of court.

(c) Final Judgment Enforcement Paragraph. In any final judgment, the judge shall include the following enforcement paragraph if requested by the prevailing party or attorney:

"It is further ordered and adjudged that the judgment debtor(s) shall complete under oath Florida Rule of Civil Procedure Form 1.977 (Fact Information Sheet), including all required attachments, and serve it on the judgment creditor's attorney, or the judgment creditor if the judgment creditor is not represented by an attorney, within 45 days from the date of this final judgment, unless the final judgment is satisfied or post-judgment discovery is stayed.

Jurisdiction of this case is retained to enter further orders that are proper to compel the judgment debtor(s) to complete form 1.977, including all required attachments, and serve it on the judgment creditor's attorney, or the judgment creditor if the judgment creditor is not represented by an attorney."

(d) Information Regarding Assets of Judgment Debtor's Spouse. In any final judgment, if requested by the judgment creditor, the court shall include the additional Spouse Related Portion of the fact information sheet upon a showing that a proper predicate exists for discovery of separate income and assets of the judgment debtor's spouse.

(e) Notice of Compliance. The judgment debtor shall file with the clerk of court a notice of compliance with the order to complete form 1.977, and serve a copy of the notice of compliance on the judgment creditor or the judgment creditor's attorney.

Committee Notes

1972 Amendment. The rule is expanded to permit discovery in any manner permitted by the rules and conforms to the 1970 change in Federal Rule of Civil Procedure 69(a).

2000 Amendment. Subdivisions (b)–(e) were added and patterned after Florida Small Claims Rule 7.221(a) and Form 7.343. Although the judgment creditor is entitled to broad discovery into the judgment debtor's finances, Fla. R. Civ. P. 1.280(b); *Jim Appley's Tru-Arc, Inc. v. Liquid Extraction Systems*, 526 So. 2d 177, 179 (Fla. 2d DCA 1988), inquiry into the individual assets of the judgment debtor's spouse may be limited until a proper predicate has been shown. *Tru-Arc, Inc.* 526 So. 2d at 179; *Rose Printing Co. v. D'Amato*, 338 So. 2d 212 (Fla. 3d DCA 1976).

Failure to complete form 1.977 as ordered may be considered contempt of court.

RULE 1.570. ENFORCEMENT OF FINAL JUDGMENTS

(a) Money Judgments. Final process to enforce a judgment solely for the payment of money shall be by execution, writ of garnishment, or other appropriate process or proceedings.

(b) Property Recovery. Final process to enforce a judgment for the recovery of property shall be by a writ of possession for real property and by a writ of replevin, distress writ, writ of garnishment, or other appropriate process or proceedings for other property.

(c) Performance of an Act. If judgment is for the performance of a specific act or contract:

(1) the judgment shall specify the time within which the act shall be performed. If the act is not performed within the time specified, the party seeking enforcement of the judgment shall make an affidavit that the judgment has not been complied with within the prescribed time and the clerk shall issue a writ of attachment against the delinquent party. The delinquent party shall not be released from the writ of attachment until that party has complied with the judgment and paid all costs accruing because of the failure to perform the act. If the delinquent party cannot be found, the party seeking enforcement of the judgment shall file an affidavit to this effect and the court shall issue a writ of sequestration against the delinquent party's property. The writ of sequestration shall not be dissolved until the delinquent party complies with the judgment;

(2) the court may hold the disobedient party in contempt; or

(3) the court may appoint some person, not a party to the action, to perform the act insofar as practicable. The performance of the act by the person appointed shall have the same effect as if performed by the party against whom the judgment was entered.

(d) Vesting Title. If the judgment is for a conveyance, transfer, release, or acquittance of real or personal property, the judgment shall have the effect of a duly executed conveyance, transfer, release, or acquittance that is recorded in the county where the judgment is recorded. A judgment under this subdivision shall be effective notwithstanding any disability of a party.

Committee Notes

1980 Amendment. This rule has been subdivided and amended to make it more easily understood. No change in the substance of the rule is intended. Subdivision (d) is partly derived from Federal Rule of Civil Procedure 70.

RULE 1.580. WRIT OF POSSESSION

(a) Issuance. When a judgment or order is for the delivery of possession of real property, the judgment or order shall direct the clerk to issue a writ of possession. The clerk shall issue the writ forthwith and deliver it to the sheriff for execution.

(b) Third-Party Claims. If a person other than the party against whom the writ of possession is issued is in possession of the property, that person may retain possession of the property by filing with the sheriff an affidavit that the person is entitled to possession of the property, specifying the nature of the claim. Thereupon the sheriff shall desist from enforcing the writ and shall serve a copy of the affidavit on the party causing issuance of the writ of possession. The party causing issuance of the writ may apply to the court for an order directing the sheriff to complete execution of the writ. The court shall determine the right of possession in the property and shall order the sheriff to continue to execute the writ or shall stay execution of the writ, if appropriate.

Committee Notes

1980 Amendment. There was inadvertently continued the difference between writs of assistance and writs of possession when law and chancery procedure was consolidated. The amendment eliminates the distinction. Writs of assistance are combined with writs of possession. The amendment provides for issuance and the determination of third-party claims. The only change is to shift the burden of the affidavit from the person causing the writ to be executed to the third person who contends that its execution is inappropriate.

RULE 1.590. PROCESS IN BEHALF OF AND AGAINST PERSONS NOT PARTIES

Every person who is not a party to the action who has obtained an order, or in whose favor an order has been made, may enforce obedience to such order by the same process as if that person were a party, and every person, not a party, against whom obedience to any order may be enforced shall be liable to the same process for enforcing obedience to such orders as if that person were a party.

RULE 1.600. DEPOSITS IN COURT

In an action in which any part of the relief sought is a judgment for a sum of money or the disposition of a sum of money or the disposition of any other thing capable of delivery, a party may deposit all or any part of such sum or thing with the court upon notice to every other party and by leave of court. Money paid into court under this rule shall be deposited and withdrawn by order of court.

RULE 1.610. INJUNCTIONS

(a) Temporary Injunction.

(1) A temporary injunction may be granted without written or oral notice to the adverse party only if:

(A) it appears from the specific facts shown by affidavit or verified pleading that immediate and irreparable injury, loss, or damage will result to the movant before the adverse party can be heard in opposition; and

(B) the movant's attorney certifies in writing any efforts that have been made to give notice and the reasons why notice should not be required.

(2) No evidence other than the affidavit or verified pleading shall be used to support the application for a temporary injunction unless the adverse party appears at the hearing or has received reasonable notice of the hearing. Every temporary injunction granted without notice shall be endorsed with the date and hour of entry and shall be filed forthwith in the clerk's office and shall define the injury, state findings by the court why the injury may be irreparable, and give the reasons why the order was granted without notice if notice was not given. The temporary injunction shall remain in effect until the further order of the court.

(b) **Bond.** No temporary injunction shall be entered unless a bond is given by the movant in an amount the court deems proper, conditioned for the payment of costs and damages sustained by the adverse party if the adverse party is wrongfully enjoined. When any injunction is issued on the pleading of a municipality or the state or any officer, agency, or political subdivision thereof, the court may require or dispense with a bond, with or without surety, and conditioned in the same manner, having due regard for the public interest. No bond shall be required for issuance of a temporary injunction issued solely to prevent physical injury or abuse of a natural person.

(c) **Form and Scope.** Every injunction shall specify the reasons for entry, shall describe in reasonable detail the act or acts restrained without reference to a pleading or another document, and shall be binding on the parties to the action, their officers, agents, servants, employees, and attorneys and on those persons in active concert or participation with them who receive actual notice of the injunction.

(d) **Motion to Dissolve.** A party against whom a temporary injunction has been granted may move to dissolve or modify it at any time. If a party moves to dissolve or modify, the motion shall be heard within 5 days after the movant applies for a hearing on the motion.

Committee Notes

1980 Amendment. This rule has been extensively amended so that it is similar to Federal Rule of Civil Procedure 65. The requirement that an injunction not be issued until a complaint was filed has been deleted as unnecessary. A pleading seeking an injunction or temporary restraining order must still be filed before either can be entered. The rule now provides for a temporary restraining order without notice that will expire automatically unless a hearing on a preliminary injunction is held and a preliminary injunction granted. The contents of an injunctive order are specified. The binding effect of an injunctive order is specified, but does not change existing law. Motions to dissolve may be made and heard at any time. The trial on the merits can be consolidated with a hearing on issuance of a preliminary injunction, and the trial can be advanced to accommodate this.

Court Commentary

1984 Amendment. Considerable dissatisfaction arose on the adoption of the 1980 rule, particularly because of the creation of the temporary restraining order with its inflexible time limits. See *Sun Tech Inc. of South Florida v. Fortune Personnel Agency of Fort Lauderdale*, 412 So. 2d 962 (Fla. 4th DCA 1982). The attempt to balance the rights of the parties in 1980 failed because of court congestion and the inability in the existing circumstances to accommodate the inflexible time limits. These changes will restore injunction procedure to substantially the same as that existing before the 1980 change. The temporary restraining order terminology and procedure is abolished. The former procedure of temporary and permanent injunctions is restored. The requirement of findings and reasons and other details in an injunctive order are retained.

Subdivision (b) eliminates the need for a bond on a temporary injunction issued to prevent physical injury or abuse of a natural person.

Subdivision (e) institutes a requirement that a motion to dissolve an injunction shall be heard within 5 days after the movant applies for it. This provision emphasizes the importance of a prompt determination of the propriety of injunctive relief granted without notice or, if the circumstances have changed since the issuance of the injunctive order, the need for speedy relief as a result of the changes. Former subdivisions (a), (b)(3), and (b)(4) have been repealed because the new procedure makes them superfluous. The right of the court to consolidate the hearing on a temporary injunction with the trial of the action is not affected because that can still be accomplished under rule 1.270(a).

RULE 1.620. RECEIVERS

(a) Notice. The provisions of rule 1.610 as to notice shall apply to applications for the appointment of receivers.

(b) Report. Every receiver shall file in the clerk's office a true and complete inventory under oath of the property coming under the receiver's control or possession under the receiver's appointment within 20 days after appointment. Every 3 months unless the court otherwise orders, the receiver shall file in the same office an inventory and account under oath of any additional property or effects which the receiver has discovered or which shall have come to the receiver's hands since appointment, and of the amount remaining in the hands of or invested by the receiver, and of the manner in which the same is secured or invested, stating the balance due from or to the receiver at the time of rendering the last account and the receipts and expenditures since that time. When a receiver neglects to file the inventory and account, the court shall enter an order requiring the receiver to file such inventory and account and to pay out of the receiver's own funds the expenses of the order and the proceedings thereon within not more than 20 days after being served with a copy of such order.

(c) Bond. The court may grant leave to put the bond of the receiver in suit against the sureties without notice to the sureties of the application for such leave.

RULE 1.625. PROCEEDINGS AGAINST SURETY ON JUDICIAL BONDS

When any rule or statute requires or permits giving of bond by a party in a judicial proceeding, the surety on the bond submits to the jurisdiction of the court when the bond is approved. The surety shall furnish the address for the service of papers affecting the surety's liability on the bond to the officer to whom the bond is given at that time. The liability of the surety may be enforced on motion without the necessity of an independent action. The motion shall be served on the surety at the address furnished to the officer. The surety shall serve a response to the motion within 20 days after service of the motion, asserting any defenses in law or in fact. If the surety fails to serve a response within the time allowed, a default may be taken. If the surety serves a response, the issues raised shall be decided by the court on reasonable notice to the parties. The right to jury trial shall not be abridged in any such proceedings.

Committee Notes

1990 Adoption. This rule is intended to avoid the necessity of an independent action against a surety on judicial bonds. It does not abolish an independent action if the obligee prefers to file one.

RULE 1.630. EXTRAORDINARY REMEDIES

(a) **Applicability.** This rule applies to actions for the issuance of writs of mandamus, prohibition, quo warranto, certiorari, and habeas corpus.

(b) **Initial Pleading.** The initial pleading shall be a complaint. It shall contain:

(1) the facts on which the plaintiff relies for relief;

(2) a request for the relief sought; and

(3) if desired, argument in support of the petition with citations of authority.

The caption shall show the action filed in the name of the plaintiff in all cases and not on the relation of the state. When the complaint seeks a writ directed to a lower court or to a governmental or administrative agency, a copy of as much of the record as is necessary to support the plaintiff's complaint shall be attached.

(c) **Time.** A complaint shall be filed within the time provided by law, except that a complaint for common law certiorari shall be filed within 30 days of rendition of the matter sought to be reviewed.

(d) **Process.** If the complaint shows a prima facie case for relief, the court shall issue:

(1) a summons in certiorari;

(2) an order nisi in prohibition;

(3) an alternative writ in mandamus that may incorporate the complaint by reference only;

(4) a writ of quo warranto; or

(5) a writ of habeas corpus.

The writ shall be served in the manner prescribed by law, except the summons in certiorari shall be served as provided in rule 1.080(b).

(e) **Response.** Defendant shall respond to the writ as provided in rule 1.140, but the answer in quo warranto shall show better title to the office when the writ seeks an adjudication of the right to an office held by the defendant.

Court Commentary

1984 Amendment. Rule 1.630 replaces rules and statutes used before 1980 when the present Florida Rules of Appellate Procedure were adopted. Experience has shown that rule 9.100 is not designed for use in trial court. The times for proceeding, the methods of proceeding, and the general nature of the procedure is appellate and presumes that the proceeding is basically an appellate proceeding. When the extraordinary remedies are sought in the trial court, these items do not usually exist and thus the rule is difficult to apply. The uniform procedure concept of rule 9.100 has been retained with changes making the procedure fit trial court procedure. The requirement of attaching a copy of the record in subdivision (b) may not be possible within the time allowed for the initial pleading because of the unavailability of the record. In that event the plaintiff should file a motion to extend the time to allow the preparation of the record and supply it when prepared. The filing of a motion to extend the time should be sufficient to extend it until the motion can be decided by the court.

RULE 1.650. MEDICAL MALPRACTICE PRESUIT SCREENING RULE

(a) Scope of Rule. This rule applies only to the procedures prescribed by section 766.106, Florida Statutes, for presuit screening of claims for medical malpractice.

(b) Notice.

(1) Notice of intent to initiate litigation sent by certified mail to and received by any prospective defendant shall operate as notice to the person and any other prospective defendant who bears a legal relationship to the prospective defendant receiving the notice. The notice shall make the recipient a party to the proceeding under this rule.

(2) The notice shall include the names and addresses of all other parties and shall be sent to each party.

(3) The court shall decide the issue of receipt of notice when raised in a motion to dismiss or to abate an action for medical malpractice.

(c) Discovery.

(1) Types. Upon receipt by a prospective defendant of a notice of intent to initiate litigation, the parties may obtain presuit screening discovery by one or more of the following methods: unsworn statements upon oral examination; production of documents or things; and physical examinations. Unless otherwise provided in this rule, the parties shall make discoverable information available without formal discovery. Evidence of failure to comply with this rule may be grounds for dismissal of claims or defenses ultimately asserted.

(2) Procedures for Conducting.

(A) Unsworn Statements. The parties may require other parties to appear for the taking of an unsworn statement. The statements shall only be used for the purpose of presuit screening and are not discoverable or admissible in any civil action for any purpose by any party. A party desiring to take the unsworn statement of any party shall give reasonable notice in writing to all parties. The notice shall state the time and place for taking the statement and the name and address of the party to be examined. Unless otherwise impractical, the examination of any party shall be done at the same time by all other parties. Any party may be represented by an attorney at the taking of an unsworn statement. Statements may be electronically or stenographically recorded, or recorded on video tape. The taking of unsworn statements of minors is subject to the provisions of rule 1.310(b)(8). The taking of unsworn statements is subject to the provisions of rule 1.310(d) and may be terminated for abuses. If abuses occur, the abuses shall be evidence of failure of that party to comply with the good faith requirements of section 766.106, Florida Statutes.

(B) Documents or Things. At any time after receipt by a party of a notice of intent to initiate litigation, a party may request discoverable documents or things. The documents or things shall be produced at the expense of the requesting party within 20 days of the date of receipt of the request. A party is required to produce discoverable documents or things within that party's possession or control. Copies of documents produced in response to the request of any party shall be served on all other parties. The party serving the documents shall list the name and address of the parties upon whom the documents were served, the date of service, the manner of service, and the identity of the document served in the certificate of service. Failure of a party to comply with the above time limits shall not relieve that party of its obligation under the statute but shall be evidence of failure of that party to comply with the good faith requirements of section 766.106, Florida Statutes.

(C) Physical Examinations. Upon receipt by a party of a notice of intent to initiate litigation and within the presuit screening period, a party may require a claimant to submit to a physical examination. The party shall give reasonable notice in writing to all parties of the time and place of the examination. Unless otherwise impractical, a claimant shall be required to submit to only one examination on behalf of all parties. The practicality of a single examination shall be determined by the nature of the claimant's condition as it relates to the potential liability of each party. The report of examination shall be made available to all parties upon payment of the reasonable cost of reproduction.

The report shall not be provided to any person not a party at any time. The report shall only be used for the purpose of presuit screening and the examining physician may not testify concerning the examination in any subsequent civil action. All requests for physical examinations or notices of unsworn statements shall be in writing and a copy served upon all parties. The requests or notices shall bear a certificate of service identifying the name and address of the person upon whom the request or notice is served, the date of the request or notice, and the manner of service. Any minor required to submit to examination pursuant to this rule shall have the right to be accompanied by a parent or guardian at all times during the examination, except upon a showing that the presence of a parent or guardian is likely to have a material, negative impact on the minor's examination.

(3) Work Product. Work product generated by the presuit screening process that is subject to exclusion in a subsequent proceeding is limited to verbal or written communications that originate pursuant to the presuit screening process.

(d) Time Requirements.

(1) The notice of intent to initiate litigation shall be served by certified mail, return receipt requested, prior to the expiration of any applicable statute of limitations or statute of repose. If an extension has been granted under section 766.104(2), Florida Statutes, or by agreement of the parties, the notice shall be served within the extended period.

(2) The action may not be filed against any defendant until 90 days after the notice of intent to initiate litigation was mailed to that party. The action may be filed against any party at any time after the notice of intent to initiate litigation has been mailed after the claimant has received a written rejection of the claim from that party.

(3) To avoid being barred by the applicable statute of limitations, an action must be filed within 60 days or within the remainder of the time of the statute of limitations after the notice of intent to initiate litigation was received, whichever is longer, after the earliest of the following:

(A) The expiration of 90 days after the date of receipt of the notice of intent to initiate litigation.

(B) The expiration of 180 days after mailing of the notice of intent to initiate litigation if the claim is controlled by section 768.28(6)(a), Florida Statutes.

(C) Receipt by claimant of a written rejection of the claim.

(D) The expiration of any extension of the 90-day presuit screening period stipulated to by the parties in accordance with section 766.106(4), Florida Statutes.

Committee Notes

2000 Amendment. The reference to the statute of repose was added to subdivision (d)(1) pursuant to *Musculoskeletal Institute Chartered v. Parham*, 745 So.2d 946 (Fla. 1999).

1988 Editor's Note: This rule was added in In re: Medical Malpractice Presuit Screening Rules — Civil Rules of Procedure, *531 So.2d 958 (Fla. 1988), revised 536 So.2d 193.*

RULE 1.700. RULES COMMON TO MEDIATION AND ARBITRATION

(a) Referral by Presiding Judge or by Stipulation. Except as hereinafter provided or as otherwise prohibited by law, the presiding judge may enter an order referring all or any part of a contested civil matter to mediation or arbitration. The parties to any contested civil matter may file a written stipulation to mediate or arbitrate any issue between them at any time. Such stipulation shall be incorporated into the order of referral.

(1) Conference or Hearing Date. Unless otherwise ordered by the court, the first mediation conference or arbitration hearing shall be held within 60 days of the order of referral. (2) Notice. Within 15 days after the designation of the mediator or the arbitrator, the court or its designee,

who may be the mediator or the chief arbitrator, shall notify the parties in writing of the date, time, and place of the conference or hearing unless the order of referral specifies the date, time, and place.

(b) Motion to Dispense with Mediation and Arbitration. A party may move, within 15 days after the order of referral, to dispense with mediation or arbitration, if:

(1) the issue to be considered has been previously mediated or arbitrated between the same parties pursuant to Florida law;

(2) the issue presents a question of law only;

(3) the order violates rule 1.710(b) or rule 1.800; or

(4) other good cause is shown.

(c) Motion to Defer Mediation or Arbitration. Within 15 days of the order of referral, any party may file a motion with the court to defer the proceeding. The movant shall set the motion to defer for hearing prior to the scheduled date for mediation or arbitration. Notice of the hearing shall be provided to all interested parties, including any mediator or arbitrator who has been appointed. The motion shall set forth, in detail, the facts and circumstances supporting the motion. Mediation or arbitration shall be tolled until disposition of the motion.

(d) Disqualification of a Mediator or Arbitrator. Any party may move to enter an order disqualifying a mediator or an arbitrator for good cause. If the court rules that a mediator or arbitrator is disqualified from hearing a case, an order shall be entered setting forth the name of a qualified replacement. Nothing in this provision shall preclude mediators or arbitrators from disqualifying themselves or refusing any assignment. The time for mediation or arbitration shall be tolled during any periods in which a motion to disqualify is pending.

1990 Editor's Note: Rules 1.700–1.830 were adopted in Rules of Civil Procedure, In re Proposed Rules for Implementation of Florida Statutes Sections 44.301–.306, *518 So.2d 908 (Fla. 1987), and amended in 563 So.2d 85 (Fla. 1990).*

RULE 1.710. MEDIATION RULES

(a) Completion of Mediation. Mediation shall be completed within 45 days of the first mediation conference unless extended by order of the court or by stipulation of the parties.

(b) Exclusions from Mediation. A civil action shall be ordered to mediation or mediation in conjunction with arbitration upon stipulation of the parties. A civil action may be ordered to mediation or mediation in conjunction with arbitration upon motion of any party or by the court, if the judge determines the action to be of such a nature that mediation could be of benefit to the litigants or the court. Under no circumstances may the following categories of actions be referred to mediation:

(1) Bond estreatures.

(2) Habeas corpus and extraordinary writs.

(3) Bond validations.

(4) Civil or criminal contempt.

(5) Other matters as may be specified by administrative order of the chief judge in the circuit.

(c) Discovery. Unless stipulated by the parties or ordered by the court, the mediation process shall not suspend discovery.

Committee Notes

1994 Amendment. The Supreme Court Committee on Mediation and Arbitration Rules encourages crafting a combination of dispute resolution processes without creating an unreasonable barrier to the traditional court system.

RULE 1.720. MEDIATION PROCEDURES

(a) Interim or Emergency Relief. A party may apply to the court for interim or emergency relief at any time. Mediation shall continue while such a motion is pending absent a contrary order of the court, or a decision of the mediator to adjourn pending disposition of the motion. Time for completing mediation shall be tolled during any periods when mediation is interrupted pending resolution of such a motion.

(b) Appearance at Mediation. Unless otherwise permitted by court order or stipulated by the parties in writing, a party is deemed to appear at a mediation conference if the following persons are physically present:

(1) The party or a party representative having full authority to settle without further consultation; and

(2) The party's counsel of record, if any; and

(3) A representative of the insurance carrier for any insured party who is not such carrier's outside counsel and who has full authority to settle in an amount up to the amount of the plaintiff's last demand or policy limits, whichever is less, without further consultation.

(c) Party Representative Having Full Authority to Settle. A "party representative having full authority to settle" shall mean the final decision maker with respect to all issues presented by the case who has the legal capacity to execute a binding settlement agreement on behalf of the party. Nothing herein shall be deemed to require any party or party representative who appears at a mediation conference in compliance with this rule to enter into a settlement agreement.

(d) Appearance by Public Entity. If a party to mediation is a public entity required to operate in compliance with chapter 286, Florida Statutes, that party shall be deemed to appear at a mediation conference by the physical presence of a representative with full authority to negotiate on behalf of the entity and to recommend settlement to the appropriate decision-making body of the entity.

(e) Certification of Authority. Unless otherwise stipulated by the parties, each party, 10 days prior to appearing at a mediation conference, shall file with the court and serve all parties a written notice identifying the person or persons who will be attending the mediation conference as a party representative or as an insurance carrier representative, and confirming that those persons have the authority required by subdivision (b).

(f) Sanctions for Failure to Appear. If a party fails to appear at a duly noticed mediation conference without good cause, the court, upon motion, shall impose sanctions, including award of mediation fees, attorneys' fees, and costs, against the party failing to appear. The failure to file a confirmation of authority required under subdivision (e) above, or failure of the persons actually identified in the confirmation to appear at the mediation conference, shall create a rebuttable presumption of a failure to appear.

(g) Adjournments. The mediator may adjourn the mediation conference at any time and may set times for reconvening the adjourned conference notwithstanding rule 1.710(a). No further notification is required for parties present at the adjourned conference.

(h) Counsel. The mediator shall at all times be in control of the mediation and the procedures to be followed in the mediation. Counsel shall be permitted to communicate privately with their clients. In the discretion of the mediator and with the agreement of the parties, mediation may proceed in the absence of counsel unless otherwise ordered by the court.

(i) Communication with Parties or Counsel. The mediator may meet and consult privately with any party or parties or their counsel.

(j) Appointment of the Mediator.

(1) Within 10 days of the order of referral, the parties may agree upon a stipulation with the court designating:

(A) a certified mediator; or

(B) a mediator, other than a senior judge, who is not certified as a mediator but who, in the opinion of the parties and upon review by the presiding judge, is otherwise qualified by training or experience to mediate all or some of the issues in the particular case.

(2) If the parties cannot agree upon a mediator within 10 days of the order of referral, the plaintiff or petitioner shall so notify the court within 10 days of the expiration of the period to agree on a mediator, and the court shall appoint a certified mediator selected by rotation or by such other procedures as may be adopted by administrative order of the chief judge in the circuit in which the action is pending. At the request of either party, the court shall appoint a certified circuit court mediator who is a member of The Florida Bar.

(3) If a mediator agreed upon by the parties or appointed by a court cannot serve, a substitute mediator can be agreed upon or appointed in the same manner as the original mediator. A mediator shall not mediate a case assigned to another mediator without the agreement of the parties or approval of the court. A substitute mediator shall have the same qualifications as the original mediator.

(k) Compensation of the Mediator. The mediator may be compensated or uncompensated. When the mediator is compensated in whole or part by the parties, the presiding judge may determine the reasonableness of the fees charged by the mediator. In the absence of a written agreement providing for the mediator's compensation, the mediator shall be compensated at the hourly rate set by the presiding judge in the referral order. Where appropriate, each party shall pay a proportionate share of the total charges of the mediator. Parties may object to the rate of the mediator's compensation within 15 days of the order of referral by serving an objection on all other parties and the mediator.

Committee Notes

2011 Amendment. Mediated settlement conferences pursuant to this rule are meant to be conducted when the participants actually engaged in the settlement negotiations have full authority to settle the case without further consultation. New language in subdivision (c) now defines "a party representative with full authority to settle" in two parts. First, the party representative must be the final decision maker with respect to all issues presented by the case in question. Second, the party representative must have the legal capacity to execute a binding agreement on behalf of the settling party. These are objective standards. Whether or not these standards have been met can be determined without reference to any confidential mediation communications. A decision by a party representative not to settle does not, in and of itself, signify the absence of full authority to settle. A party may delegate full authority to settle to more than one person, each of whom can serve as the final decision maker. A party may also designate multiple persons to serve together as the final decision maker, all of whom must appear at mediation.

New subdivision (e) provides a process for parties to identify party representative and representatives of insurance carriers who will be attending the mediation conference on behalf of parties and insurance carriers and to confirm their respective settlement authority by means of a direct representation to the court. If necessary, any verification of this representation would be upon motion by a party or inquiry by the court without involvement of the mediator and would not require disclosure of confidential mediation communications. Nothing in this rule shall be deemed to impose any duty or obligation on the mediator selected by the parties or appointed by the court to ensure compliance.

The concept of self determination in mediation also contemplates the parties' free choice in structuring and organizing their mediation sessions, including those who are to participate.

Accordingly, elements of this rule are subject to revision or qualification with the mutual consent of the parties.

RULE 1.730. COMPLETION OF MEDIATION

(a) No Agreement. If the parties do not reach an agreement as to any matter as a result of mediation, the mediator shall report the lack of an agreement to the court without comment or recommendation. With the consent of the parties, the mediator's report may also identify any pending motions or outstanding legal issues, discovery process, or other action by any party which, if resolved or completed, would facilitate the possibility of a settlement.

(b) Agreement. If a partial or final agreement is reached, it shall be reduced to writing and signed by the parties and their counsel, if any. The agreement shall be filed when required by law or with the parties' consent. A report of the agreement shall be submitted to the court or a stipulation of dismissal shall be filed. By stipulation of the parties, the agreement may be electronically or stenographically recorded. In such event, the transcript may be filed with the court. The mediator shall report the existence of the signed or transcribed agreement to the court without comment within 10 days thereof. No agreement under this rule shall be reported to the court except as provided herein.

(c) Imposition of Sanctions. In the event of any breach or failure to perform under the agreement, the court upon motion may impose sanctions, including costs, attorneys' fees, or other appropriate remedies including entry of judgment on the agreement.

Committee Notes

1996 Amendment. Subdivision (b) is amended to provide for partial settlements, to clarify the procedure for concluding mediation by report or stipulation of dismissal, and to specify the procedure for reporting mediated agreements to the court. The reporting requirements are intended to ensure the confidentiality provided for in section 44.102(3), Florida Statutes, and to prevent premature notification to the court.

RULE 1.750. COUNTY COURT ACTIONS

(a) Applicability. This rule applies to the mediation of county court matters and issues only and controls over conflicting provisions in rules 1.700, 1.710, 1.720, and 1.730.

(b) Limitation on Referral to Mediation. When a mediation program utilizing volunteer mediators is unavailable or otherwise inappropriate, county court matters may be referred to a mediator or mediation program which charges a fee. Such order of referral shall advise the parties that they may object to mediation on grounds of financial hardship or on any ground set forth in rule 1.700(b). If a party objects, mediation shall not be conducted until the court rules on the objection. The court may consider the amount in controversy, the objecting party's ability to pay, and any other pertinent information in determining the propriety of the referral. When appropriate, the court shall apportion mediation fees between the parties.

(c) Scheduling. In small claims actions, the mediator shall be appointed and the mediation conference held during or immediately after the pretrial conference unless otherwise ordered by the court. In no event shall the mediation conference be held more than 14 days after the pretrial conference.

(d) Appointment of the Mediator. In county court actions not subject to the Florida Small Claims Rules, rule 1.720(f) shall apply unless the case is sent to a mediation program provided at no cost to the parties.

(e) Appearance at Mediation. In small claims actions, an attorney may appear on behalf of a party at mediation provided that the attorney has full authority to settle without further consultation. Unless otherwise ordered by the court, a nonlawyer representative may appear on behalf of a party to a small claims mediation if the representative has the party's signed written authority to appear and has full authority to settle without further consultation. In either event, the party need not appear in person.

In any other county court action, a party will be deemed to appear if the persons set forth in rule 1.720(b) are physically present.

(f) Agreement. Any agreements reached as a result of small claims mediation shall be written in the form of a stipulation. The stipulation may be entered as an order of the court.

RULE 1.800. EXCLUSIONS FROM ARBITRATION

A civil action shall be ordered to arbitration or arbitration in conjunction with mediation upon stipulation of the parties. A civil action may be ordered to arbitration or arbitration in conjunction with mediation upon motion of any party or by the court, if the judge determines the action to be of such a nature that arbitration could be of benefit to the litigants or the court. Under no circumstances may the following categories of actions be referred to arbitration:

(1) Bond estreatures.

(2) Habeas corpus or other extraordinary writs.

(3) Bond validations.

(4) Civil or criminal contempt.

(5) Such other matters as may be specified by order of the chief judge in the circuit.

Committee Notes

1994 Amendment. The Supreme Court Committee on Mediation and Arbitration Rules encourages crafting a combination of dispute resolution processes without creating an unreasonable barrier to the traditional court system.

RULE 1.810. SELECTION AND COMPENSATION OF ARBITRATORS

(a) Selection. The chief judge of the circuit or a designee shall maintain a list of qualified persons who have agreed to serve as arbitrators. Cases assigned to arbitration shall be assigned to an arbitrator or to a panel of 3 arbitrators. The court shall determine the number of arbitrators and designate them within 15 days after service of the order of referral in the absence of an agreement by the parties. In the case of a panel, one of the arbitrators shall be appointed as the chief arbitrator. Where there is only one arbitrator, that person shall be the chief arbitrator.

(b) Compensation. The chief judge of each judicial circuit shall establish the compensation of arbitrators subject to the limitations in section 44.103(3), Florida Statutes.

Committee Notes

2003 Amendment. The statutory reference in subdivision (b) is changed to reflect changes in the statutory numbering.

RULE 1.820. HEARING PROCEDURES FOR NON-BINDING ARBITRATION

(a) Authority of the Chief Arbitrator. The chief arbitrator shall have authority to commence and adjourn the arbitration hearing and carry out other such duties as are prescribed by section 44.103, Florida Statutes. The chief arbitrator shall not have authority to hold any person in contempt or to in any way impose sanctions against any person.

(b) Conduct of the Arbitration Hearing.

(1) The chief judge of each judicial circuit shall set procedures for determining the time and place of the arbitration hearing and may establish other procedures for the expeditious and orderly operation of the arbitration hearing to the extent such procedures are not in conflict with any rules of court.

(2) Hearing procedures shall be included in the notice of arbitration hearing sent to the parties and arbitration panel.

(3) Individual parties or authorized representatives of corporate parties shall attend the arbitration hearing unless excused in advance by the chief arbitrator for good cause shown.

(c) Rules of Evidence. The hearing shall be conducted informally. Presentation of testimony shall be kept to a minimum, and matters shall be presented to the arbitrator(s) primarily through the statements and arguments of counsel.

(d) Orders. The chief arbitrator may issue instructions as are necessary for the expeditious and orderly conduct of the hearing. The chief arbitrator's instructions are not appealable. Upon notice to all parties the chief arbitrator may apply to the presiding judge for orders directing compliance with such instructions. Instructions enforced by a court order are appealable as are other orders of the court.

(e) Default of a Party. When a party fails to appear at a hearing, the chief arbitrator may proceed with the hearing and the arbitration panel shall render a decision based upon the facts and circumstances as presented by the parties present.

(f) Record and Transcript. Any party may have a record and transcript made of the arbitration hearing at that party's expense.

(g) Completion of the Arbitration Process.

(1) Arbitration shall be completed within 30 days of the first arbitration hearing unless extended by order of the court on motion of the chief arbitrator or of a party. No extension of time shall be for a period exceeding 60 days from the date of the first arbitration hearing.

(2) Upon the completion of the arbitration process, the arbitrator(s) shall render a decision. In the case of a panel, a decision shall be final upon a majority vote of the panel.

(3) Within 10 days of the final adjournment of the arbitration hearing, the arbitrator(s) shall notify the parties, in writing, of their decision. The arbitration decision may set forth the issues in controversy and the arbitrator('s)(s') conclusions and findings of fact and law. The arbitrator('s)(s') decision and the originals of any transcripts shall be sealed and filed with the clerk at the time the parties are notified of the decision.

(h) Time for Filing Motion for Trial. Any party may file a motion for trial. If a motion for trial is filed by any party, any party having a third-party claim at issue at the time of arbitration may file a motion for trial within 10 days of service of the first motion for trial. If a motion for trial is not made within 20 days of service on the parties of the decision, the decision shall be referred to the presiding judge, who shall enter such orders and judgments as may be required to carry out the terms of the decision as provided by section 44.103(5), Florida Statutes.

Committee Notes

1988 Adoption. Arbitration proceedings should be informal and expeditious. The court should take into account the nature of the proceedings when determining whether to award costs and attorneys' fees after a trial de novo. Counsel are free to file exceptions to an arbitration decision or award at the time it is to be considered by the court. The court should consider such exceptions when determining whether to award costs and attorneys' fees. The court should consider rule 1.442 concerning offers of judgment and section 45.061, Florida Statutes (1985), concerning offers of settlement, as statements of public policy in deciding whether fees should be awarded.

1994 Amendment. The Supreme Court Committee on Mediation and Arbitration Rules recommends that a copy of the local arbitration procedures be disseminated to the local bar.

2003 Amendment. The statutory reference in subdivision (h) is changed to reflect changes in the statutory numbering.

2007 Amendment. Subdivision (h) is amended to avoid the unintended consequences for defendants with third-party claims who prevailed at arbitration but could not pursue those claims in a circuit court action because no motion for trial was filed despite a plaintiff or plaintiffs having filed a motion for trial that covered those claims. See *State Dept. of Transportation v. BellSouth Telecommunications, Inc.*, 859 So. 2d 1278 (Fla. 4th DCA 2003).

RULE 1.830. VOLUNTARY BINDING ARBITRATION

(a) Absence of Party Agreement.

(1) Compensation. In the absence of an agreement by the parties as to compensation of the arbitrator(s), the court shall determine the amount of compensation subject to the provisions of section 44.104(3), Florida Statutes.

(2) Hearing Procedures. Subject to these rules and section 44.104, Florida Statutes, the parties may, by written agreement before the hearing, establish the hearing procedures for voluntary binding arbitration. In the absence of such agreement, the court shall establish the hearing procedures.

(b) Record and Transcript.
A record and transcript may be made of the arbitration hearing if requested by any party or at the direction of the chief arbitrator. The record and transcript may be used in subsequent legal proceedings subject to the Florida Rules of Evidence.

(c) Arbitration Decision and Appeal.

(1) The arbitrator(s) shall serve the parties with notice of the decision and file the decision with the court within 10 days of the final adjournment of the arbitration hearing.

(2) A voluntary binding arbitration decision may be appealed within 30 days after service of the decision on the parties. Appeal is limited to the grounds specified in section 44.104(10), Florida Statutes.

(3) If no appeal is filed within the time period set out in subdivision (2) of this rule, the decision shall be referred to the presiding judge who shall enter such orders and judgments as required to carry out the terms of the decision as provided under section 44.104(11), Florida Statutes.

RULE 1.900. FORMS

(a) Process.
The following forms of process, notice of lis pendens, and notice of action are sufficient. Variations from the forms do not void process or notices that are otherwise sufficient.

(b) Other Forms.
The other forms are sufficient for the matters that are covered by them. So long as the substance is expressed without prolixity, the forms may be varied to meet the facts of a particular case.

(c) Formal Matters.
Captions, except for the designation of the paper, are omitted from the forms. A general form of caption is the first form. Signatures are omitted from pleadings and motions.

Editor's Note: Fla.R.Jud.Admin. *2.540 requires that a notice to persons with disabilities be included in "[a]ll notices of court proceedings to be held in a public facility, and all process compelling appearance at such proceedings." The content of the notice is set forth in that rule.*

End of Florida Rules of Civil Procedure 2012

Florida Evidence Code 2012

TITLE VII

EVIDENCE

CHAPTER 90

EVIDENCE CODE

90.101   Short title.—This chapter shall be known and may be cited as the "Florida Evidence Code."

History.—s. 1, ch. 76-237; s. 1, ch. 77-77; s. 22, ch. 78-361; s. 1, ch. 78-379.

90.102   Construction.—This chapter shall replace and supersede existing statutory or common law in conflict with its provisions.

History.—s. 1, ch. 76-237; s. 1, ch. 77-77; s. 22, ch. 78-361; s. 1, ch. 78-379.

90.103   Scope; applicability.—

(1)   Unless otherwise provided by statute, this code applies to the same proceedings that the general law of evidence applied to before the effective date of this code.

(2)   This act shall apply to criminal proceedings related to crimes committed after the effective date of this code and to civil actions and all other proceedings pending on or brought after October 1, 1981.

(3)   Nothing in this act shall operate to repeal or modify the parol evidence rule.

History.—ss. 1, 5, 7, ch. 76-237; s. 1, ch. 77-77; ss. 1, 22, ch. 78-361; ss. 1, 2, ch. 78-379; s. 1, ch. 81-93.

90.104   Rulings on evidence.—

(1)   A court may predicate error, set aside or reverse a judgment, or grant a new trial on the basis of admitted or excluded evidence when a substantial right of the party is adversely affected and:

(a)   When the ruling is one admitting evidence, a timely objection or motion to strike appears on the record, stating the specific ground of objection if the specific ground was not apparent from the context; or

(b)   When the ruling is one excluding evidence, the substance of the evidence was made known to the court by offer of proof or was apparent from the context within which the questions were asked.

If the court has made a definitive ruling on the record admitting or excluding evidence, either at or before trial, a party need not renew an objection or offer of proof to preserve a claim of error for appeal.

(2)   In cases tried by a jury, a court shall conduct proceedings, to the maximum extent practicable, in such a manner as to prevent inadmissible evidence from being suggested to the jury by any means.

(3)   Nothing in this section shall preclude a court from taking notice of fundamental errors affecting substantial rights, even though such errors were not brought to the attention of the trial judge.

History.—s. 1, ch. 76-237; s. 1, ch. 77-77; s. 1, ch. 77-174; s. 22, ch. 78-361; s. 1, ch. 78-379; s. 1, ch. 2003-259.

90.105 Preliminary questions.—

(1) Except as provided in subsection (2), the court shall determine preliminary questions concerning the qualification of a person to be a witness, the existence of a privilege, or the admissibility of evidence.

(2) When the relevancy of evidence depends upon the existence of a preliminary fact, the court shall admit the proffered evidence when there is prima facie evidence sufficient to support a finding of the preliminary fact. If prima facie evidence is not introduced to support a finding of the preliminary fact, the court may admit the proffered evidence subject to the subsequent introduction of prima facie evidence of the preliminary fact.

(3) Hearings on the admissibility of confessions shall be conducted out of the hearing of the jury. Hearings on other preliminary matters shall be similarly conducted when the interests of justice require or when an accused is a witness, if he or she so requests.

History.—s. 1, ch. 76-237; s. 1, ch. 77-77; s. 22, ch. 78-361; s. 1, ch. 78-379; s. 471, ch. 95-147.

90.106 Summing up and comment by judge.—A judge may not sum up the evidence or comment to the jury upon the weight of the evidence, the credibility of the witnesses, or the guilt of the accused.

History.—s. 1, ch. 76-237; s. 1, ch. 77-77; s. 22, ch. 78-361; s. 1, ch. 78-379.

90.107 Limited admissibility.—When evidence that is admissible as to one party or for one purpose, but inadmissible as to another party or for another purpose, is admitted, the court, upon request, shall restrict such evidence to its proper scope and so inform the jury at the time it is admitted.

History.—s. 1, ch. 76-237; s. 1, ch. 77-77; s. 22, ch. 78-361; s. 1, ch. 78-379.

90.108 Introduction of related writings or recorded statements.—

(1) When a writing or recorded statement or part thereof is introduced by a party, an adverse party may require him or her at that time to introduce any other part or any other writing or recorded statement that in fairness ought to be considered contemporaneously. An adverse party is not bound by evidence introduced under this section.

(2) The report of a court reporter, when certified to by the court reporter as being a correct transcript of the testimony and proceedings in the case, is prima facie a correct statement of such testimony and proceedings.

History.—s. 1, ch. 76-237; s. 1, ch. 77-77; ss. 2, 22, ch. 78-361; ss. 1, 2, ch. 78-379; s. 472, ch. 95-147; s. 5, ch. 95-286.

90.201 Matters which must be judicially noticed.—A court shall take judicial notice of:

(1) Decisional, constitutional, and public statutory law and resolutions of the Florida Legislature and the Congress of the United States.

(2)   Florida rules of court that have statewide application, its own rules, and the rules of United States courts adopted by the United States Supreme Court.

(3)   Rules of court of the United States Supreme Court and of the United States Courts of Appeal.

History.—s. 1, ch. 76-237; s. 1, ch. 77-77; ss. 21, 22, ch. 78-361; ss. 1, 2, ch. 78-379.

90.202 Matters which may be judicially noticed.—A court may take judicial notice of the following matters, to the extent that they are not embraced within s. 90.201:

(1)   Special, local, and private acts and resolutions of the Congress of the United States and of the Florida Legislature.

(2)   Decisional, constitutional, and public statutory law of every other state, territory, and jurisdiction of the United States.

(3)   Contents of the Federal Register.

(4)   Laws of foreign nations and of an organization of nations.

(5)   Official actions of the legislative, executive, and judicial departments of the United States and of any state, territory, or jurisdiction of the United States.

(6)   Records of any court of this state or of any court of record of the United States or of any state, territory, or jurisdiction of the United States.

(7)   Rules of court of any court of this state or of any court of record of the United States or of any other state, territory, or jurisdiction of the United States.

(8)   Provisions of all municipal and county charters and charter amendments of this state, provided they are available in printed copies or as certified copies.

(9)   Rules promulgated by governmental agencies of this state which are published in the Florida Administrative Code or in bound written copies.

(10)   Duly enacted ordinances and resolutions of municipalities and counties located in Florida, provided such ordinances and resolutions are available in printed copies or as certified copies.

(11)   Facts that are not subject to dispute because they are generally known within the territorial jurisdiction of the court.

(12)   Facts that are not subject to dispute because they are capable of accurate and ready determination by resort to sources whose accuracy cannot be questioned.

(13)   Official seals of governmental agencies and departments of the United States and of any state, territory, or jurisdiction of the United States.

History.—s. 1, ch. 76-237; s. 1, ch. 77-77; s. 1, ch. 77-174; ss. 3, 22, ch. 78-361; ss. 1, 2, ch. 78-379.

90.203 Compulsory judicial notice upon request.—A court shall take judicial notice of any matter in s. 90.202 when a party requests it and:

(1)   Gives each adverse party timely written notice of the request, proof of which is filed with the court, to enable the adverse party to prepare to meet the request.

(2)   Furnishes the court with sufficient information to enable it to take judicial notice of the matter.

History.—s. 1, ch. 76-237; s. 1, ch. 77-77; s. 22, ch. 78-361; s. 1, ch. 78-379.

90.204 Determination of propriety of judicial notice and nature of matter noticed.—

(1) When a court determines upon its own motion that judicial notice of a matter should be taken or when a party requests such notice and shows good cause for not complying with s. 90.203(1), the court shall afford each party reasonable opportunity to present information relevant to the propriety of taking judicial notice and to the nature of the matter noticed.

(2) In determining the propriety of taking judicial notice of a matter or the nature thereof, a court may use any source of pertinent and reliable information, whether or not furnished by a party, without regard to any exclusionary rule except a valid claim of privilege and except for the exclusions provided in s. 90.403.

(3) If a court resorts to any documentary source of information not received in open court, the court shall make the information and its source a part of the record in the action and shall afford each party reasonable opportunity to challenge such information, and to offer additional information, before judicial notice of the matter is taken.

History.—s. 1, ch. 76-237; s. 1, ch. 77-77; s. 22, ch. 78-361; s. 1, ch. 78-379.

90.205 Denial of a request for judicial notice.—Upon request of counsel, when a court denies a request to take judicial notice of any matter, the court shall inform the parties at the earliest practicable time and shall indicate for the record that it has denied the request.

History.—s. 1, ch. 76-237; s. 1, ch. 77-77; s. 22, ch. 78-361; s. 1, ch. 78-379.

90.206 Instructing jury on judicial notice.—The court may instruct the jury during the trial to accept as a fact a matter judicially noticed.

History.—s. 1, ch. 76-237; s. 1, ch. 77-77; ss. 4, 22, ch. 78-361; ss. 1, 2, ch. 78-379.

90.207 Judicial notice by trial court in subsequent proceedings.—The failure or refusal of a court to take judicial notice of a matter does not preclude a court from taking judicial notice of the matter in subsequent proceedings, in accordance with the procedure specified in ss. 90.201-90.206.

History.—s. 1, ch. 76-237; s. 1, ch. 77-77; s. 22, ch. 78-361; s. 1, ch. 78-379.

90.301 Presumption defined; inferences.—

(1) For the purposes of this chapter, a presumption is an assumption of fact which the law makes from the existence of another fact or group of facts found or otherwise established.

(2) Except for presumptions that are conclusive under the law from which they arise, a presumption is rebuttable.

(3) Nothing in this chapter shall prevent the drawing of an inference that is appropriate.

(4) Sections 90.301-90.304 are applicable only in civil actions or proceedings.

History.—s. 1, ch. 76-237; s. 1, ch. 77-77; ss. 5, 22, ch. 78-361; ss. 1, 2, ch. 78-379.

90.302 Classification of rebuttable presumptions.—Every rebuttable presumption is either:

(1) A presumption affecting the burden of producing evidence and requiring the trier of fact to assume the existence of the presumed fact, unless credible evidence sufficient to sustain a finding of the nonexistence of the presumed fact is introduced, in which event, the existence or nonexistence of the presumed fact shall be determined from the evidence without regard to the presumption; or

(2) A presumption affecting the burden of proof that imposes upon the party against whom it operates the burden of proof concerning the nonexistence of the presumed fact.

History.—s. 1, ch. 76-237; s. 1, ch. 77-77; s. 22, ch. 78-361; s. 1, ch. 78-379.

90.303 Presumption affecting the burden of producing evidence defined.—In a civil action or proceeding, unless otherwise provided by statute, a presumption established primarily to facilitate the determination of the particular action in which the presumption is applied, rather than to implement public policy, is a presumption affecting the burden of producing evidence.

History.—s. 1, ch. 76-237; s. 1, ch. 77-77; s. 22, ch. 78-361; s. 1, ch. 78-379.

90.304 Presumption affecting the burden of proof defined.—In civil actions, all rebuttable presumptions which are not defined in s. 90.303 are presumptions affecting the burden of proof.

History.—s. 1, ch. 76-237; s. 1, ch. 77-77; s. 22, ch. 78-361; s. 1, ch. 78-379.

90.401 Definition of relevant evidence.—Relevant evidence is evidence tending to prove or disprove a material fact.

History.—s. 1, ch. 76-237; s. 1, ch. 77-77; s. 22, ch. 78-361; s. 1, ch. 78-379.

90.402 Admissibility of relevant evidence.—All relevant evidence is admissible, except as provided by law.

History.—s. 1, ch. 76-237; s. 1, ch. 77-77; s. 22, ch. 78-361; s. 1, ch. 78-379.

90.4025 Admissibility of paternity determination in certain criminal prosecutions.—If a person less than 18 years of age gives birth to a child and the paternity of that child is established under chapter 742, such evidence of paternity is admissible in a criminal prosecution under ss. 794.011, 794.05, 800.04, and 827.04(3).

History.—s. 8, ch. 96-215; s. 2, ch. 96-409; s. 27, ch. 99-2.

90.4026 Statements expressing sympathy; admissibility; definitions.—

(1) As used in this section:

(a) "Accident" means an occurrence resulting in injury or death to one or more persons which is not the result of willful action by a party.

(b) "Benevolent gestures" means actions that convey a sense of compassion or commiseration emanating from human impulses.

(c) "Family" means the spouse, parent, grandparent, stepmother, stepfather, child, grandchild, brother, sister, half-brother, half-sister, adopted child of parent, or spouse's parent of an injured party.

(2) The portion of statements, writings, or benevolent gestures expressing sympathy or a general sense of benevolence relating to the pain, suffering, or death of a person involved in an accident and made to that person or to the family of that person shall be inadmissible as evidence in a civil action. A statement of fault, however, which is part of, or in addition to, any of the above shall be admissible pursuant to this section.

History.—s. 1, ch. 2001-132.

90.403 Exclusion on grounds of prejudice or confusion.—Relevant evidence is inadmissible if its probative value is substantially outweighed by the danger of unfair prejudice, confusion of issues, misleading the jury, or needless presentation of cumulative evidence. This section shall not be construed to mean that evidence of the existence of available third-party benefits is inadmissible.

History.—s. 1, ch. 76-237; s. 1, ch. 77-77; ss. 6, 22, ch. 78-361; ss. 1, 2, ch. 78-379.

90.404 Character evidence; when admissible.—

(1) CHARACTER EVIDENCE GENERALLY.—Evidence of a person's character or a trait of character is inadmissible to prove action in conformity with it on a particular occasion, except:

(a) Character of accused.—Evidence of a pertinent trait of character offered by an accused, or by the prosecution to rebut the trait.

(b) Character of victim.—

1. Except as provided in s. 794.022, evidence of a pertinent trait of character of the victim of the crime offered by an accused, or by the prosecution to rebut the trait; or

2. Evidence of a character trait of peacefulness of the victim offered by the prosecution in a homicide case to rebut evidence that the victim was the aggressor.

(c) Character of witness.—Evidence of the character of a witness, as provided in ss. 90.608-90.610.

(2) OTHER CRIMES, WRONGS, OR ACTS.—

(a) Similar fact evidence of other crimes, wrongs, or acts is admissible when relevant to prove a material fact in issue, including, but not limited to, proof of motive, opportunity, intent, preparation, plan, knowledge, identity, or absence of mistake or accident, but it is inadmissible when the evidence is relevant solely to prove bad character or propensity.

(b) 1. In a criminal case in which the defendant is charged with a crime involving child molestation, evidence of the defendant's commission of other crimes, wrongs, or acts of child molestation is admissible and may be considered for its bearing on any matter to which it is relevant.

2. For the purposes of this paragraph, the term "child molestation" means conduct proscribed by s. 787.025(2)(c), s. 794.011, excluding s. 794.011(10), s. 794.05, s. 796.03, s. 796.035, s. 796.045, s. 800.04, s. 827.071, s. 847.0135(5), s. 847.0145, or s. 985.701(1) when committed against a person 16 years of age or younger.

(c)   1.   In a criminal case in which the defendant is charged with a sexual offense, evidence of the defendant's commission of other crimes, wrongs, or acts involving a sexual offense is admissible and may be considered for its bearing on any matter to which it is relevant.

2.   For the purposes of this paragraph, the term "sexual offense" means conduct proscribed by s. 787.025(2)(c), s. 794.011, excluding s. 794.011(10), s. 794.05, s. 796.03, s. 796.035, s. 796.045, s. 825.1025(2)(b), s. 827.071, s. 847.0135(5), s. 847.0145, or s. 985.701(1).

(d)   1.   When the state in a criminal action intends to offer evidence of other criminal offenses under paragraph (a), paragraph (b), or paragraph (c), no fewer than 10 days before trial, the state shall furnish to the defendant or to the defendant's counsel a written statement of the acts or offenses it intends to offer, describing them with the particularity required of an indictment or information. No notice is required for evidence of offenses used for impeachment or on rebuttal.

2.   When the evidence is admitted, the court shall, if requested, charge the jury on the limited purpose for which the evidence is received and is to be considered. After the close of the evidence, the jury shall be instructed on the limited purpose for which the evidence was received and that the defendant cannot be convicted for a charge not included in the indictment or information.

(3)   Nothing in this section affects the admissibility of evidence under s. 90.610.

History.—s. 1, ch. 76-237; s. 1, ch. 77-77; s. 22, ch. 78-361; s. 1, ch. 78-379; s. 2, ch. 90-40; s. 26, ch. 93-156; s. 473, ch. 95-147; s. 1, ch. 2001-221; s. 9, ch. 2008-172; s. 2, ch. 2011-220.

90.405   Methods of proving character.—

(1)   REPUTATION.—When evidence of the character of a person or of a trait of that person's character is admissible, proof may be made by testimony about that person's reputation.

(2)   SPECIFIC INSTANCES OF CONDUCT.—When character or a trait of character of a person is an essential element of a charge, claim, or defense, proof may be made of specific instances of that person's conduct.

History.—s. 1, ch. 76-237; s. 1, ch. 77-77; ss. 7, 22, ch. 78-361; ss. 1, 2, ch. 78-379; s. 474, ch. 95-147.

90.406   Routine practice.—Evidence of the routine practice of an organization, whether corroborated or not and regardless of the presence of eyewitnesses, is admissible to prove that the conduct of the organization on a particular occasion was in conformity with the routine practice.

History.—s. 1, ch. 76-237; s. 1, ch. 77-77; s. 22, ch. 78-361; s. 1, ch. 78-379.

90.407   Subsequent remedial measures.—Evidence of measures taken after an injury or harm caused by an event, which measures if taken before the event would have made injury or harm less likely to occur, is not admissible to prove negligence, the existence of a product defect, or culpable conduct in connection with the event. This rule does not require the exclusion of evidence of subsequent remedial measures when offered for another purpose, such as proving ownership, control, or the feasibility of precautionary measures, if controverted, or impeachment.

History.—s. 1, ch. 76-237; s. 1, ch. 77-77; s. 1, ch. 77-174; s. 22, ch. 78-361; s. 1, ch. 78-379; s. 13, ch. 99-225.

90.408   Compromise and offers to compromise.—Evidence of an offer to compromise a claim which was disputed as to validity or amount, as well as any relevant conduct or statements made in negotiations concerning a compromise, is inadmissible to prove liability or absence of liability for the claim or its value.

History.—s. 1, ch. 76-237; s. 1, ch. 77-77; s. 22, ch. 78-361; s. 1, ch. 78-379.

90.409 Payment of medical and similar expenses.—Evidence of furnishing, or offering or promising to pay, medical or hospital expenses or other damages occasioned by an injury or accident is inadmissible to prove liability for the injury or accident.

History.—s. 1, ch. 76-237; s. 1, ch. 77-77; s. 22, ch. 78-361; s. 1, ch. 78-379.

90.410 Offer to plead guilty; nolo contendere; withdrawn pleas of guilty.—Evidence of a plea of guilty, later withdrawn; a plea of nolo contendere; or an offer to plead guilty or nolo contendere to the crime charged or any other crime is inadmissible in any civil or criminal proceeding. Evidence of statements made in connection with any of the pleas or offers is inadmissible, except when such statements are offered in a prosecution under chapter 837.

History.—s. 1, ch. 76-237; s. 1, ch. 77-77; ss. 8, 22, ch. 78-361; ss. 1, 2, ch. 78-379.

90.501 Privileges recognized only as provided.—Except as otherwise provided by this chapter, any other statute, or the Constitution of the United States or of the State of Florida, no person in a legal proceeding has a privilege to:

(1) Refuse to be a witness.

(2) Refuse to disclose any matter.

(3) Refuse to produce any object or writing.

(4) Prevent another from being a witness, from disclosing any matter, or from producing any object or writing.

History.—s. 1, ch. 76-237; s. 1, ch. 77-77; ss. 9, 22, ch. 78-361; ss. 1, 2, ch. 78-379.

90.5015 Journalist's privilege.—

(1) DEFINITIONS.—For purposes of this section, the term:

(a) "Professional journalist" means a person regularly engaged in collecting, photographing, recording, writing, editing, reporting, or publishing news, for gain or livelihood, who obtained the information sought while working as a salaried employee of, or independent contractor for, a newspaper, news journal, news agency, press association, wire service, radio or television station, network, or news magazine. Book authors and others who are not professional journalists, as defined in this paragraph, are not included in the provisions of this section.

(b) "News" means information of public concern relating to local, statewide, national, or worldwide issues or events.

(2) PRIVILEGE.—A professional journalist has a qualified privilege not to be a witness concerning, and not to disclose the information, including the identity of any source, that the professional journalist has obtained while actively gathering news. This privilege applies only to information or eyewitness observations obtained within the normal scope of employment and does not apply to physical evidence,

eyewitness observations, or visual or audio recording of crimes. A party seeking to overcome this privilege must make a clear and specific showing that:

(a) The information is relevant and material to unresolved issues that have been raised in the proceeding for which the information is sought;

(b) The information cannot be obtained from alternative sources; and

(c) A compelling interest exists for requiring disclosure of the information.

(3) DISCLOSURE.—A court shall order disclosure pursuant to subsection (2) only of that portion of the information for which the showing under subsection (2) has been made and shall support such order with clear and specific findings made after a hearing.

(4) WAIVER.—A professional journalist does not waive the privilege by publishing or broadcasting information.

(5) CONSTRUCTION.—This section must not be construed to limit any privilege or right provided to a professional journalist under law.

(6) AUTHENTICATION.—Photographs, diagrams, video recordings, audio recordings, computer records, or other business records maintained, disclosed, provided, or produced by a professional journalist, or by the employer or principal of a professional journalist, may be authenticated for admission in evidence upon a showing, by affidavit of the professional journalist, or other individual with personal knowledge, that the photograph, diagram, video recording, audio recording, computer record, or other business record is a true and accurate copy of the original, and that the copy truly and accurately reflects the observations and facts contained therein.

(7) ACCURACY OF EVIDENCE.—If the affidavit of authenticity and accuracy, or other relevant factual circumstance, causes the court to have clear and convincing doubts as to the authenticity or accuracy of the proffered evidence, the court may decline to admit such evidence.

(8) SEVERABILITY.—If any provision of this section or its application to any particular person or circumstance is held invalid, that provision or its application is severable and does not affect the validity of other provisions or applications of this section.

History.—s. 1, ch. 98-48.

90.502 Lawyer-client privilege.—

(1) For purposes of this section:

(a) A "lawyer" is a person authorized, or reasonably believed by the client to be authorized, to practice law in any state or nation.

(b) A "client" is any person, public officer, corporation, association, or other organization or entity, either public or private, who consults a lawyer with the purpose of obtaining legal services or who is rendered legal services by a lawyer.

(c) A communication between lawyer and client is "confidential" if it is not intended to be disclosed to third persons other than:

1. Those to whom disclosure is in furtherance of the rendition of legal services to the client.

2. Those reasonably necessary for the transmission of the communication.

(2)   A client has a privilege to refuse to disclose, and to prevent any other person from disclosing, the contents of confidential communications when such other person learned of the communications because they were made in the rendition of legal services to the client.

(3)   The privilege may be claimed by:

(a)   The client.

(b)   A guardian or conservator of the client.

(c)   The personal representative of a deceased client.

(d)   A successor, assignee, trustee in dissolution, or any similar representative of an organization, corporation, or association or other entity, either public or private, whether or not in existence.

(e)   The lawyer, but only on behalf of the client. The lawyer's authority to claim the privilege is presumed in the absence of contrary evidence.

(4)   There is no lawyer-client privilege under this section when:

(a)   The services of the lawyer were sought or obtained to enable or aid anyone to commit or plan to commit what the client knew was a crime or fraud.

(b)   A communication is relevant to an issue between parties who claim through the same deceased client.

(c)   A communication is relevant to an issue of breach of duty by the lawyer to the client or by the client to the lawyer, arising from the lawyer-client relationship.

(d)   A communication is relevant to an issue concerning the intention or competence of a client executing an attested document to which the lawyer is an attesting witness, or concerning the execution or attestation of the document.

(e)   A communication is relevant to a matter of common interest between two or more clients, or their successors in interest, if the communication was made by any of them to a lawyer retained or consulted in common when offered in a civil action between the clients or their successors in interest.

(5)   Communications made by a person who seeks or receives services from the Department of Revenue under the child support enforcement program to the attorney representing the department shall be confidential and privileged as provided for in this section. Such communications shall not be disclosed to anyone other than the agency except as provided for in this section. Such disclosures shall be protected as if there were an attorney-client relationship between the attorney for the agency and the person who seeks services from the department.

(6)   A discussion or activity that is not a meeting for purposes of s. 286.011 shall not be construed to waive the attorney-client privilege established in this section. This shall not be construed to constitute an exemption to either s. 119.07 or s. 286.011.

History.—s. 1, ch. 76-237; s. 1, ch. 77-77; s. 22, ch. 78-361; s. 1, ch. 78-379; s. 16, ch. 92-138; s. 12, ch. 94-124; s. 1378, ch. 95-147; s. 1, ch. 2000-316.

[1]90.5021   **Fiduciary lawyer-client privilege.—**

(1)   For the purpose of this section, a client acts as a fiduciary when serving as a personal representative or a trustee as defined in ss. 731.201 and 736.0103, an administrator ad litem as described in s. 733.308, a curator as described in s. 733.501, a guardian or guardian ad litem as defined in s. 744.102, a conservator as defined in s. 710.102, or an attorney in fact as described in chapter 709.

(2)   A communication between a lawyer and a client acting as a fiduciary is privileged and protected from disclosure under s. 90.502 to the same extent as if the client were not acting as a fiduciary. In applying s. 90.502 to a communication under this section, only the person or entity acting as a fiduciary is considered a client of the lawyer.

(3)   This section does not affect the crime or fraud exception to the lawyer-client privilege provided in s. 90.502(4)(a).

History.—s. 1, ch. 2011-183.

[1]Note.—Section 14, ch. 2011-183, provides that "[e]xcept as otherwise expressly provided in this act, this act shall take effect upon becoming a law and shall apply to all proceedings pending before such date and all cases commenced on or after the effective date."

90.503   Psychotherapist-patient privilege.—

(1)   For purposes of this section:

(a)   A "psychotherapist" is:

1.   A person authorized to practice medicine in any state or nation, or reasonably believed by the patient so to be, who is engaged in the diagnosis or treatment of a mental or emotional condition, including alcoholism and other drug addiction;

2.   A person licensed or certified as a psychologist under the laws of any state or nation, who is engaged primarily in the diagnosis or treatment of a mental or emotional condition, including alcoholism and other drug addiction;

3.   A person licensed or certified as a clinical social worker, marriage and family therapist, or mental health counselor under the laws of this state, who is engaged primarily in the diagnosis or treatment of a mental or emotional condition, including alcoholism and other drug addiction;

4.   Treatment personnel of facilities licensed by the state pursuant to chapter 394, chapter 395, or chapter 397, of facilities designated by the Department of Children and Family Services pursuant to chapter 394 as treatment facilities, or of facilities defined as community mental health centers pursuant to s. 394.907(1), who are engaged primarily in the diagnosis or treatment of a mental or emotional condition, including alcoholism and other drug addiction; or

5.   An advanced registered nurse practitioner certified under s. 464.012, whose primary scope of practice is the diagnosis or treatment of mental or emotional conditions, including chemical abuse, and limited only to actions performed in accordance with part I of chapter 464.

(b)   A "patient" is a person who consults, or is interviewed by, a psychotherapist for purposes of diagnosis or treatment of a mental or emotional condition, including alcoholism and other drug addiction.

(c)   A communication between psychotherapist and patient is "confidential" if it is not intended to be disclosed to third persons other than:

1.   Those persons present to further the interest of the patient in the consultation, examination, or interview.

2.   Those persons necessary for the transmission of the communication.

3.   Those persons who are participating in the diagnosis and treatment under the direction of the psychotherapist.

(2)   A patient has a privilege to refuse to disclose, and to prevent any other person from disclosing, confidential communications or records made for the purpose of diagnosis or treatment of the patient's mental or emotional condition, including alcoholism and other drug addiction, between the patient and the psychotherapist, or persons who are participating in the diagnosis or treatment under the direction of the psychotherapist. This privilege includes any diagnosis made, and advice given, by the psychotherapist in the course of that relationship.

(3)   The privilege may be claimed by:

(a)   The patient or the patient's attorney on the patient's behalf.

(b)   A guardian or conservator of the patient.

(c)   The personal representative of a deceased patient.

(d)   The psychotherapist, but only on behalf of the patient. The authority of a psychotherapist to claim the privilege is presumed in the absence of evidence to the contrary.

(4)   There is no privilege under this section:

(a)   For communications relevant to an issue in proceedings to compel hospitalization of a patient for mental illness, if the psychotherapist in the course of diagnosis or treatment has reasonable cause to believe the patient is in need of hospitalization.

(b)   For communications made in the course of a court-ordered examination of the mental or emotional condition of the patient.

(c)   For communications relevant to an issue of the mental or emotional condition of the patient in any proceeding in which the patient relies upon the condition as an element of his or her claim or defense or, after the patient's death, in any proceeding in which any party relies upon the condition as an element of the party's claim or defense.

History.—s. 1, ch. 76-237; s. 1, ch. 77-77; s. 22, ch. 78-361; s. 1, ch. 78-379; s. 40, ch. 90-347; s. 1, ch. 92-57; s. 19, ch. 93-39; s. 475, ch. 95-147; s. 28, ch. 99-2; s. 5, ch. 99-8; s. 1, ch. 2006-204.

90.5035   Sexual assault counselor-victim privilege.—

(1)   For purposes of this section:

(a)   A "rape crisis center" is any public or private agency that offers assistance to victims of sexual assault or sexual battery and their families.

(b)   A "sexual assault counselor" is any employee of a rape crisis center whose primary purpose is the rendering of advice, counseling, or assistance to victims of sexual assault or sexual battery.

(c)   A "trained volunteer" is a person who volunteers at a rape crisis center, has completed 30 hours of training in assisting victims of sexual violence and related topics provided by the rape crisis center, is supervised by members of the staff of the rape crisis center, and is included on a list of volunteers that is maintained by the rape crisis center.

(d)   A "victim" is a person who consults a sexual assault counselor or a trained volunteer for the purpose of securing advice, counseling, or assistance concerning a mental, physical, or emotional condition caused by a sexual assault or sexual battery, an alleged sexual assault or sexual battery, or an attempted sexual assault or sexual battery.

(e)   A communication between a sexual assault counselor or trained volunteer and a victim is "confidential" if it is not intended to be disclosed to third persons other than:

    1. Those persons present to further the interest of the victim in the consultation, examination, or interview.

    2. Those persons necessary for the transmission of the communication.

    3. Those persons to whom disclosure is reasonably necessary to accomplish the purposes for which the sexual assault counselor or the trained volunteer is consulted.

(2) A victim has a privilege to refuse to disclose, and to prevent any other person from disclosing, a confidential communication made by the victim to a sexual assault counselor or trained volunteer or any record made in the course of advising, counseling, or assisting the victim. Such confidential communication or record may be disclosed only with the prior written consent of the victim. This privilege includes any advice given by the sexual assault counselor or trained volunteer in the course of that relationship.

(3) The privilege may be claimed by:

    (a) The victim or the victim's attorney on his or her behalf.

    (b) A guardian or conservator of the victim.

    (c) The personal representative of a deceased victim.

    (d) The sexual assault counselor or trained volunteer, but only on behalf of the victim. The authority of a sexual assault counselor or trained volunteer to claim the privilege is presumed in the absence of evidence to the contrary.

History.—s. 1, ch. 83-284; s. 476, ch. 95-147; s. 1, ch. 2002-246.

90.5036   Domestic violence advocate-victim privilege.—

(1) For purposes of this section:

    (a) A "domestic violence center" is any public or private agency that offers assistance to victims of domestic violence, as defined in s. 741.28, and their families.

    (b) A "domestic violence advocate" means any employee or volunteer who has 30 hours of training in assisting victims of domestic violence and is an employee of or volunteer for a program for victims of domestic violence whose primary purpose is the rendering of advice, counseling, or assistance to victims of domestic violence.

    (c) A "victim" is a person who consults a domestic violence advocate for the purpose of securing advice, counseling, or assistance concerning a mental, physical, or emotional condition caused by an act of domestic violence, an alleged act of domestic violence, or an attempted act of domestic violence.

    (d) A communication between a domestic violence advocate and a victim is "confidential" if it relates to the incident of domestic violence for which the victim is seeking assistance and if it is not intended to be disclosed to third persons other than:

    1. Those persons present to further the interest of the victim in the consultation, assessment, or interview.

    2. Those persons to whom disclosure is reasonably necessary to accomplish the purpose for which the domestic violence advocate is consulted.

(2) A victim has a privilege to refuse to disclose, and to prevent any other person from disclosing, a confidential communication made by the victim to a domestic violence advocate or any record made in the course of advising, counseling, or assisting the victim. The privilege applies to confidential

communications made between the victim and the domestic violence advocate and to records of those communications only if the advocate is registered under s. 39.905 at the time the communication is made. This privilege includes any advice given by the domestic violence advocate in the course of that relationship.

(3)   The privilege may be claimed by:

(a)   The victim or the victim's attorney on behalf of the victim.

(b)   A guardian or conservator of the victim.

(c)   The personal representative of a deceased victim.

(d)   The domestic violence advocate, but only on behalf of the victim. The authority of a domestic violence advocate to claim the privilege is presumed in the absence of evidence to the contrary.

History.—s. 7, ch. 95-187; s. 127, ch. 98-403.

90.504   Husband-wife privilege.—

(1)   A spouse has a privilege during and after the marital relationship to refuse to disclose, and to prevent another from disclosing, communications which were intended to be made in confidence between the spouses while they were husband and wife.

(2)   The privilege may be claimed by either spouse or by the guardian or conservator of a spouse. The authority of a spouse, or guardian or conservator of a spouse, to claim the privilege is presumed in the absence of contrary evidence.

(3)   There is no privilege under this section:

(a)   In a proceeding brought by or on behalf of one spouse against the other spouse.

(b)   In a criminal proceeding in which one spouse is charged with a crime committed at any time against the person or property of the other spouse, or the person or property of a child of either.

(c)   In a criminal proceeding in which the communication is offered in evidence by a defendant-spouse who is one of the spouses between whom the communication was made.

History.—s. 1, ch. 76-237; s. 1, ch. 77-77; ss. 10, 22, ch. 78-361; ss. 1, 2, ch. 78-379.

90.505   Privilege with respect to communications to clergy.—

(1)   For the purposes of this section:

(a)   A "member of the clergy" is a priest, rabbi, practitioner of Christian Science, or minister of any religious organization or denomination usually referred to as a church, or an individual reasonably believed so to be by the person consulting him or her.

(b)   A communication between a member of the clergy and a person is "confidential" if made privately for the purpose of seeking spiritual counsel and advice from the member of the clergy in the usual course of his or her practice or discipline and not intended for further disclosure except to other persons present in furtherance of the communication.

(2)   A person has a privilege to refuse to disclose, and to prevent another from disclosing, a confidential communication by the person to a member of the clergy in his or her capacity as spiritual adviser.

(3)   The privilege may be claimed by:

    (a)   The person.

    (b)   The guardian or conservator of a person.

    (c)   The personal representative of a deceased person.

    (d)   The member of the clergy, on behalf of the person. The member of the clergy's authority to do so is presumed in the absence of evidence to the contrary.

History.—s. 1, ch. 76-237; s. 1, ch. 77-77; s. 1, ch. 77-174; ss. 11, 22, ch. 78-361; ss. 1, 2, ch. 78-379; s. 477, ch. 95-147.

90.5055   Accountant-client privilege.—

(1)   For purposes of this section:

    (a)   An "accountant" is a certified public accountant or a public accountant.

    (b)   A "client" is any person, public officer, corporation, association, or other organization or entity, either public or private, who consults an accountant with the purpose of obtaining accounting services.

    (c)   A communication between an accountant and the accountant's client is "confidential" if it is not intended to be disclosed to third persons other than:

        1.   Those to whom disclosure is in furtherance of the rendition of accounting services to the client.

        2.   Those reasonably necessary for the transmission of the communication.

(2)   A client has a privilege to refuse to disclose, and to prevent any other person from disclosing, the contents of confidential communications with an accountant when such other person learned of the communications because they were made in the rendition of accounting services to the client. This privilege includes other confidential information obtained by the accountant from the client for the purpose of rendering accounting advice.

(3)   The privilege may be claimed by:

    (a)   The client.

    (b)   A guardian or conservator of the client.

    (c)   The personal representative of a deceased client.

    (d)   A successor, assignee, trustee in dissolution, or any similar representative of an organization, corporation, or association or other entity, either public or private, whether or not in existence.

    (e)   The accountant, but only on behalf of the client. The accountant's authority to claim the privilege is presumed in the absence of contrary evidence.

(4)   There is no accountant-client privilege under this section when:

    (a)   The services of the accountant were sought or obtained to enable or aid anyone to commit or plan to commit what the client knew or should have known was a crime or fraud.

(b) A communication is relevant to an issue of breach of duty by the accountant to the accountant's client or by the client to his or her accountant.

(c) A communication is relevant to a matter of common interest between two or more clients, if the communication was made by any of them to an accountant retained or consulted in common when offered in a civil action between the clients.

History.—s. 12, ch. 78-361; s. 2, ch. 78-379; s. 478, ch. 95-147.

90.506 Privilege with respect to trade secrets.—A person has a privilege to refuse to disclose, and to prevent other persons from disclosing, a trade secret owned by that person if the allowance of the privilege will not conceal fraud or otherwise work injustice. When the court directs disclosure, it shall take the protective measures that the interests of the holder of the privilege, the interests of the parties, and the furtherance of justice require. The privilege may be claimed by the person or the person's agent or employee.

History.—s. 1, ch. 76-237; s. 1, ch. 77-77; s. 22, ch. 78-361; s. 1, ch. 78-379; s. 479, ch. 95-147.

90.507 Waiver of privilege by voluntary disclosure.—A person who has a privilege against the disclosure of a confidential matter or communication waives the privilege if the person, or the person's predecessor while holder of the privilege, voluntarily discloses or makes the communication when he or she does not have a reasonable expectation of privacy, or consents to disclosure of, any significant part of the matter or communication. This section is not applicable when the disclosure is itself a privileged communication.

History.—s. 1, ch. 76-237; s. 1, ch. 77-77; ss. 13, 22, ch. 78-361; ss. 1, 2, ch. 78-379; s. 480, ch. 95-147.

90.508 Privileged matter disclosed under compulsion or without opportunity to claim privilege.—Evidence of a statement or other disclosure of privileged matter is inadmissible against the holder of the privilege if the statement or disclosure was compelled erroneously by the court or made without opportunity to claim the privilege.

History.—s. 1, ch. 76-237; s. 1, ch. 77-77; s. 22, ch. 78-361; s. 1, ch. 78-379.

90.509 Application of privileged communication.—Nothing in this act shall abrogate a privilege for any communication which was made prior to July 1, 1979, if such communication was privileged at the time it was made.

History.—s. 1, ch. 76-237; s. 1, ch. 77-77; s. 22, ch. 78-361; s. 1, ch. 78-379; s. 41, ch. 81-259.

90.510 Privileged communication necessary to adverse party.—In any civil case or proceeding in which a party claims a privilege as to a communication necessary to an adverse party, the court, upon motion, may dismiss the claim for relief or the affirmative defense to which the privileged testimony would relate. In making its determination, the court may engage in an in camera inquiry into the privilege.

History.—s. 1, ch. 76-237; s. 1, ch. 77-77; s. 22, ch. 78-361; s. 1, ch. 78-379.

90.601 General rule of competency.—Every person is competent to be a witness, except as otherwise provided by statute.

History.—s. 1, ch. 76-237; s. 1, ch. 77-77; s. 22, ch. 78-361, s. 1, ch. 78-379.

90.603 Disqualification of witness.—A person is disqualified to testify as a witness when the court determines that the person is:

(1) Incapable of expressing himself or herself concerning the matter in such a manner as to be understood, either directly or through interpretation by one who can understand him or her.

(2) Incapable of understanding the duty of a witness to tell the truth.

History.—s. 1, ch. 76-237; s. 1, ch. 77-77; s. 22, ch. 78-361; s. 1, ch. 78-379; s. 482, ch. 95-147.

90.604 Lack of personal knowledge.—Except as otherwise provided in s. 90.702, a witness may not testify to a matter unless evidence is introduced which is sufficient to support a finding that the witness has personal knowledge of the matter. Evidence to prove personal knowledge may be given by the witness's own testimony.

History.—s. 1, ch. 76-237; s. 1, ch. 77-77; s. 22, ch. 78-361; s. 1, ch. 78-379; s. 483, ch. 95-147.

90.605 Oath or affirmation of witness.—

(1) Before testifying, each witness shall declare that he or she will testify truthfully, by taking an oath or affirmation in substantially the following form: "Do you swear or affirm that the evidence you are about to give will be the truth, the whole truth, and nothing but the truth?" The witness's answer shall be noted in the record.

(2) In the court's discretion, a child may testify without taking the oath if the court determines the child understands the duty to tell the truth or the duty not to lie.

History.—s. 1, ch. 76-237; s. 1, ch. 77-77; s. 22, ch. 78-361; s. 1, ch. 78-379; s. 3, ch. 85-53; s. 484, ch. 95-147.

90.606 Interpreters and translators.—

(1) (a) When a judge determines that a witness cannot hear or understand the English language, or cannot express himself or herself in English sufficiently to be understood, an interpreter who is duly qualified to interpret for the witness shall be sworn to do so.

(b) This section is not limited to persons who speak a language other than English, but applies also to the language and descriptions of any person, such as a child or a person who is mentally or developmentally disabled, who cannot be reasonably understood, or who cannot understand questioning, without the aid of an interpreter.

(2) A person who serves in the role of interpreter or translator in any action or proceeding is subject to all the provisions of this chapter relating to witnesses.

(3) An interpreter shall take an oath that he or she will make a true interpretation of the questions asked and the answers given and that the interpreter will make a true translation into English of any writing which he or she is required by his or her duties to decipher or translate.

History.—s. 1, ch. 76-237; s. 1, ch. 77-77; s. 22, ch. 78-361; s. 1, ch. 78-379; s. 2, ch. 85-53; s. 485, ch. 95-147.

90.6063   Interpreter services for deaf persons.—

(1)   The Legislature finds that it is an important concern that the rights of deaf citizens be protected. It is the intent of the Legislature to ensure that appropriate and effective interpreter services be made available to Florida's deaf citizens.

(2)   In all judicial proceedings and in sessions of a grand jury wherein a deaf person is a complainant, defendant, witness, or otherwise a party, or wherein a deaf person is a juror or grand juror, the court or presiding officer shall appoint a qualified interpreter to interpret the proceedings or deliberations to the deaf person and to interpret the deaf person's testimony, statements, or deliberations to the court, jury, or grand jury. A qualified interpreter shall be appointed, or other auxiliary aid provided as appropriate, for the duration of the trial or other proceeding in which a deaf juror or grand juror is seated.

(3)   (a)   "Deaf person" means any person whose hearing is so seriously impaired as to prohibit the person from understanding oral communications when spoken in a normal, conversational tone.

(b)   For the purposes of this section, the term "qualified interpreter" means an interpreter certified by the National Registry of Interpreters for the Deaf or the Florida Registry of Interpreters for the Deaf or an interpreter whose qualifications are otherwise determined by the appointing authority.

(4)   Every deaf person whose appearance before a proceeding entitles him or her to an interpreter shall notify the appointing authority of his or her disability not less than 5 days prior to any appearance and shall request at such time the services of an interpreter. Whenever a deaf person receives notification of the time of an appearance before a proceeding less than 5 days prior to the proceeding, the deaf person shall provide his or her notification and request as soon thereafter as practicable. In any case, nothing in this subsection shall operate to relieve an appointing authority's duty to provide an interpreter for a deaf person so entitled, and failure to strictly comply with the notice requirement will not be deemed a waiver of the right to an interpreter. An appointing authority may require a person requesting the appointment of an interpreter to furnish reasonable proof of the person's disability when the appointing authority has reason to believe that the person is not so disabled.

(5)   The appointing authority may channel requests for qualified interpreters through:

(a)   The Florida Registry of Interpreters for the Deaf;

(b)   The Division of Vocational Rehabilitation of the Department of Education; or

(c)   Any other resource wherein the appointing authority knows that qualified interpreters can be found.

(6)   No qualified interpreter shall be appointed unless the appointing authority and the deaf person make a preliminary determination that the interpreter is able to communicate readily with the deaf person and is able to repeat and translate statements to and from the deaf person accurately.

(7)   Before a qualified interpreter may participate in any proceedings subsequent to an appointment under the provisions of this act, such interpreter shall make an oath or affirmation that he or she will make a true interpretation in an understandable manner to the deaf person for whom the interpreter is appointed and that he or she will repeat the statements of the deaf person in the English language to the best of his or her skill and judgment. Whenever a deaf person communicates through an interpreter to any person under such circumstances that the communication would be privileged, and the recipient of the communication could not be compelled to testify as to the communication, this privilege shall apply to the interpreter.

(8) An interpreter appointed by the court in a criminal matter or in a civil matter shall be entitled to a reasonable fee for such service, in addition to actual expenses for travel, to be paid out of general county funds.

History.—ss. 1, 2, 3, 4, 5, 7, 8, 9, ch. 80-155; s. 42, ch. 81-259; s. 1, ch. 90-123; s. 2, ch. 93-125; s. 486, ch. 95-147; s. 6, ch. 99-8; s. 18, ch. 2002-22.

90.607 Competency of certain persons as witnesses.—

(1) (a) Except as provided in paragraph (b), the judge presiding at the trial of an action is not competent to testify as a witness in that trial. An objection is not necessary to preserve the point.

(b) By agreement of the parties, the trial judge may give evidence on a purely formal matter to facilitate the trial of the action.

(2) (a) A member of the jury is not competent to testify as a witness in a trial when he or she is sitting as a juror. If the juror is called to testify, the opposing party shall be given an opportunity to object out of the presence of the jury.

(b) Upon an inquiry into the validity of a verdict or indictment, a juror is not competent to testify as to any matter which essentially inheres in the verdict or indictment.

History.—s. 1, ch. 76-237; s. 1, ch. 77-77; s. 22, ch. 78-361; s. 1, ch. 78-379; s. 487, ch. 95-147.

90.608 Who may impeach.—Any party, including the party calling the witness, may attack the credibility of a witness by:

(1) Introducing statements of the witness which are inconsistent with the witness's present testimony.

(2) Showing that the witness is biased.

(3) Attacking the character of the witness in accordance with the provisions of s. 90.609 or s. 90.610.

(4) Showing a defect of capacity, ability, or opportunity in the witness to observe, remember, or recount the matters about which the witness testified.

(5) Proof by other witnesses that material facts are not as testified to by the witness being impeached.

History.—s. 1, ch. 76-237; s. 1, ch. 77-77; ss. 14, 22, ch. 78-361; ss. 1, 2, ch. 78-379; s. 1, ch. 90-174; s. 488, ch. 95-147.

90.609 Character of witness as impeachment.—A party may attack or support the credibility of a witness, including an accused, by evidence in the form of reputation, except that:

(1) The evidence may refer only to character relating to truthfulness.

(2) Evidence of a truthful character is admissible only after the character of the witness for truthfulness has been attacked by reputation evidence.

History.—s. 1, ch. 76-237; s. 1, ch. 77-77; ss. 15, 22, ch. 78-361; ss. 1, 2, ch. 78-379.

90.610 Conviction of certain crimes as impeachment.—

(1) A party may attack the credibility of any witness, including an accused, by evidence that the witness has been convicted of a crime if the crime was punishable by death or imprisonment in excess of 1 year under the law under which the witness was convicted, or if the crime involved dishonesty or a false statement regardless of the punishment, with the following exceptions:

(a) Evidence of any such conviction is inadmissible in a civil trial if it is so remote in time as to have no bearing on the present character of the witness.

(b) Evidence of juvenile adjudications are inadmissible under this subsection.

(2) The pendency of an appeal or the granting of a pardon relating to such crime does not render evidence of the conviction from which the appeal was taken or for which the pardon was granted inadmissible. Evidence of the pendency of the appeal is admissible.

(3) Nothing in this section affects the admissibility of evidence under s. 90.404 or s. 90.608.

History.—s. 1, ch. 76-237; s. 1, ch. 77-77; ss. 16, 22, ch. 78-361; ss. 1, 2, ch. 78-379; s. 489, ch. 95-147.

90.611 Religious beliefs or opinions.—Evidence of the beliefs or opinions of a witness on matters of religion is inadmissible to show that the witness's credibility is impaired or enhanced thereby.

History.—s. 1, ch. 76-237; s. 1, ch. 77-77; s. 22, ch. 78-361; s. 1, ch. 78-379; s. 490, ch. 95-147.

90.612 Mode and order of interrogation and presentation.—

(1) The judge shall exercise reasonable control over the mode and order of the interrogation of witnesses and the presentation of evidence, so as to:

(a) Facilitate, through effective interrogation and presentation, the discovery of the truth.

(b) Avoid needless consumption of time.

(c) Protect witnesses from harassment or undue embarrassment.

(2) Cross-examination of a witness is limited to the subject matter of the direct examination and matters affecting the credibility of the witness. The court may, in its discretion, permit inquiry into additional matters.

(3) Leading questions should not be used on the direct examination of a witness except as may be necessary to develop the witness's testimony. Ordinarily, leading questions should be permitted on cross-examination. When a party calls a hostile witness, an adverse party, or a witness identified with an adverse party, interrogation may be by leading questions.

The judge shall take special care to protect a witness under age 14 from questions that are in a form that cannot reasonably be understood by a person of the age and understanding of the witness, and shall take special care to restrict the unnecessary repetition of questions.

History.—s. 1, ch. 76-237; s. 1, ch. 77-77; s. 22, ch. 78-361; s. 1, ch. 78-379; s. 1, ch. 95-179; s. 2, ch. 2000-316.

90.613 Refreshing the memory of a witness.—When a witness uses a writing or other item to refresh memory while testifying, an adverse party is entitled to have such writing or other item produced at the hearing, to inspect it, to cross-examine the witness thereon, and to introduce it, or, in the case of a writing, to introduce those portions which relate to the testimony of the witness, in evidence. If it is claimed that the writing contains matters not related to the subject matter of the testimony, the judge shall examine the writing in camera, excise any portions not so related, and order delivery of the remainder to the party entitled thereto. Any portion withheld over objection shall be preserved and made available to the appellate court in the event of an appeal. If a writing or other item is not produced or delivered pursuant to order under this section, the testimony of the witness concerning those matters shall be stricken.

History.—s. 1, ch. 76-237; s. 1, ch. 77-77; s. 22, ch. 78-361; s. 1, ch. 78-379; s. 491, ch. 95-147.

90.614 Prior statements of witnesses.—

(1) When a witness is examined concerning the witness's prior written statement or concerning an oral statement that has been reduced to writing, the court, on motion of the adverse party, shall order the statement to be shown to the witness or its contents disclosed to him or her.

(2) Extrinsic evidence of a prior inconsistent statement by a witness is inadmissible unless the witness is first afforded an opportunity to explain or deny the prior statement and the opposing party is afforded an opportunity to interrogate the witness on it, or the interests of justice otherwise require. If a witness denies making or does not distinctly admit making the prior inconsistent statement, extrinsic evidence of such statement is admissible. This subsection is not applicable to admissions of a party-opponent as defined in s. 90.803(18).

History.—s. 1, ch. 76-237; s. 1, ch. 77-77; ss. 17, 22, ch. 78-361; ss. 1, 2, ch. 78-379; s. 492, ch. 95-147.

90.615 Calling witnesses by the court.—

(1) The court may call witnesses whom all parties may cross-examine.

(2) When required by the interests of justice, the court may interrogate witnesses, whether called by the court or by a party.

History.—s. 1, ch. 76-237; s. 1, ch. 77-77; s. 22, ch. 78-361; s. 1, ch. 78-379.

90.616 Exclusion of witnesses.—

(1) At the request of a party the court shall order, or upon its own motion the court may order, witnesses excluded from a proceeding so that they cannot hear the testimony of other witnesses except as provided in subsection (2).

(2) A witness may not be excluded if the witness is:

(a) A party who is a natural person.

(b) In a civil case, an officer or employee of a party that is not a natural person. The party's attorney shall designate the officer or employee who shall be the party's representative.

(c) A person whose presence is shown by the party's attorney to be essential to the presentation of the party's cause.

(d) In a criminal case, the victim of the crime, the victim's next of kin, the parent or guardian of a minor child victim, or a lawful representative of such person, unless, upon motion, the court determines such person's presence to be prejudicial.

History.—s. 2, ch. 90-174; s. 1, ch. 92-107; s. 493, ch. 95-147.

90.701 Opinion testimony of lay witnesses.—If a witness is not testifying as an expert, the witness's testimony about what he or she perceived may be in the form of inference and opinion when:

(1) The witness cannot readily, and with equal accuracy and adequacy, communicate what he or she has perceived to the trier of fact without testifying in terms of inferences or opinions and the witness's use of inferences or opinions will not mislead the trier of fact to the prejudice of the objecting party; and

(2) The opinions and inferences do not require a special knowledge, skill, experience, or training.

History.—s. 1, ch. 76-237; s. 1, ch. 77-77; s. 22, ch. 78-361; s. 1, ch. 78-379; s. 494, ch. 95-147.

90.702 Testimony by experts.—If scientific, technical, or other specialized knowledge will assist the trier of fact in understanding the evidence or in determining a fact in issue, a witness qualified as an expert by knowledge, skill, experience, training, or education may testify about it in the form of an opinion; however, the opinion is admissible only if it can be applied to evidence at trial.

History.—s. 1, ch. 76-237; s. 1, ch. 77-77; s. 22, ch. 78-361; s. 1, ch. 78-379.

90.703 Opinion on ultimate issue.—Testimony in the form of an opinion or inference otherwise admissible is not objectionable because it includes an ultimate issue to be decided by the trier of fact.

History.—s. 1, ch. 76-237; s. 1, ch. 77-77; s. 22, ch. 78-361; s. 1, ch. 78-379.

90.704 Basis of opinion testimony by experts.—The facts or data upon which an expert bases an opinion or inference may be those perceived by, or made known to, the expert at or before the trial. If the facts or data are of a type reasonably relied upon by experts in the subject to support the opinion expressed, the facts or data need not be admissible in evidence.

History.—s. 1, ch. 76-237; s. 1, ch. 77-77; s. 22, ch. 78-361; s. 1, ch. 78-379; s. 495, ch. 95-147.

90.705 Disclosure of facts or data underlying expert opinion.—

(1) Unless otherwise required by the court, an expert may testify in terms of opinion or inferences and give reasons without prior disclosure of the underlying facts or data. On cross-examination the expert shall be required to specify the facts or data.

(2) Prior to the witness giving the opinion, a party against whom the opinion or inference is offered may conduct a voir dire examination of the witness directed to the underlying facts or data for the witness's opinion. If the party establishes prima facie evidence that the expert does not have a sufficient basis for the opinion, the opinions and inferences of the expert are inadmissible unless the party offering the testimony establishes the underlying facts or data.

History.—s. 1, ch. 76-237; s. 1, ch. 77-77; s. 22, ch. 78-361; s. 1, ch. 78-379; s. 496, ch. 95-147.

90.706 Authoritativeness of literature for use in cross-examination.—Statements of facts or opinions on a subject of science, art, or specialized knowledge contained in a published treatise, periodical, book, dissertation, pamphlet, or other writing may be used in cross-examination of an expert witness if the expert witness recognizes the author or the treatise, periodical, book, dissertation, pamphlet, or other writing to be authoritative, or, notwithstanding nonrecognition by the expert witness, if the trial court finds the author or the treatise, periodical, book, dissertation, pamphlet, or other writing to be authoritative and relevant to the subject matter.

History.—s. 18, ch. 78-361; s. 2, ch. 78-379.

90.801 Hearsay; definitions; exceptions.—

(1) The following definitions apply under this chapter:

    (a) A "statement" is:

        1. An oral or written assertion; or

        2. Nonverbal conduct of a person if it is intended by the person as an assertion.

    (b) A "declarant" is a person who makes a statement.

    (c) "Hearsay" is a statement, other than one made by the declarant while testifying at the trial or hearing, offered in evidence to prove the truth of the matter asserted.

(2) A statement is not hearsay if the declarant testifies at the trial or hearing and is subject to cross-examination concerning the statement and the statement is:

    (a) Inconsistent with the declarant's testimony and was given under oath subject to the penalty of perjury at a trial, hearing, or other proceeding or in a deposition;

    (b) Consistent with the declarant's testimony and is offered to rebut an express or implied charge against the declarant of improper influence, motive, or recent fabrication; or

    (c) One of identification of a person made after perceiving the person.

History.—s. 1, ch. 76-237; s. 1, ch. 77-77; ss. 19, 22, ch. 78-361; ss. 1, 2, ch. 78-379; s. 2, ch. 81-93; s. 497, ch. 95-147.

90.802 Hearsay rule.—Except as provided by statute, hearsay evidence is inadmissible.

History.—s. 1, ch. 76-237; s. 1, ch. 77-77; s. 22, ch. 78-361; s. 1, ch. 78-379.

90.803 Hearsay exceptions; availability of declarant immaterial.—The provision of s. 90.802 to the contrary notwithstanding, the following are not inadmissible as evidence, even though the declarant is available as a witness:

    (1) SPONTANEOUS STATEMENT.—A spontaneous statement describing or explaining an event or condition made while the declarant was perceiving the event or condition, or immediately thereafter, except when such statement is made under circumstances that indicate its lack of trustworthiness.

    (2) EXCITED UTTERANCE.—A statement or excited utterance relating to a startling event or condition made while the declarant was under the stress of excitement caused by the event or condition.

(3) THEN-EXISTING MENTAL, EMOTIONAL, OR PHYSICAL CONDITION.—

(a) A statement of the declarant's then-existing state of mind, emotion, or physical sensation, including a statement of intent, plan, motive, design, mental feeling, pain, or bodily health, when such evidence is offered to:

1. Prove the declarant's state of mind, emotion, or physical sensation at that time or at any other time when such state is an issue in the action.

2. Prove or explain acts of subsequent conduct of the declarant.

(b) However, this subsection does not make admissible:

1. An after-the-fact statement of memory or belief to prove the fact remembered or believed, unless such statement relates to the execution, revocation, identification, or terms of the declarant's will.

2. A statement made under circumstances that indicate its lack of trustworthiness.

(4) STATEMENTS FOR PURPOSES OF MEDICAL DIAGNOSIS OR TREATMENT.— Statements made for purposes of medical diagnosis or treatment by a person seeking the diagnosis or treatment, or made by an individual who has knowledge of the facts and is legally responsible for the person who is unable to communicate the facts, which statements describe medical history, past or present symptoms, pain, or sensations, or the inceptions or general character of the cause or external source thereof, insofar as reasonably pertinent to diagnosis or treatment.

(5) RECORDED RECOLLECTION.—A memorandum or record concerning a matter about which a witness once had knowledge, but now has insufficient recollection to enable the witness to testify fully and accurately, shown to have been made by the witness when the matter was fresh in the witness's memory and to reflect that knowledge correctly. A party may read into evidence a memorandum or record when it is admitted, but no such memorandum or record is admissible as an exhibit unless offered by an adverse party.

(6) RECORDS OF REGULARLY CONDUCTED BUSINESS ACTIVITY.—

(a) A memorandum, report, record, or data compilation, in any form, of acts, events, conditions, opinion, or diagnosis, made at or near the time by, or from information transmitted by, a person with knowledge, if kept in the course of a regularly conducted business activity and if it was the regular practice of that business activity to make such memorandum, report, record, or data compilation, all as shown by the testimony of the custodian or other qualified witness, or as shown by a certification or declaration that complies with paragraph (c) and s. 90.902(11), unless the sources of information or other circumstances show lack of trustworthiness. The term "business" as used in this paragraph includes a business, institution, association, profession, occupation, and calling of every kind, whether or not conducted for profit.

(b) Evidence in the form of an opinion or diagnosis is inadmissible under paragraph (a) unless such opinion or diagnosis would be admissible under ss. 90.701-90.705 if the person whose opinion is recorded were to testify to the opinion directly.

(c) A party intending to offer evidence under paragraph (a) by means of a certification or declaration shall serve reasonable written notice of that intention upon every other party and shall make the evidence available for inspection sufficiently in advance of its offer in evidence to provide to any other party a fair opportunity to challenge the admissibility of the evidence. If the evidence is maintained in a foreign country, the party intending to offer the evidence must provide written notice of that intention at the arraignment or as soon after the arraignment as is practicable or, in a civil case, 60 days before the trial. A motion opposing the admissibility of such evidence must be made by the opposing party and determined by the court before trial. A party's failure to file such a motion before trial constitutes a waiver of objection to the evidence, but the court for good cause shown may grant relief from the waiver.

(7) ABSENCE OF ENTRY IN RECORDS OF REGULARLY CONDUCTED ACTIVITY.—Evidence that a matter is not included in the memoranda, reports, records, or data compilations, in any form, of a regularly conducted activity to prove the nonoccurrence or nonexistence of the matter, if the matter was of a kind of which a memorandum, report, record, or data compilation was regularly made and preserved, unless the sources of information or other circumstances show lack of trustworthiness.

(8) PUBLIC RECORDS AND REPORTS.—Records, reports, statements reduced to writing, or data compilations, in any form, of public offices or agencies, setting forth the activities of the office or agency, or matters observed pursuant to duty imposed by law as to matters which there was a duty to report, excluding in criminal cases matters observed by a police officer or other law enforcement personnel, unless the sources of information or other circumstances show their lack of trustworthiness. The criminal case exclusion shall not apply to an affidavit otherwise admissible under s. 316.1934 or s. 327.354.

(9) RECORDS OF VITAL STATISTICS.—Records or data compilations, in any form, of births, fetal deaths, deaths, or marriages, if a report was made to a public office pursuant to requirements of law. However, nothing in this section shall be construed to make admissible any other marriage of any party to any cause of action except for the purpose of impeachment as set forth in s. 90.610.

(10) ABSENCE OF PUBLIC RECORD OR ENTRY.—Evidence, in the form of a certification in accord with s. 90.902, or in the form of testimony, that diligent search failed to disclose a record, report, statement, or data compilation or entry, when offered to prove the absence of the record, report, statement, or data compilation or the nonoccurrence or nonexistence of a matter of which a record, report, statement, or data compilation would regularly have been made and preserved by a public office and agency.

(11) RECORDS OF RELIGIOUS ORGANIZATIONS.—Statements of births, marriages, divorces, deaths, parentage, ancestry, relationship by blood or marriage, or other similar facts of personal or family history contained in a regularly kept record of a religious organization.

(12) MARRIAGE, BAPTISMAL, AND SIMILAR CERTIFICATES.—Statements of facts contained in a certificate that the maker performed a marriage or other ceremony or administered a sacrament, when such statement was certified by a member of the clergy, public official, or other person authorized by the rules or practices of a religious organization or by law to perform the act certified, and when such certificate purports to have been issued at the time of the act or within a reasonable time thereafter.

(13) FAMILY RECORDS.—Statements of fact concerning personal or family history in family Bibles, charts, engravings in rings, inscriptions on family portraits, engravings on urns, crypts, or tombstones, or the like.

(14) RECORDS OF DOCUMENTS AFFECTING AN INTEREST IN PROPERTY.—The record of a document purporting to establish or affect an interest in property, as proof of the contents of the original recorded or filed document and its execution and delivery by each person by whom it purports to have been executed, if the record is a record of a public office and an applicable statute authorized the recording or filing of the document in the office.

(15) STATEMENTS IN DOCUMENTS AFFECTING AN INTEREST IN PROPERTY.—A statement contained in a document purporting to establish or affect an interest in property, if the matter stated was relevant to the purpose of the document, unless dealings with the property since the document was made have been inconsistent with the truth of the statement or the purport of the document.

(16) STATEMENTS IN ANCIENT DOCUMENTS.—Statements in a document in existence 20 years or more, the authenticity of which is established.

(17) MARKET REPORTS, COMMERCIAL PUBLICATIONS.—Market quotations, tabulations, lists, directories, or other published compilations, generally used and relied upon by the

public or by persons in particular occupations if, in the opinion of the court, the sources of information and method of preparation were such as to justify their admission.

(18) ADMISSIONS.—A statement that is offered against a party and is:

(a) The party's own statement in either an individual or a representative capacity;

(b) A statement of which the party has manifested an adoption or belief in its truth;

(c) A statement by a person specifically authorized by the party to make a statement concerning the subject;

(d) A statement by the party's agent or servant concerning a matter within the scope of the agency or employment thereof, made during the existence of the relationship; or

(e) A statement by a person who was a coconspirator of the party during the course, and in furtherance, of the conspiracy. Upon request of counsel, the court shall instruct the jury that the conspiracy itself and each member's participation in it must be established by independent evidence, either before the introduction of any evidence or before evidence is admitted under this paragraph.

(19) REPUTATION CONCERNING PERSONAL OR FAMILY HISTORY.—Evidence of reputation:

(a) Among members of a person's family by blood, adoption, or marriage;

(b) Among a person's associates; or

(c) In the community,

concerning a person's birth, adoption, marriage, divorce, death, relationship by blood, adoption, or marriage, ancestry, or other similar fact of personal or family history.

(20) REPUTATION CONCERNING BOUNDARIES OR GENERAL HISTORY.—Evidence of reputation:

(a) In a community, arising before the controversy about the boundaries of, or customs affecting lands in, the community.

(b) About events of general history which are important to the community, state, or nation where located.

(21) REPUTATION AS TO CHARACTER.—Evidence of reputation of a person's character among associates or in the community.

(22) FORMER TESTIMONY.—Former testimony given by the declarant which testimony was given as a witness at another hearing of the same or a different proceeding, or in a deposition taken in compliance with law in the course of the same or another proceeding, if the party against whom the testimony is now offered, or, in a civil action or proceeding, a predecessor in interest, or a person with a similar interest, had an opportunity and similar motive to develop the testimony by direct, cross, or redirect examination; provided, however, the court finds that the testimony is not inadmissible pursuant to s. 90.402 or s. 90.403.

(23) HEARSAY EXCEPTION; STATEMENT OF CHILD VICTIM.—

(a) Unless the source of information or the method or circumstances by which the statement is reported indicates a lack of trustworthiness, an out-of-court statement made by a child victim with a physical, mental, emotional, or developmental age of 11 or less describing any act of child abuse or neglect, any act of sexual abuse against a child, the offense of child abuse, the offense of aggravated child abuse, or any offense involving an unlawful sexual act, contact, intrusion, or penetration performed in the presence of, with, by, or on the declarant child, not otherwise admissible, is admissible in evidence in any civil or criminal proceeding if:

1. The court finds in a hearing conducted outside the presence of the jury that the time, content, and circumstances of the statement provide sufficient safeguards of reliability. In making its determination, the court may consider the mental and physical age and maturity of the child, the nature and duration of the abuse or offense, the relationship of the child to the offender, the reliability of the assertion, the reliability of the child victim, and any other factor deemed appropriate; and

2. The child either:

    a. Testifies; or

    b. Is unavailable as a witness, provided that there is other corroborative evidence of the abuse or offense. Unavailability shall include a finding by the court that the child's participation in the trial or proceeding would result in a substantial likelihood of severe emotional or mental harm, in addition to findings pursuant to s. 90.804(1).

(b) In a criminal action, the defendant shall be notified no later than 10 days before trial that a statement which qualifies as a hearsay exception pursuant to this subsection will be offered as evidence at trial. The notice shall include a written statement of the content of the child's statement, the time at which the statement was made, the circumstances surrounding the statement which indicate its reliability, and such other particulars as necessary to provide full disclosure of the statement.

(c) The court shall make specific findings of fact, on the record, as to the basis for its ruling under this subsection.

(24) HEARSAY EXCEPTION; STATEMENT OF ELDERLY PERSON OR DISABLED ADULT.—

(a) Unless the source of information or the method or circumstances by which the statement is reported indicates a lack of trustworthiness, an out-of-court statement made by an elderly person or disabled adult, as defined in s. 825.101, describing any act of abuse or neglect, any act of exploitation, the offense of battery or aggravated battery or assault or aggravated assault or sexual battery, or any other violent act on the declarant elderly person or disabled adult, not otherwise admissible, is admissible in evidence in any civil or criminal proceeding if:

1. The court finds in a hearing conducted outside the presence of the jury that the time, content, and circumstances of the statement provide sufficient safeguards of reliability. In making its determination, the court may consider the mental and physical age and maturity of the elderly person or disabled adult, the nature and duration of the abuse or offense, the relationship of the victim to the offender, the reliability of the assertion, the reliability of the elderly person or disabled adult, and any other factor deemed appropriate; and

2. The elderly person or disabled adult either:

    a. Testifies; or

    b. Is unavailable as a witness, provided that there is corroborative evidence of the abuse or offense. Unavailability shall include a finding by the court that the elderly person's or disabled adult's participation in the trial or proceeding would result in a substantial likelihood of severe emotional, mental, or physical harm, in addition to findings pursuant to s. 90.804(1).

(b) In a criminal action, the defendant shall be notified no later than 10 days before the trial that a statement which qualifies as a hearsay exception pursuant to this subsection will be offered as evidence at trial. The notice shall include a written statement of the content of the elderly person's or disabled adult's statement, the time at which the statement was made, the circumstances surrounding the statement which indicate its reliability, and such other particulars as necessary to provide full disclosure of the statement.

(c) The court shall make specific findings of fact, on the record, as to the basis for its ruling under this subsection.

History.—s. 1, ch. 76-237; s. 1, ch. 77-77; s. 1, ch. 77-174; ss. 20, 22, ch. 78-361; ss. 1, 2, ch. 78-379; s. 4, ch. 85-53; s. 11, ch. 87-224; s. 2, ch. 90-139; s. 3, ch. 90-174; s. 12, ch. 91-255; s. 498, ch. 95-147; s. 1, ch. 95-158; s. 2, ch. 96-330; s. 1, ch. 98-2; s. 2, ch. 2003-259.

90.804 Hearsay exceptions; declarant unavailable.—

(1) DEFINITION OF UNAVAILABILITY.—"Unavailability as a witness" means that the declarant:

(a) Is exempted by a ruling of a court on the ground of privilege from testifying concerning the subject matter of the declarant's statement;

(b) Persists in refusing to testify concerning the subject matter of the declarant's statement despite an order of the court to do so;

(c) Has suffered a lack of memory of the subject matter of his or her statement so as to destroy the declarant's effectiveness as a witness during the trial;

(d) Is unable to be present or to testify at the hearing because of death or because of then-existing physical or mental illness or infirmity; or

(e) Is absent from the hearing, and the proponent of a statement has been unable to procure the declarant's attendance or testimony by process or other reasonable means.

However, a declarant is not unavailable as a witness if such exemption, refusal, claim of lack of memory, inability to be present, or absence is due to the procurement or wrongdoing of the party who is the proponent of his or her statement in preventing the witness from attending or testifying.

(2) HEARSAY EXCEPTIONS.—The following are not excluded under s. 90.802, provided that the declarant is unavailable as a witness:

(a) Former testimony.—Testimony given as a witness at another hearing of the same or a different proceeding, or in a deposition taken in compliance with law in the course of the same or another proceeding, if the party against whom the testimony is now offered, or, in a civil action or proceeding, a predecessor in interest, had an opportunity and similar motive to develop the testimony by direct, cross, or redirect examination.

(b) Statement under belief of impending death.—In a civil or criminal trial, a statement made by a declarant while reasonably believing that his or her death was imminent, concerning the physical cause or instrumentalities of what the declarant believed to be impending death or the circumstances surrounding impending death.

(c) Statement against interest.—A statement which, at the time of its making, was so far contrary to the declarant's pecuniary or proprietary interest or tended to subject the declarant to liability or to render invalid a claim by the declarant against another, so that a person in the declarant's position would not have made the statement unless he or she believed it to be true. A statement tending to expose the declarant to criminal liability and offered to exculpate the accused is inadmissible, unless corroborating circumstances show the trustworthiness of the statement.

(d) Statement of personal or family history.—A statement concerning the declarant's own birth, adoption, marriage, divorce, parentage, ancestry, or other similar fact of personal or family history, including relationship by blood, adoption, or marriage, even though the declarant had no means of acquiring personal knowledge of the matter stated.

(e) Statement by deceased or ill declarant similar to one previously admitted.—In an action or proceeding brought against the personal representative, heir at law, assignee, legatee, devisee, or survivor of a deceased person, or against a trustee of a trust created by a deceased person, or against the assignee, committee, or guardian of a mentally incompetent person, when a declarant is unavailable as provided in paragraph (1)(d), a written or oral statement made regarding the same subject matter as another statement made by the declarant that has previously been offered by an adverse party and admitted in evidence.

History.—s. 1, ch. 76-237; s. 1, ch. 77-77; s. 22, ch. 78-361; s. 1, ch. 78-379; s. 3, ch. 90-139; s. 4, ch. 90-174; s. 499, ch. 95-147; s. 2, ch. 2005-46.

90.805 Hearsay within hearsay.—Hearsay within hearsay is not excluded under s. 90.802, provided each part of the combined statements conforms with an exception to the hearsay rule as provided in s. 90.803 or s. 90.804.

History.—s. 1, ch. 76-237; s. 1, ch. 77-77; s. 22, ch. 78-361; s. 1, ch. 78-379.

90.806 Attacking and supporting credibility of declarant.—

(1) When a hearsay statement has been admitted in evidence, credibility of the declarant may be attacked and, if attacked, may be supported by any evidence that would be admissible for those purposes if the declarant had testified as a witness. Evidence of a statement or conduct by the declarant at any time inconsistent with the declarant's hearsay statement is admissible, regardless of whether or not the declarant has been afforded an opportunity to deny or explain it.

(2) If the party against whom a hearsay statement has been admitted calls the declarant as a witness, the party is entitled to examine the declarant on the statement as if under cross-examination.

History.—s. 1, ch. 76-237; s. 1, ch. 77-77; s. 22, ch. 78-361; s. 1, ch. 78-379; s. 500, ch. 95-147.

90.901 Requirement of authentication or identification.—Authentication or identification of evidence is required as a condition precedent to its admissibility. The requirements of this section are satisfied by evidence sufficient to support a finding that the matter in question is what its proponent claims.

History.—s. 1, ch. 76-237; s. 1, ch. 77-77; s. 22, ch. 78-361; s. 1, ch. 78-379.

90.902 Self-authentication.—Extrinsic evidence of authenticity as a condition precedent to admissibility is not required for:

(1) A document bearing:

(a) A seal purporting to be that of the United States or any state, district, commonwealth, territory, or insular possession thereof; the Panama Canal Zone; the Trust Territory of the Pacific Islands; or a court, political subdivision, department, officer, or agency of any of them; and

(b) A signature by the custodian of the document attesting to the authenticity of the seal.

(2) A document not bearing a seal but purporting to bear a signature of an officer or employee of any entity listed in subsection (1), affixed in the officer's or employee's official capacity.

(3) An official foreign document, record, or entry that is:

(a) Executed or attested to by a person in the person's official capacity authorized by the laws of a foreign country to make the execution or attestation; and

(b) Accompanied by a final certification, as provided herein, of the genuineness of the signature and official position of:

1. The executing person; or

2. Any foreign official whose certificate of genuineness of signature and official position relates to the execution or attestation or is in a chain of certificates of genuineness of signature and official position relating to the execution or attestation.

The final certification may be made by a secretary of an embassy or legation, consul general, consul, vice consul, or consular agent of the United States or a diplomatic or consular official of the foreign country assigned or accredited to the United States. When the parties receive reasonable opportunity to investigate the authenticity and accuracy of official foreign documents, the court may order that they be treated as presumptively authentic without final certification or permit them in evidence by an attested summary with or without final certification.

(4) A copy of an official public record, report, or entry, or of a document authorized by law to be recorded or filed and actually recorded or filed in a public office, including data compilations in any form, certified as correct by the custodian or other person authorized to make the certification by certificate complying with subsection (1), subsection (2), or subsection (3) or complying with any act of the Legislature or rule adopted by the Supreme Court.

(5) Books, pamphlets, or other publications purporting to be issued by a governmental authority.

(6) Printed materials purporting to be newspapers or periodicals.

(7) Inscriptions, signs, tags, or labels purporting to have been affixed in the course of business and indicating ownership, control, or origin.

(8) Commercial papers and signatures thereon and documents relating to them, to the extent provided in the Uniform Commercial Code.

(9) Any signature, document, or other matter declared by the Legislature to be presumptively or prima facie genuine or authentic.

(10) Any document properly certified under the law of the jurisdiction where the certification is made.

(11) An original or a duplicate of evidence that would be admissible under s. 90.803(6), which is maintained in a foreign country or domestic location and is accompanied by a certification or declaration from the custodian of the records or another qualified person certifying or declaring that the record:

(a) Was made at or near the time of the occurrence of the matters set forth by, or from information transmitted by, a person having knowledge of those matters;

(b) Was kept in the course of the regularly conducted activity; and

(c) Was made as a regular practice in the course of the regularly conducted activity,

provided that falsely making such a certification or declaration would subject the maker to criminal penalty under the laws of the foreign or domestic location in which the certification or declaration was signed.

History.—s. 1, ch. 76-237; s. 1, ch. 77-77; s. 1, ch. 77-174; s. 22, ch. 78-361; s. 1, ch. 78-379; s. 501, ch. 95-147; s. 3, ch. 2003-259.

90.903 Testimony of subscribing witness unnecessary.—The testimony of a subscribing witness is not necessary to authenticate a writing unless the statute requiring attestation requires it.

History.—s. 1, ch. 76-237; s. 1, ch. 77-77; s. 22, ch. 78-361; s. 1, ch. 78-379.

90.91 Photographs of property wrongfully taken; use in prosecution, procedure; return of property to owner.—In any prosecution for a crime involving the wrongful taking of property, a photograph of the property alleged to have been wrongfully taken may be deemed competent evidence of such property and may be admissible in the prosecution to the same extent as if such property were introduced as evidence. Such photograph shall bear a written description of the property alleged to have been wrongfully taken, the name of the owner of the property, the location where the alleged wrongful taking occurred, the name of the investigating law enforcement officer, the date the photograph was taken, and the name of the photographer. Such writing shall be made under oath by the investigating law enforcement officer, and the photograph shall be identified by the signature of the photographer. Upon the filing of such photograph and writing with the law enforcement authority or court holding such property as evidence, the property may be returned to the owner from whom the property was taken.

History.—s. 4, ch. 84-363.

90.951 Definitions.—For purposes of this chapter:

(1) "Writings" and "recordings" include letters, words, or numbers, or their equivalent, set down by handwriting, typewriting, printing, photostating, photography, magnetic impulse, mechanical or electronic recording, or other form of data compilation, upon paper, wood, stone, recording tape, or other materials.

(2) "Photographs" include still photographs, X-ray films, videotapes, and motion pictures.

(3) An "original" of a writing or recording means the writing or recording itself, or any counterpart intended to have the same effect by a person executing or issuing it. An "original" of a photograph includes the negative or any print made from it. If data are stored in a computer or similar device, any printout or other output readable by sight and shown to reflect the data accurately is an "original."

(4) "Duplicate" includes:

(a) A counterpart produced by the same impression as the original, from the same matrix; by means of photography, including enlargements and miniatures; by mechanical or electronic rerecording; by chemical reproduction; or by other equivalent technique that accurately reproduces the original; or

(b) An executed carbon copy not intended by the parties to be an original.

History.—s. 1, ch. 76-237; s. 1, ch. 77-77; s. 22, ch. 78-361; s. 1, ch. 78-379.

90.952 Requirement of originals.—Except as otherwise provided by statute, an original writing, recording, or photograph is required in order to prove the contents of the writing, recording, or photograph.

History.—s. 1, ch. 76-237; s. 1, ch. 77-77; s. 1, ch. 77-174; s. 22, ch. 78-361; s. 1, ch. 78-379.

90.953 Admissibility of duplicates.—A duplicate is admissible to the same extent as an original, unless:

(1) The document or writing is a negotiable instrument as defined in s. 673.1041, a security as defined in s. 678.1021, or any other writing that evidences a right to the payment of money, is not itself a security agreement or lease, and is of a type that is transferred by delivery in the ordinary course of business with any necessary endorsement or assignment.

(2)   A genuine question is raised about the authenticity of the original or any other document or writing.

(3)   It is unfair, under the circumstance, to admit the duplicate in lieu of the original.

History.—s. 1, ch. 76-237; s. 1, ch. 77-77; s. 22, ch. 78-361; s. 1, ch. 78-379; s. 57, ch. 92-82; s. 29, ch. 99-2.

90.954   Admissibility of other evidence of contents.—The original of a writing, recording, or photograph is not required, except as provided in s. 90.953, and other evidence of its contents is admissible when:

(1)   All originals are lost or destroyed, unless the proponent lost or destroyed them in bad faith.

(2)   An original cannot be obtained in this state by any judicial process or procedure.

(3)   An original was under the control of the party against whom offered at a time when that party was put on notice by the pleadings or by written notice from the adverse party that the contents of such original would be subject to proof at the hearing, and such original is not produced at the hearing.

(4)   The writing, recording, or photograph is not related to a controlling issue.

History.—s. 1, ch. 76-237; s. 1, ch. 77-77; s. 1, ch. 77-174; s. 22, ch. 78-361; s. 1, ch. 78-379; s. 502, ch. 95-147.

90.955   Public records.—

(1)   The contents of an official record or of a document authorized to be recorded or filed, and actually recorded or filed, with a governmental agency, either federal, state, county, or municipal, in a place where official records or documents are ordinarily filed, including data compilations in any form, may be proved by a copy authenticated as provided in s. 90.902, if otherwise admissible.

(2)   If a party cannot obtain, by the exercise of reasonable diligence, a copy that complies with subsection (1), other evidence of the contents is admissible.

History.—s. 1, ch. 76-237; s. 1, ch. 77-77; s. 22, ch. 78-361; s. 1, ch. 78-379.

90.956   Summaries.—When it is not convenient to examine in court the contents of voluminous writings, recordings, or photographs, a party may present them in the form of a chart, summary, or calculation by calling a qualified witness. The party intending to use such a summary must give timely written notice of his or her intention to use the summary, proof of which shall be filed with the court, and shall make the summary and the originals or duplicates of the data from which the summary is compiled available for examination or copying, or both, by other parties at a reasonable time and place. A judge may order that they be produced in court.

History.—s. 1, ch. 76-237; s. 1, ch. 77-77; s. 22, ch. 78-361; s. 1, ch. 78-379; s. 503, ch. 95-147.

90.957   Testimony or written admissions of a party.—A party may prove the contents of writings, recordings, or photographs by the testimony or deposition of the party against whom they are offered or by that party's written admission, without accounting for the nonproduction of the original.

History.—s. 1, ch. 76-237; s. 1, ch. 77-77; s. 22, ch. 78-361; s. 1, ch. 78-379; s. 504, ch. 95-147.

90.958 Functions of court and jury.—

(1) Except as provided in subsection (2), when the admissibility under this chapter of other evidence of the contents of writings, recordings, or photographs depends upon the existence of a preliminary fact, the question as to whether the preliminary fact exists is for the court to determine.

(2) The trier of fact shall determine whether:

(a) The asserted writing ever existed.

(b) Another writing, recording, or photograph produced at the trial is the original.

(c) Other evidence of the contents correctly reflects the contents.

History.—s. 1, ch. 76-237; s. 1, ch. 77-77; s. 22, ch. 78-361; s. 1, ch. 78-379.

TITLE VII

EVIDENCE

CHAPTER 92

WITNESSES, RECORDS, AND DOCUMENTS

92.05   Final judgments and decrees of courts of record.—All final judgments and decrees heretofore or hereafter rendered and entered in courts of record of this state, and certified copies thereof, shall be admissible as prima facie evidence in the several courts of this state of the entry and validity of such judgments and decrees. For the purposes of this section, a court of record shall be taken and construed to mean any court other than a municipal court or the Metropolitan Court of Miami-Dade County.

History.—s. 1, ch. 4723, 1899; GS 1522; RGS 2722; CGL 4390; s. 7, ch. 22858, 1945; s. 1, ch. 67-362; s. 15, ch. 73-334; s. 13, ch. 2008-4.

92.06   Judgments and decrees of United States District Courts.—All final judgments and decrees heretofore or hereafter to be rendered and entered in the United States District Courts of this state and certified copies thereof are declared to be admissible as prima facie evidence in the several courts of this state of the entry and validity of such judgments and decrees.

History.—s. 1, ch. 14748, 1931; CGL 1936 Supp. 4391(1).

92.07   Judgments and decrees of this state.—The recitals in all judgments and decrees of the Supreme Court and of the several circuit courts of this state, when such judgment or decree appears regular and has been recorded as provided by law for more than 20 years, shall be admissible in evidence as prima facie proof of the truth of the facts so recited. Either party to any suit at law or equity may offer a properly certified copy of such judgment or decree entered and recorded more than 20 years prior to the institution of the suit in which the same is offered, and such copy shall be admissible in evidence as prima facie proof of the facts in said judgment or decree set forth; provided, however, the party offering the same shall at least 10 days before the trial of the suit in which this copy is offered in evidence give notice to the opposite side of the intention to offer such copy in evidence and the purpose for which the same will be offered, and deliver with such notice a copy of the judgment or decree; provided, that nothing in this law shall render admissible in evidence any instrument of writing based on any judgment, deed of conveyance or power of attorney included in this law where any such instrument of writing has heretofore been brought in question in any action at law or in equity in any suit now pending or heretofore decided.

History.—s. 1, ch. 10111, 1925; CGL 4391.

92.08   Deeds and powers of attorney of record for 20 years or more.—The recitals in any deed of conveyance or power of attorney shall be admissible in evidence when offered in evidence by either party to any suit at law or in equity as prima facie proof of the truth of the facts therein recited, provided such deed of conveyance or power of attorney appears regular on its face and is a muniment in the chain of title under which the party offering the deed claims, and has been recorded as provided by law for more than 20 years prior to the institution of the suit in which it is offered; and provided further, that the party offering the deed of conveyance or power of attorney for such purposes shall at least 10 days before the trial of the suit in which the said copy is offered in evidence give notice to the opposite side of the intention to offer such copy in evidence and the purpose for which the same will be offered, and deliver with such notice a copy of the deed or power of attorney. The original deed or power of attorney shall be offered unless the party offering the certified copy shall show that the original is not within the custody or control of the party offering the copy.

History.—s. 2, ch. 10111, 1925; CGL 4392.

92.09 Effect of reversal, etc., of judgment or successful attack on deed.—No copy of a judgment or decree shall be admitted in evidence as aforesaid when it shall be made to appear that such decree has been reversed, annulled, vacated, or set aside, or that the same in collateral proceedings has been successfully attacked. No deed shall be admitted in evidence as hereinbefore provided if it shall appear that the execution or validity of said deed has been successfully attacked in any proceedings to which the grantee therein named or those or any of them holding under such grantee has been a party or parties.

History.—s. 3, ch. 10111, 1925; CGL 4393.

92.13 Certified copies of records of certified copies.—Certified copies of the record of certified copies of deeds, mortgages, powers of attorney and other instruments referred to in s. 695.19 shall have the same effect as to notice and all other purposes whatsoever as the record of the original has or can have; and certified copies of the record of such certified copies shall be admissible and may be used in evidence in the same manner and with like effect and under the same conditions as certified copies of the record of the original instrument.

History.—s. 2, ch. 11989, 1927; CGL 4388, 5718.

92.14 United States deeds and patents and copies thereof.—Deeds and patents issued by the United States Government and photographic copies made by authority of said government from its records thereof in the General Land Office, embracing lands in this state, and certified copies of the record thereof made in this state may be used in evidence in the courts of this state subject to the same rules that are applicable to the admission in evidence of other deeds and certified copies of the record thereof.

History.—s. 3, ch. 8565, 1921; CGL 5716.

92.141 Law enforcement employees; travel expenses; compensation as witness.—Any employee of a law enforcement agency of a municipality or county or the state who appears as an official witness to testify at any hearing or law action in any court of this state as a direct result of his or her employment in the law enforcement agency is entitled to per diem and travel expenses at the same rate provided for state employees under s. 112.061, except that if the employee travels by privately owned vehicle he or she is entitled to such travel expenses for the actual distance traveled to and from court. In addition thereto, such employee is entitled to receive the daily witness pay, exclusive of the mileage allowance, provided by s. 92.142, except when the employee is appearing as a witness during time compensated as a part of his or her normal duties.

History.—s. 1, ch. 63-508; s. 1, ch. 67-427; s. 3, ch. 76-237; s. 1, ch. 77-77; s. 22, ch. 78-361; s. 1, ch. 78-379; s. 43, ch. 81-259; s. 1, ch. 84-153; s. 505, ch. 95-147.

Note.—Former s. 90.141.

92.142 Witnesses; pay.—

(1) Witnesses in all cases, civil and criminal, in all courts, now or hereafter created, and witnesses summoned before any arbitrator or general or special magistrate appointed by the court shall receive for each day's actual attendance $5 and also 6 cents per mile for actual distance traveled to and from the courts. A witness in a criminal case required to appear in a county other than the county of his or her residence and residing more than 50 miles from the location of the trial shall be entitled to per diem and travel expenses at the same rate provided for state employees under s. 112.061, in lieu of any other witness fee.

(2) An employee of the state who is required, as a direct result of employment, to appear as an official witness to testify in the course of any action in any court of this state, or before an administrative law judge, a hearing officer, hearing examiner, or any board or commission of the state or of its agencies, instrumentalities, or political subdivisions, shall be considered to be on duty during such appearance and shall be entitled to per diem and travel expenses as provided in s. 112.061. Except as provided in s. 92.141 and as provided in this subsection, such employee shall be required to tender to the employing agency any witness fee and other expense reimbursement received by the employee for such appearance.

(3) Any witness subpoenaed to testify on behalf of the state in any action brought pursuant to s. 895.05 or chapter 542 who is required to travel outside his or her county of residence and more than 50 miles from his or her residence, or who is required to travel from out of state, shall be entitled to per diem and travel expenses at the same rate provided for state employees under s. 112.061 in lieu of any state witness fee.

History.—s. 5, ch. 3106, 1879; RS 1103; s. 1, ch. 4387, 1895; GS 1512; s. 2, ch. 5649, 1907; s. 1, ch. 6905, 1915; s. 1, ch. 7280, 1917; RGS 2712; CGL 4379; s. 1, ch. 29927, 1955; s. 8, ch. 65-483; s. 1, ch. 67-401; s. 15, ch. 73-334; s. 3, ch. 76-237; s. 1, ch. 77-77; s. 1, ch. 78-175; s. 22, ch. 78-361; ss. 1, 2, ch. 78-379; s. 1, ch. 83-36; s. 506, ch. 95-147; s. 9, ch. 96-410; s. 59, ch. 2004-11; s. 36, ch. 2005-236.

Note.—Former s. 90.14.

92.143 Compensation to traffic court witnesses.—Any party who secures the attendance of a witness in traffic court shall bear all costs of calling the witness, including witness fees. If the witness is required to testify on behalf of the prosecution, the office of the state attorney of the respective judicial circuit shall pay the fees and costs of calling the witness.

History.—s. 66, ch. 2005-236.

92.15 Receipts in cases involving title from United States.—A receipt of a receiver of a United States Land Office shall in all cases be prima facie evidence that the title to the land covered by said receipt has passed from the United States to the person named in the receipt as having paid for the said land.

History.—s. 1, ch. 3915, 1889; RS 1119; GS 1537; RGS 2737; CGL 4409.

92.151 Witness compensation; payment; overcharges.—Compensation shall be paid to the witness by the party in whose behalf the witness is summoned, and the prevailing party may tax the same as costs against the prevailing party's adversary; but no person shall be compelled to attend court as a witness in any civil cause unless the party in whose behalf the person is summoned shall first pay the person the amount of compensation to which he or she would be entitled for mileage and per diem for 1 day, or the same is deposited with the executive officer of said court, and the person shall not be compelled to attend thereafter unless paid in advance. But if any witness should serve without payment in advance, at the completion of his or her services the witness may exhibit his or her account for compensation, and when the same shall have been taxed and approved by the court wherein the services have been rendered, such bill shall have the force and effect of judgment and execution against the party in whose behalf the witness was summoned, and be collected by the sheriff as in other cases of execution. Any witness who shall charge and receive more than is really due shall forfeit and pay to the party injured 4 times the amount so unjustly claimed; and if the witness shall willfully make out the account for more than is lawfully due, the witness shall forfeit the compensation.

History.—s. 41, Nov. 11, 1828; RS 1104; s. 4, ch. 4387, 1895; GS 1513; RGS 2713; CGL 4380; s. 3, ch. 76-237; s. 1, ch. 77-77; s. 22, ch. 78-361; s. 1, ch. 78-379; s. 507, ch. 95-147.

Note.—Former s. 90.15.

92.153 Production of documents by witnesses; reimbursement of costs.—

(1) DEFINITIONS.—As used in this section:

(a) "Disinterested witness" means a person to whom a summons is issued with respect to documents involving or relating to transactions of others and who has not initiated a proceeding, is not a party to a proceeding, and is not the subject of investigation in a proceeding and who, at the time the summons is issued, is not an officer, employee, accountant, or attorney, or acting as such, for a person who has initiated, is a party to, or is the subject of investigation in a proceeding.

(b) "Document" means any book, paper, record, or other data, or a reproduction thereof.

(c) "Proceeding" means any civil or criminal action before a court; any investigation, inquiry, or proceeding before a grand jury, a state attorney, or a state, county, municipal, or other governmental department, division, bureau, commission or other body, or any officer thereof; any action before an officer or person authorized to issue a summons; or any administrative action authorized by law.

(d) "Summons" means any subpoena, subpoena duces tecum, order, or other legal process which requires the production of documents.

(2) REIMBURSEMENT OF A DISINTERESTED WITNESS.—

(a) In any proceeding, a disinterested witness shall be paid for any costs the witness reasonably incurs either directly or indirectly in producing, searching for, reproducing, or transporting documents pursuant to a summons; however, the cost of documents produced pursuant to a subpoena or records request by a state attorney or public defender may not exceed 15 cents per page and $10 per hour for research or retrieval.

(b) In a proceeding before a court or an administrative agency or officer, which is not an investigation or inquiry and which by law or rule includes the right to a public trial or hearing in the same proceeding and which involves adversary parties, responsibility for payment to the disinterested witness shall be fixed by the court, agency, or officer before which the proceeding is pending. Payment shall be enforced by the court, agency, or officer upon motion by the disinterested witness.

(c) In all other proceedings, payment to the disinterested witness shall be made by the person or governmental authority requesting the summons. Any disinterested witness who desires reimbursement of such costs shall submit a request for reimbursement, supported by an affidavit, to the person or governmental authority responsible for payment. Payment shall be made within 30 days from the date the request is submitted. If payment is not made within such time, the witness may enforce payment by bringing a separate action in a court which has jurisdiction of the total amount of such costs and which is located in the judicial circuit where the witness resides.

History.—ss. 1, 2, ch. 81-196; s. 508, ch. 95-147; s. 77, ch. 2003-402.

92.16 Certificates of Board of Trustees of the Internal Improvement Trust Fund respecting the ownership, conveyance of, and other facts in connection with public lands.—A certificate of the Board of Trustees of the Internal Improvement Trust Fund under its official seal, with respect to the present or past ownership by the state or by the school, seminary or internal improvement funds of any lands in this state, or of the conveyance or transfer of any such lands by said Board of Trustees of the Internal Improvement Trust Fund or of the State Board of Education or other officers or boards of the state having power to convey any such lands, or any facts shown by the public records of his or her office with respect to any of such lands, or the transfer, ownership, or conveyance of the same, shall be prima facie evidence of the facts therein certified, and every such certificate shall be admissible in evidence in all of the courts of this state. All such certificates shall, without other or further proof, be admitted to record and recorded in the deed books of the respective counties of this state where the lands mentioned in such certificates lie, and the record of every such certificate shall have the same force and effect for all purposes as the record of deeds.

History.—s. 1, ch. 2063, 1875; RS 1112; GS 1524; s. 1, ch. 7381, 1917; RGS 2724; CGL 4395; s. 7, ch. 22858, 1945; s. 3, ch. 63-294; ss. 27, 35, ch. 69-106; s. 509, ch. 95-147.

92.17 Effect of seal of Board of Trustees of the Internal Improvement Trust Fund.—The impression of the seal of the Board of Trustees of the Internal Improvement Trust Fund upon any deed, agreement or contract, purporting to have been made by the Board of Trustees of the Internal Improvement Trust Fund, or by the members of the State Board of Education, shall entitle the same to be received in evidence in all courts and in all proceedings in this state.

History.—s. 1, ch. 3127, 1879; ss. 1, 2, ch. 3877, 1889; RS 1114; GS 1526; RGS 2726; CGL 4397; s. 4, ch. 63-294; ss. 27, 35, ch. 69-106.

92.18 Certificate of state officer.—The certificate of any state officer, under seal of office, as to any official act occurring in the course of the official business of the office in which the state officer presides, shall be prima facie evidence of such fact.

History.—s. 1, ch. 3250, 1881; RS 1113; GS 1525; RGS 2725; CGL 4396; s. 510, ch. 95-147.

92.19 Portions of records.—In all cases where any certified copy of any record, pleading, document, deed, conveyance, paper or instrument in writing, involving the title to real estate shall be lawfully admissible in evidence in any of the courts of this state, a certified copy of such portions of such instrument as shall contain the essential parts thereof and only such portion of the descriptive matter thereof as shall be involved in the case on trial, shall likewise be admissible in evidence; and in no case shall it be necessary to include in such certified copies descriptive matter not involved in the case in which such copy is offered in evidence.

History.—s. 1, ch. 10237, 1925; CGL 4400.

92.20 Certificates issued under authority of Congress.—Every certificate issued under authority of the Congress and every duly certified copy thereof under the seal of the United States governmental department having the authority to issue such certified copy, relating to the grade, classification, quality or condition of agricultural products shall be accepted in any court of this state as prima facie evidence of the true grade, classification, condition or quality of such agricultural product at the time of its inspection.

History.—s. 1, ch. 13568, 1929; CGL 1936 Supp. 4400(1).

92.21 Certificate as to sanitary condition of buildings.—Every owner, agent, or lessee of any building or buildings used for the purpose of providing board and lodgings for the entertainment of guests, containing 10 rooms or more, who shall have obtained and posted a certificate as provided by law, may present the same as evidence in the owner's, agent's, or lessee's defense in any suit in any of the courts in this state in which damages are claimed for injuries from alleged unsanitary conditions of said buildings and premises.

History.—s. 4, ch. 4606, 1899; GS 1527; RGS 2727; CGL 4398; s. 511, ch. 95-147.

92.23 Rule of evidence in suits on fire policies for loss or damage to building.—In all suits or proceedings brought upon policies of insurance on buildings against loss or damage by fire, hereafter issued or renewed, the insurer shall not be permitted to deny that the property insured was worth, at the time of insuring it by the policy, the full sum insured therein on such property.

History.—s. 2, ch. 4677, 1899; GS 1528; RGS 2728; CGL 4399.

92.231 Expert witnesses; fee.—

(1) The term "expert witness" as used herein shall apply to any witness who offers himself or herself in the trial of any action as an expert witness or who is subpoenaed to testify in such capacity before a state attorney in the investigation of a criminal matter, or before a grand jury, and who is permitted by the court to qualify and testify as such, upon any matter pending before any court.

(2) Any expert or skilled witness who shall have testified in any cause shall be allowed a witness fee including the cost of any exhibits used by such witness in an amount agreed to by the parties, and the same shall be taxed as costs. In instances where services are provided for the state, including for state-paid private court-appointed counsel, payment from state funds shall be in accordance with standards adopted by the Legislature.

(3) In a criminal case in which the state or an indigent defendant requires the services of an expert witness whose opinion is relevant to the issues of the case, the expert witness shall be compensated in accordance with standards adopted by the Legislature.

History.—ss. 1, 2, ch. 25090, 1949; s. 19, ch. 29737, 1955; s. 1, ch. 59-201; s. 3, ch. 76-237; s. 1, ch. 77-77; s. 22, ch. 78-361; s. 1, ch. 78-379; s. 512, ch. 95-147; s. 78, ch. 2003-402; s. 37, ch. 2005-236.

Note.—Former s. 90.231.

92.233 Compensation of witness summoned in two or more criminal cases.—A witness subpoenaed in two or more criminal cases pending at the same time shall be paid one charge for per diem and mileage, but when the costs are taxed against the defendant, a witness may charge the full amount in each case.

History.—s. 4, ch. 159, 1848; RS 2865; s. 1, ch. 5133, 1903; GS 3921; RGS 6020; CGL 8314; s. 102, ch. 70-339; s. 79, ch. 2003-402.

Note.—Former s. 932.34; s. 914.09.

92.24 Certain tax deeds prima facie evidence of title.—All tax deeds issued under and pursuant to the provisions and in the form prescribed in and by the following acts and statutes of this state, to wit: s. 10, chapter 4888, Acts, 1901 and said section as amended by s. 1, chapter 5152, Acts, 1903; s. 577 of the General Statutes of Florida, 1906; s. 779 of the Revised General Statutes of Florida, 1920, and said section as amended by s. 12, chapter 14572, Acts, 1929; are declared to be prima facie evidence of the regularity of the proceedings from the valuation of the land described in such deeds respectively, by the assessors, to the date of the deed or deeds inclusive, and shall be so received in evidence in any and all the courts of this state, without regard to date of execution.

History.—s. 1, ch. 5150, 1903; GS 1521; RGS 2721; CGL 4389.

92.25 Records destroyed by fire; use of abstracts.—Whenever in the trial of any suit, or in any proceeding in any court of this state, it shall be made to appear that the original of any deed or other instrument of writing, or of any record of any court relating to any land, the title thereof or any interest therein being in controversy in such suit or proceeding, is lost or destroyed, or not within the power of the party to produce the same, and that the record thereof has been heretofore destroyed by fire, and that no certified copy of such record is in the possession or control of such party, it is lawful for such party, and the court shall receive as evidence, any abstract of title, or letter-press copy thereof made in the ordinary course of business prior to such loss or destruction; and it is also lawful for any such party to offer, and the court shall receive as evidence, any copy, extract or minutes from such destroyed records, or from the original thereof, which were at the date of such destruction in the possession of any person or persons then engaged in the business of making abstracts of titles for others for hire.

History.—s. 1, ch. 4951, 1901; GS 1529; RGS 2729; CGL 4401.

92.251 Uniform Foreign Depositions Law.—

(1) This section may be cited as the "Uniform Foreign Depositions Law."

(2) Whenever any mandate, writ or commission is issued out of any court of record in any other state, territory, district, or foreign jurisdiction, or whenever upon notice or agreement it is required to take the testimony of a witness or witnesses in this state, witnesses may be compelled to appear and testify in the same manner and by the same process and proceeding as may be employed for the purpose of taking testimony in proceedings pending in this state.

(3) This section shall be so interpreted and construed as to effectuate its general purposes to make uniform the law of those states which enact it.

History.—ss. 1, 2, 3, ch. 59-250; s. 3, ch. 76-237; s. 1, ch. 77-77; s. 22, ch. 78-361; s. 1, ch. 78-379.

Note.—Former s. 90.25.

92.26 Records destroyed by fire; use of sworn copies.—A sworn copy of any writing admissible under s. 92.25 made by the person or persons having possession of such writing shall be admissible in evidence; provided, the party desiring to use such sworn copy, as aforesaid, shall have given the opposite party a reasonable opportunity to verify the correctness of such copy; and provided, that no abstract of title or letter-press copy thereof, extract or minutes or copy made admissible in evidence by this section, shall be so admitted by virtue hereof unless a copy thereof shall have been served on the opposite party, or the opposite party's attorney or counsel, at least 10 days before the same is offered in evidence. Nothing herein shall be construed to prevent the impeachment of such evidence, or its exclusion by the court for good and sufficient cause.

History.—s. 1, ch. 4951, 1901; GS 1530; RGS 2730; CGL 4402; s. 513, ch. 95-147; s. 12, ch. 95-280.

92.27 Records destroyed by fire; effect of abstracts in evidence.—In all cases in which any destroyed abstracts, copies, minutes, extracts, maps or plats, or copies thereof, purchased and placed in the clerk's office, as provided by law, or which are made admissible in evidence under any of the provisions of this revision, whether purchased or placed in such office or not, shall be received in evidence under this law, all deeds or other instruments of writing appearing thereby to have been executed by any person or persons, or in which they appear to have joined, shall (except as against any person or persons in actual possession of the land or lot described therein at the time of the destruction of the record of such county, claiming title thereto, otherwise than under sale for taxes or special assessments) be presumed to have been executed and acknowledged according to law; and all sales under powers, and all judgments, decrees and legal proceedings, and all sales thereunder (sale for taxes and assessments, and judgments and proceedings for the enforcement of taxes and assessments excepted) shall be presumed to be regular and correct, except as against the person or persons in this section above-mentioned and excepted.

History.—s. 4, ch. 4951, 1901; GS 1531; RGS 2731; CGL 4403.

92.28 Records destroyed by fire; land title suits; what may be received in evidence.—In all suits or proceedings concerning any land, or any estate, interest or right in, or any lien or encumbrance upon the same, when it shall be made to appear that the original of any deed, conveyance, map, plat or other written or record evidence has been lost or destroyed, or is not in the power, custody or control of the party wishing to use it on the trial to produce same, and the record thereof has been heretofore destroyed by fire, the court shall receive all such evidence as may have a bearing on the case to establish the execution or contents of any deed, conveyance, map, plat record, or other written evidence so lost or destroyed; provided, that the testimony of the parties themselves shall be received only in such cases, and subject to all the qualifications in respect to such testimony as now provided by law; and provided further, that any writing in the hands of any person or persons, which may become admissible in evidence under the provisions of this section, or any part of this law, shall be rejected and not admitted as evidence, unless the same appear upon the face thereof without erasure, blemish, alteration, interlineation or interpolation in any material part, unless the same shall be explained to the satisfaction of the court, and appear fairly and honestly made in the ordinary course of business.

History.—s. 5, ch. 4951, 1901; GS 1532; RGS 2732; CGL 4404.

92.29 Photographic or electronic copies.—Photographic reproductions or reproductions through electronic recordkeeping systems made by any federal, state, county, or municipal governmental board, department or agency, in the regular course of business, of any original record, document, paper or instrument in writing or in an electronic recordkeeping system, which is, or may be, required or authorized to be made, filed, or recorded with that board, department or agency shall in all cases and in all courts and places be admitted and received as evidence with a like force and effect as the original would be, whether the original record, document, paper, or instrument in writing or in an electronic recordkeeping system is in existence or not.

History.—s. 1, ch. 20866, 1941; s. 7, ch. 94-348.

92.295 Copies of voter registration records.—Any reproduction of an original voter registration record stored pursuant to s. 98.461, whether microfilmed or maintained digitally or on electronic, magnetic, or optic media, which reproduction is certified by the supervisor of elections who is the custodian of the record, is admissible as evidence in any judicial or administrative proceeding in this state with the same effect as the original voter registration record, whether the original voter registration record exists or not.

History.—s. 1, ch. 88-45; s. 7, ch. 90-315.

92.30 Presumption of death; official findings.—A written finding of presumed death, made by the Secretary of the Army, the Secretary of the Navy, or other officer or employee of the United States authorized to make such findings, pursuant to the [1]Federal Missing Persons Act (56 Stat. 143, 1092, and Pub. L. No. 408, Ch. 371, 2d Sess. 78th Cong.; 50 U.S.C. App. Supp. 1001-17), as now or hereafter amended, or a duly certified copy of such finding, shall be received in any court, office, or other place in this state as evidence of the death of the person therein found to be dead, and the date, circumstances, and place of the person's disappearance.

History.—s. 1, ch. 22866, 1945; s. 22, ch. 77-104; s. 514, ch. 95-147.

[1]Note.—Repealed by Act Sept. 6, 1966, Pub. L. No. 89-554, s. 8(a), 80 Stat. 632, 651-654, 656, 657, 659, 662.

92.31 Missing persons and persons imprisoned or interned in foreign countries; official reports.—An official written report or record, or duly certified copy thereof, that a person is missing, missing in action, interned in a neutral country, or beleaguered, besieged, or captured by an enemy, or is dead, or is alive, made by any officer or employee of the United States authorized by the act referred to in s. 92.30, or by any other law of the United States to make same, shall be received in any court, office, or other place in this state as evidence that such person is missing, missing in action, interned in a neutral country, or beleaguered, besieged, or captured by an enemy, or is dead, or is alive, as the case may be.

History.—s. 2, ch. 22866, 1945.

92.32 Official findings and reports; presumption of authority to issue or execute.—For the purposes of this law, any finding, report, or record, or duly certified copy thereof, purporting to have been signed by such an officer or employee of the United States as is described above, shall prima facie be deemed to have been signed and issued by such an officer or employee pursuant to law, and the person signing same shall prima facie be deemed to have acted within the scope of the person's authority. If a copy purports to have been certified by a person authorized by law to certify the same, such certified copy shall be prima facie evidence of the person's authority so to certify.

History.—s. 3, ch. 22866, 1945; s. 515, ch. 95-147.

92.33 Written statement concerning injury to person or property; furnishing copies; admission as evidence.—Every person who shall take a written statement by any injured person with respect to any accident or with respect to any injury to person or property shall, at the time of taking such statement, furnish to the person making such statement a true and complete copy thereof. Any person having taken, or having possession of any written statement or a copy of such statement, by any injured person with respect to any accident or with respect to any injury to person or property shall, at the request of the person who made such statement or his or her personal representative, furnish the person who made such statement or his or her personal representative a true and complete copy thereof. No written statement by an injured person shall be admissible in evidence or otherwise used in any manner in any civil action relating to the subject matter thereof unless it shall be made to appear that a true and complete copy thereof was furnished to the person making such statement at the time of the making thereof, or, if it shall be made to appear that thereafter a person having possession of such statement refused, upon request of the person who made the statement or his or her personal representatives, to furnish him or her a true and complete copy thereof.

History.—s. 1, ch. 26482, 1951; s. 516, ch. 95-147.

92.351 Prohibition against prisoners submitting nondocumentary physical evidence without authorization of court; prisoner mailings to courts.—

(1) No prisoner as defined by s. 57.085 who is a party to a judicial proceeding may submit evidence or any other item that is not in paper document form to a court or clerk of court without first obtaining authorization from the court. This prohibition includes, but is not limited to, all nondocumentary evidence or items offered in support of a motion, pleading, or other document filed with the court. This prohibition does not preclude a prisoner who is appearing in person or through counsel before a court at a trial or hearing from submitting physical evidence to the court at the appropriate time.

(2) A corrections or detention facility for prisoners may conduct a cursory examination of the outside of any package or other mailing from a prisoner to a court or clerk of court of this state to determine whether the package or mailing contains materials other than paper documents. If such package or mailing appears to contain materials other than paper documents, the facility shall refuse to forward it until the sender presents a court order authorizing the mailing of such nondocumentary items or demonstrates that the contents are not prohibited by this section.

History.—s. 3, ch. 96-106.

92.38 Comparison of disputed writings.—Comparison of a disputed writing with any writing proved to the satisfaction of the judge to be genuine, shall be permitted to be made by the witnesses; and such writings, and the evidence of witnesses respecting the same, may be submitted to the jury, or to the court in case of a trial by the court, as evidence of the genuineness, or otherwise, of the writing in dispute.

History.—s. 55, ch. 1096, 1861; RS 1121; GS 1539; RGS 2739; CGL 4411.

Note.—Former s. 90.20.

92.39 Evidence of individual's claim against the state in suits between them.—In suits between the state and individuals, no claim for a credit shall be allowed upon trial, but such as shall appear to have been presented to the Chief Financial Officer for his or her examination, and by him or her disallowed in whole or in part, unless it shall be proved to the satisfaction of the court that the defendant is, at the time of the trial, in possession of vouchers not before in the defendant's power to procure, and that the defendant was prevented from exhibiting a claim for such credit at the Chief Financial Officer's office by unavoidable accident.

History.—s. 4, Feb. 10, 1837; RS 1122; GS 1540; RGS 2740; CGL 4412; s. 517, ch. 95-147; s. 108, ch. 2003-261.

Note.—Former s. 90.22.

92.40 Reports of building, housing, or health code violations; admissibility.—A copy of a report, notice, or citation of a violation of any building, housing, or health code by a governmental agency charged with the enforcement of such codes, certified by the agency, if otherwise material shall be admissible as evidence.

History.—s. 11, ch. 73-330.

92.50 Oaths, affidavits, and acknowledgments; who may take or administer; requirements.—

(1) IN THIS STATE.—Oaths, affidavits, and acknowledgments required or authorized under the laws of this state (except oaths to jurors and witnesses in court and such other oaths, affidavits and acknowledgments as are required by law to be taken or administered by or before particular officers) may be taken or administered by or before any judge, clerk, or deputy clerk of any court of record within this state, including federal courts, or before any United States commissioner or any notary public within this state. The jurat, or certificate of proof or acknowledgment, shall be authenticated by the signature and official seal of such officer or person taking or administering the same; however, when taken or administered before any judge, clerk, or deputy clerk of a court of record, the seal of such court may be affixed as the seal of such officer or person.

(2) IN OTHER STATES, TERRITORIES, AND DISTRICTS OF THE UNITED STATES.—Oaths, affidavits, and acknowledgments required or authorized under the laws of this state, may be taken or administered in any other state, territory, or district of the United States, before any judge, clerk or deputy clerk of any court of record, within such state, territory, or district, having a seal, or before any notary public or justice of the peace, having a seal, in such state, territory, or district; provided, however, such officer or person is authorized under the laws of such state, territory, or district to take or administer oaths, affidavits and acknowledgments. The jurat, or certificate of proof or acknowledgment, shall be authenticated by the signature and official seal of such officer or person taking or administering the same; provided, however, when taken or administered by or before any judge, clerk, or deputy clerk of a court of record, the seal of such court may be affixed as the seal of such officer or person.

(3) IN FOREIGN COUNTRIES.—Oaths, affidavits, and acknowledgments, required or authorized by the laws of this state, may be taken or administered in any foreign country, by or before any judge or justice of a court of last resort, any notary public of such foreign country, any minister, consul general, charge d'affaires, or consul of the United States resident in such country. The jurat, or certificate of proof or acknowledgment, shall be authenticated by the signature and official seal of the officer or person taking or administering the same; provided, however, when taken or administered by or before any judge or justice of a court of last resort, the seal of such court may be affixed as the seal of such judge or justice.

History.—s. 1, ch. 48, 1845; RS 1299; GS 1730; RGS 2945; CGL 4669; s. 1, ch. 23156, 1945; s. 7, ch. 24337, 1947; s. 15, ch. 73-334; s. 3, ch. 76-237; s. 1, ch. 77-77; s. 22, ch. 78-361; s. 1, ch. 78-379.

Note.—Former s. 90.01.

92.51 Oaths, affidavits, and acknowledgments; taken or administered by commissioned officer of United States Armed Forces.—

(1) Oaths, affidavits, and acknowledgments required or authorized by the laws of this state may be taken or administered within or without the United States by or before any commissioned officer in active service of the Armed Forces of the United States with the rank of second lieutenant or higher in the Army, Air Force or Marine Corps or ensign or higher in the Navy or Coast Guard when the person required or authorized to make and execute the oath, affidavit, or acknowledgment is a member of the Armed Forces of the United States, the spouse of such member or a person whose duties require the person's presence with the Armed Forces of the United States.

(2) A certificate endorsed upon the instrument which shows the date of the oath, affidavit, or acknowledgment and which states in substance that the person appearing before the officer acknowledged the instrument as the person's act or made or signed the instrument under oath shall be sufficient for all intents and purposes. The instrument shall not be rendered invalid by the failure to state the place of execution or acknowledgment.

(3) If the signature, rank, and branch of service or subdivision thereof of any commissioned officer appears upon such instrument, document or certificate no further proof of the authority of such officer

so to act shall be required and such action by such commissioned officer shall be prima facie evidence that the person making such oath, affidavit or acknowledgment is within the purview of this act.

History.—ss. 1, 2, 3, ch. 61-196; s. 3, ch. 76-237; s. 1, ch. 77-77; s. 22, ch. 78-361; s. 1, ch. 78-379; s. 518, ch. 95-147.

Note.—Former s. 90.011.

92.52 Affirmation equivalent to oath.—Whenever an oath shall be required by any law of this state in any proceeding, an affirmation may be substituted therefor.

History.—RS 1300; GS 1731; RGS 2946; CGL 4670; s. 3, ch. 76-237; s. 1, ch. 77-77; s. 22, ch. 78-361; s. 1, ch. 78-379.

Note.—Former s. 90.02.

92.525 Verification of documents; perjury by false written declaration, penalty.—

(1) When it is authorized or required by law, by rule of an administrative agency, or by rule or order of court that a document be verified by a person, the verification may be accomplished in the following manner:

(a) Under oath or affirmation taken or administered before an officer authorized under s. 92.50 to administer oaths; or

(b) By the signing of the written declaration prescribed in subsection (2).

(2) A written declaration means the following statement: "Under penalties of perjury, I declare that I have read the foregoing [document] and that the facts stated in it are true," followed by the signature of the person making the declaration, except when a verification on information or belief is permitted by law, in which case the words "to the best of my knowledge and belief" may be added. The written declaration shall be printed or typed at the end of or immediately below the document being verified and above the signature of the person making the declaration.

(3) A person who knowingly makes a false declaration under subsection (2) is guilty of the crime of perjury by false written declaration, a felony of the third degree, punishable as provided in s. 775.082, s. 775.083, or s. 775.084.

(4) As used in this section:

(a) The term "administrative agency" means any department or agency of the state or any county, municipality, special district, or other political subdivision.

(b) The term "document" means any writing including, without limitation, any form, application, claim, notice, tax return, inventory, affidavit, pleading, or paper.

(c) The requirement that a document be verified means that the document must be signed or executed by a person and that the person must state under oath or affirm that the facts or matters stated or recited in the document are true, or words of that import or effect.

History.—s. 12, ch. 86-201.

92.53 Videotaping of testimony of victim or witness under age 16 or person with mental retardation.—

(1) On motion and hearing in camera and a finding that there is a substantial likelihood that a victim or witness who is under the age of 16 or who is a person with mental retardation as defined in s. 393.063 would suffer at least moderate emotional or mental harm due to the presence of the defendant if the child or person with mental retardation is required to testify in open court, or that such victim or witness is otherwise unavailable as defined in s. 90.804(1), the trial court may order the videotaping of the testimony of the victim or witness in a case, whether civil or criminal in nature, in which videotaped testimony is to be utilized at trial in lieu of trial testimony in open court.

(2) The motion may be filed by:

(a) The victim or witness, or the victim's or witness's attorney, parent, legal guardian, or guardian ad litem;

(b) A trial judge on his or her own motion;

(c) Any party in a civil proceeding; or

(d) The prosecuting attorney or the defendant, or the defendant's counsel.

(3) The judge shall preside, or shall appoint a special master to preside, at the videotaping unless the following conditions are met:

(a) The child or person with mental retardation is represented by a guardian ad litem or counsel;

(b) The representative of the victim or witness and the counsel for each party stipulate that the requirement for the presence of the judge or special master may be waived; and

(c) The court finds at a hearing on the motion that the presence of a judge or special master is not necessary to protect the victim or witness.

(4) The defendant and the defendant's counsel shall be present at the videotaping, unless the defendant has waived this right. The court may require the defendant to view the testimony from outside the presence of the child or person with mental retardation by means of a two-way mirror or another similar method that will ensure that the defendant can observe and hear the testimony of the victim or witness in person, but that the victim or witness cannot hear or see the defendant. The defendant and the attorney for the defendant may communicate by any appropriate private method.

(5) Any party, or the court on its own motion, may request the aid of an interpreter, as provided in s. 90.606, to aid the parties in formulating methods of questioning the child or person with mental retardation and in interpreting the answers of the child or person with mental retardation throughout proceedings conducted under this section.

(6) The motion referred to in subsection (1) may be made at any time with reasonable notice to each party to the cause, and videotaping of testimony may be made any time after the court grants the motion. The videotaped testimony shall be admissible as evidence in the trial of the cause; however, such testimony shall not be admissible in any trial or proceeding in which such witness testifies by use of closed circuit television pursuant to s. 92.54.

(7) The court shall make specific findings of fact, on the record, as to the basis for its ruling under this section.

History.—ss. 1, 2, ch. 79-69; s. 1, ch. 84-36; ss. 5, 9, ch. 85-53; s. 9, ch. 85-80; s. 1, ch. 93-131; s. 21, ch. 94-154; s. 1379, ch. 95-147; s. 30, ch. 99-2; s. 4, ch. 2000-338; s. 89, ch. 2004-267.

Note.—Former ss. 918.17, 90.90.

92.54   Use of closed circuit television in proceedings involving victims or witnesses under the age of 16 or persons with mental retardation.—

(1)   Upon motion and hearing in camera and upon a finding that there is a substantial likelihood that the child or person with mental retardation will suffer at least moderate emotional or mental harm due to the presence of the defendant if the child or person with mental retardation is required to testify in open court, or that such victim or witness is unavailable as defined in s. 90.804(1), the trial court may order that the testimony of a child under the age of 16 or person with mental retardation who is a victim or witness be taken outside of the courtroom and shown by means of closed circuit television.

(2)   The motion may be filed by the victim or witness; the attorney, parent, legal guardian, or guardian ad litem of the victim or witness; the prosecutor; the defendant or the defendant's counsel; or the trial judge on his or her own motion.

(3)   Only the judge, the prosecutor, the defendant, the attorney for the defendant, the operators of the videotape equipment, an interpreter, and some other person who, in the opinion of the court, contributes to the well-being of the child or person with mental retardation and who will not be a witness in the case may be in the room during the recording of the testimony.

(4)   During the child's or person's with mental retardation testimony by closed circuit television, the court may require the defendant to view the testimony from the courtroom. In such a case, the court shall permit the defendant to observe and hear the testimony of the child or person with mental retardation, but shall ensure that the child or person with mental retardation cannot hear or see the defendant. The defendant's right to assistance of counsel, which includes the right to immediate and direct communication with counsel conducting cross-examination, must be protected and, upon the defendant's request, such communication shall be provided by any appropriate electronic method.

(5)   The court shall make specific findings of fact, on the record, as to the basis for its ruling under this section.

History.—s. 6, ch. 85-53; s. 12, ch. 87-224; s. 2, ch. 93-131; s. 22, ch. 94-154; s. 1380, ch. 95-147.

92.55   Judicial or other proceedings involving victim or witness under the age of 16 or person with mental retardation; special protections; use of registered service or therapy animals.—

(1)   Upon motion of any party, upon motion of a parent, guardian, attorney, or guardian ad litem for a child under the age of 16 or person with mental retardation, or upon its own motion, the court may enter any order necessary to protect a child under the age of 16 or person with mental retardation who is a victim or witness in any judicial proceeding or other official proceeding from severe emotional or mental harm due to the presence of the defendant if the child or person with mental retardation is required to testify in open court. Such orders shall relate to the taking of testimony and shall include, but not be limited to:

(a)   Interviewing or the taking of depositions as part of a civil or criminal proceeding.

(b)   Examination and cross-examination for the purpose of qualifying as a witness or testifying in any proceeding.

(c)   The use of testimony taken outside of the courtroom, including proceedings under ss. 92.53 and 92.54.

(2)   In ruling upon the motion, the court shall take into consideration:

(a)   The age of the child, the nature of the offense or act, the relationship of the child to the parties in the case or to the defendant in a criminal action, the degree of emotional trauma that will result to the child as a consequence of the defendant's presence, and any other fact that the court deems relevant; or

(b) The age of the person with mental retardation, the functional capacity of the person with mental retardation, the nature of the offenses or act, the relationship of the person with mental retardation to the parties in the case or to the defendant in a criminal action, the degree of emotional trauma that will result to the person with mental retardation as a consequence of the defendant's presence, and any other fact that the court deems relevant.

(3) In addition to such other relief as is provided by law, the court may enter orders limiting the number of times that a child or person with mental retardation may be interviewed, prohibiting depositions of a child or person with mental retardation, requiring the submission of questions prior to examination of a child or person with mental retardation, setting the place and conditions for interviewing a child or person with mental retardation or for conducting any other proceeding, or permitting or prohibiting the attendance of any person at any proceeding. The court shall enter any order necessary to protect the rights of all parties, including the defendant in any criminal action.

(4) The court may set any other conditions it finds just and appropriate on the taking of testimony by a child, including the use of a service or therapy animal that has been evaluated and registered according to national standards, in any proceeding involving a sexual offense. When deciding whether to permit a child to testify with the assistance of a registered service or therapy animal, the court shall take into consideration the age of the child, the interests of the child, the rights of the parties to the litigation, and any other relevant factor that would facilitate the testimony by the child.

History.—s. 7, ch. 85-53; s. 3, ch. 93-131; s. 23, ch. 94-154; s. 8, ch. 2000-336; s. 3, ch. 2011-220.

92.56   Judicial proceedings and court records involving sexual offenses.—

(1)   (a)   The confidential and exempt status of criminal intelligence information or criminal investigative information made confidential and exempt pursuant to s. 119.071(2)(h) must be maintained in court records pursuant to s. 119.0714(1)(h) and in court proceedings, including testimony from witnesses.

(b)   If a petition for access to such confidential and exempt records is filed with the trial court having jurisdiction over the alleged offense, the confidential and exempt status of such information shall be maintained by the court if the state or the victim demonstrates that:

1.   The identity of the victim is not already known in the community;

2.   The victim has not voluntarily called public attention to the offense;

3.   The identity of the victim has not otherwise become a reasonable subject of public concern;

4.   The disclosure of the victim's identity would be offensive to a reasonable person; and

5.   The disclosure of the victim's identity would:

a.   Endanger the victim because the assailant has not been apprehended and is not otherwise known to the victim;

b.   Endanger the victim because of the likelihood of retaliation, harassment, or intimidation;

c.   Cause severe emotional or mental harm to the victim;

d.   Make the victim unwilling to testify as a witness; or

e.   Be inappropriate for other good cause shown.

(2)   A defendant charged with a crime described in chapter 794 or chapter 800, or with child abuse, aggravated child abuse, or sexual performance by a child as described in chapter 827, may apply to the

trial court for an order of disclosure of information in court records held confidential and exempt pursuant to s. 119.0714(1)(h) or maintained as confidential and exempt pursuant to court order under this section. Such identifying information concerning the victim may be released to the defendant or his or her attorney in order to prepare the defense. The confidential and exempt status of this information may not be construed to prevent the disclosure of the victim's identity to the defendant; however, the defendant may not disclose the victim's identity to any person other than the defendant's attorney or any other person directly involved in the preparation of the defense. A willful and knowing disclosure of the identity of the victim to any other person by the defendant constitutes contempt.

(3)   The state may use a pseudonym instead of the victim's name to designate the victim of a crime described in chapter 794 or chapter 800, or of child abuse, aggravated child abuse, or sexual performance by a child as described in chapter 827, or any crime involving the production, possession, or promotion of child pornography as described in chapter 847, in all court records and records of court proceedings, both civil and criminal.

(4)   The protection of this section may be waived by the victim of the alleged offense in a writing filed with the court, in which the victim consents to the use or release of identifying information during court proceedings and in the records of court proceedings.

(5)   This section does not prohibit the publication or broadcast of the substance of trial testimony in a prosecution for an offense described in chapter 794 or chapter 800, or a crime of child abuse, aggravated child abuse, or sexual performance by a child, as described in chapter 827, but the publication or broadcast may not include an identifying photograph, an identifiable voice, or the name or address of the victim, unless the victim has consented in writing to the publication and filed such consent with the court or unless the court has declared such records not confidential and exempt as provided for in subsection (1).

(6)   A willful and knowing violation of this section or a willful and knowing failure to obey any court order issued under this section constitutes contempt.

History.—s. 3, ch. 95-207; s. 1, ch. 2008-172; s. 4, ch. 2008-234; s. 3, ch. 2011-83.

92.561   Prohibition on reproduction of child pornography.—

(1)   In a criminal proceeding, any property or material that portrays sexual performance by a child as defined in s. 827.071, or constitutes child pornography as defined in s. 847.001, must remain secured or locked in the care, custody, and control of a law enforcement agency, the state attorney, or the court.

(2)   Notwithstanding any law or rule of court, a court shall deny, in a criminal proceeding, any request by the defendant to copy, photograph, duplicate, or otherwise reproduce any property or material that portrays sexual performance by a child or constitutes child pornography so long as the state attorney makes the property or material reasonably available to the defendant.

(3)   For purposes of this section, property or material is deemed to be reasonably available to the defendant if the state attorney provides ample opportunity at a designated facility for the inspection, viewing, and examination of the property or material that portrays sexual performance by a child or constitutes child pornography by the defendant, his or her attorney, or any individual whom the defendant uses as an expert during the discovery process or at a court proceeding.

History.—s. 4, ch. 2011-220.

92.565   Admissibility of confession in sexual abuse cases.—

(1)   As used in this section, the term "sexual abuse" means an act of a sexual nature or sexual act that may be prosecuted under any law of this state, including those offenses specifically designated in subsection (2).

(2) In any criminal action in which the defendant is charged with a crime against a victim under s. 794.011; s. 794.05; s. 800.04; s. 826.04; s. 827.03, involving sexual abuse; s. 827.04, involving sexual abuse; s. 827.071; or s. 847.0135(5), or any other crime involving sexual abuse of another, or with any attempt, solicitation, or conspiracy to commit any of these crimes, the defendant's memorialized confession or admission is admissible during trial without the state having to prove a corpus delicti of the crime if the court finds in a hearing conducted outside the presence of the jury that the state is unable to show the existence of each element of the crime, and having so found, further finds that the defendant's confession or admission is trustworthy. Factors which may be relevant in determining whether the state is unable to show the existence of each element of the crime include, but are not limited to, the fact that, at the time the crime was committed, the victim was:

    (a) Physically helpless, mentally incapacitated, or mentally defective, as those terms are defined in s. 794.011;

    (b) Physically incapacitated due to age, infirmity, or any other cause; or

    (c) Less than 12 years of age.

(3) Before the court admits the defendant's confession or admission, the state must prove by a preponderance of evidence that there is sufficient corroborating evidence that tends to establish the trustworthiness of the statement by the defendant. Hearsay evidence is admissible during the presentation of evidence at the hearing. In making its determination, the court may consider all relevant corroborating evidence, including the defendant's statements.

(4) The court shall make specific findings of fact, on the record, for the basis of its ruling.

History.—s. 1, ch. 2000-204; s. 10, ch. 2008-172.

92.57 Termination of employment of witness prohibited.—A person who testifies in a judicial proceeding in response to a subpoena may not be dismissed from employment because of the nature of the person's testimony or because of absences from employment resulting from compliance with the subpoena. In any civil action arising out of a violation of this section, the court may award attorney's fees and punitive damages to the person unlawfully dismissed, in addition to actual damages suffered by such person.

History.—s. 1, ch. 90-185.

92.60 Foreign records of regularly conducted business activity.—

(1) For the purposes of this section:

    (a) "Foreign record of regularly conducted business activity" means a memorandum, report, record, or data compilation, in any form, of acts, events, conditions, opinions, or diagnoses, maintained in a foreign country.

    (b) "Foreign certification" means a written declaration made and signed in a foreign country by the custodian of a foreign record of regularly conducted business activity or another qualified person that, if falsely made, would subject the maker to criminal penalty under the laws of that country.

    (c) "Business" means any business, institution, association, profession, occupation, or calling of any kind, whether or not conducted for profit.

(2) In a criminal or civil proceeding in a court of the State of Florida, a foreign record of regularly conducted business activity, or a copy of such record, shall not be excluded as evidence by the hearsay rule if a foreign certification attests that:

(a)   Such record was made at or near the time of the occurrence of the matters set forth by, or from information transmitted by, a person with knowledge of those matters;

(b)   Such record was kept in the course of a regularly conducted business activity;

(c)   The business activity made such a record as a regular practice; and

(d)   If such record is not the original, it is a duplicate of the original;

unless the source of information or the method or circumstances of preparation indicate lack of trustworthiness.

(3)   A foreign certification under this section shall authenticate such record or duplicate.

(4)   No evidence in such records in the form of opinion or diagnosis is admissible under subsection (2) unless such opinion or diagnosis would be admissible under ss. 90.701-90.705 if the person whose opinion is recorded were to testify to the opinion directly.

(5)   At the arraignment or as soon after the arraignment as practicable, or 60 days prior to a civil trial, a party intending to offer in evidence under this section a foreign record of regularly conducted business activity shall provide written notice of that intention to each other party. A motion opposing admission in evidence of such record shall be made by the opposing party and determined by the court before trial. Failure by a party to file such motion before trial shall constitute a waiver of objection to such record or duplicate, but the court for cause shown may grant relief from the waiver.

History.—s. 17, ch. 88-381; s. 1, ch. 97-189.

92.605   Production of certain records by Florida businesses and out-of-state corporations.—

(1)   For the purposes of this section, the term:

(a)   "Adverse result" includes one of the following consequences to notification of the existence of a court order, a subpoena, or a search warrant:

1.   Danger to the life or physical safety of an individual.

2.   A flight from prosecution.

3.   The destruction of or tampering with evidence.

4.   The intimidation of potential witnesses.

5.   Serious jeopardy to an investigation or undue delay of a trial.

(b)   "Applicant" means a law enforcement officer who is seeking a court order or subpoena under s. 16.56, s. 27.04, s. 905.185, or s. 914.04 or who is issued a search warrant under s. 933.01, or anyone who is authorized to issue a subpoena under the Florida Rules of Criminal Procedure.

(c)   "Business" means any business, institution, association, profession, occupation, or calling of any kind, whether or not conducted for profit.

(d)   "Electronic communication services" and "remote computing services" have the same meaning as provided in the Electronic Communications Privacy Act in chapter 121 (commencing with s. 2701) of part I of Title 18 of the United States Code Annotated. This section does not apply to corporations that do not provide those services to the public.

(e)   "Out-of-state corporation" means any corporation that is qualified to do business in this state under s. 607.1501.

(f) "Out-of-state record of regularly conducted business activity" means a memorandum, report, record, or data compilation, in any form, of acts, events, conditions, opinions, or diagnoses, maintained in another state or country.

(g) "Out-of-state certification" means a written declaration made and signed in another state or country by the custodian of an out-of-state record of regularly conducted business activity or another qualified person that, if falsely made, would subject the declarant to criminal penalty under the laws of another state or country.

(h) "Properly served" means delivery by hand or in a manner reasonably allowing for proof of delivery if delivered by United States mail, overnight delivery service, or facsimile to a person or entity properly registered to do business in any state. In order for an out-of-state corporation to be properly served, the service described in this paragraph must be effected on the corporation's registered agent.

(2) The following provisions apply to any subpoena, court order, or search warrant issued in compliance with the Electronic Communications Privacy Act in chapter 121 (commencing with s. 2701) of part I of Title 18 of the United States Code and that is subject to this chapter, which allows a search for records that are in the actual or constructive possession of an out-of-state corporation that provides electronic communication services or remote computing services to the public, when those records would reveal the identity of the customers using those services; data stored by, or on behalf of, the customers; the customers' usage of those services; or the recipients or destinations of communications sent to or from those customers.

(a) Any subpoena, court order, or warrant issued under this subsection must contain the following language in bold type on the first page of the document: "This (subpoena, order, warrant) is issued pursuant to Florida Statute s. 92.605. A response is due within 20 business days of receipt of this (subpoena, order, warrant) unless a longer time period is stated herein."

(b) When properly served with a subpoena, court order, or search warrant issued by a Florida court or other applicant, an out-of-state corporation subject to this section shall provide to the applicant all records sought pursuant to such subpoena, court order, or warrant within 20 business days after receipt, or the date indicated within the subpoena, if later, including those records maintained or located outside the State of Florida. If the records cannot be produced within the 20-day time period, the out-of-state corporation shall notify the applicant within the 20-day time period and agree to produce the documents at the earliest possible time. The applicant shall pay the out-of-state corporation the reasonable expenses associated with compliance.

(c) When the applicant makes a showing and the court finds that failure to produce records within 20 business days would cause an adverse result, the subpoena, court order, or warrant may require production of records within less than 20 business days. A court may reasonably extend the time required for production of the records upon finding that the out-of-state corporation needs the extension and that an extension of time would not cause an adverse result.

(d) An out-of-state corporation seeking to quash or object to the subpoena, court order, or warrant must seek relief from the court issuing such subpoena, court order, or warrant within the time required for production of records under this section. The issuing court shall hear and decide that motion within 5 court days after the motion is filed.

(e) Upon written request from the applicant or if ordered by the court, the out-of-state corporation shall verify the authenticity of records that it produces by providing an affidavit that complies with the requirements set forth in this section. Records produced in compliance with this section are admissible in evidence as set forth in subsection (5).

(3) A Florida business that provides electronic communication services or remote computing services to the public, when served with a subpoena, court order, or warrant issued by another state to produce records that would reveal the identity of the customers using those services; data stored by, or on behalf of, the customers; the customers' usage of those services; or the recipients or destinations of communications sent to or from those customers shall produce those records as if that subpoena, court order, or warrant had been issued by a Florida court.

Florida Evidence Code 2012

(4)   A cause of action does not arise against any out-of-state corporation or Florida business subject to this section, or its officers, employees, agents, or other specified persons, for providing records, information, facilities, or assistance in accordance with the terms of a subpoena, court order, or warrant subject to this section.

(5)   In a criminal proceeding in a court of this state, an out-of-state record of regularly conducted business activity, or a copy of such record, shall not be excluded as hearsay evidence by s. 90.802, if an out-of-state certification attests that:

(a)   Such record was made at or near the time of the occurrence of the matters set forth by, or from information transmitted by, a person with knowledge of those matters.

(b)   Such record was kept in the course of a regularly conducted business activity.

(c)   The business activity made such a record as a regular practice.

(d)   If such record is not the original, it is a duplicate of the original, unless the source of information or the method or circumstances of preparation indicate lack of trustworthiness.

(6)   An out-of-state certification under this section shall authenticate such record or duplicate.

(7)   No evidence in such records in the form of opinion or diagnosis is admissible under subsection (5) unless such opinion or diagnosis would be admissible under ss. 90.701-90.705 if the person whose opinion is recorded were to testify to the opinion directly.

(8)   As soon after the arraignment as practicable, or 60 days prior to trial, a party intending to offer in evidence under this section an out-of-state record of regularly conducted business activity shall provide written notice of that intention to each other party. A motion opposing admission in evidence of such record shall be made by the opposing party and determined by the court before trial. Failure by a party to file such motion before trial shall constitute a waiver of objection to such record or duplicate, but the court for cause shown may grant relief from the waiver.

(9)   In any criminal case, the content of any electronic communication may be obtained under this section only by court order or by the issuance of a search warrant, unless otherwise provided under the Electronic Communications Privacy Act or other provision of law.

History.—s. 3, ch. 2003-71.

135

22207176R00084

Made in the USA
Lexington, KY
17 April 2013